PET-ORIENTED CHILD PSYCHOTHERAPY

ABOUT THE AUTHORS

Gerald P. Mallon is Assistant Professor at the Columbia University School of Social Work in New York City. Prior to his appointment at Columbia, Dr. Mallon was the Associate Executive Director at Green Chimneys Children's Services. He has written extensively about and has conducted research on the efficacy of Animal-Assisted Therapy with children and youth.

Boris M. Levinson was Professor of Psychology at the Ferkauf Graduate School of Humanities and Social Sciences at Yeshiva University in New York City. Dr. Levinson was also a Diplomat in Clinical Psychology and a member of the American Board of Examiners in Professional Psychology. After his retirement from full-time teaching, Dr. Levinson was appointed Professor Emeritus and accepted a position as Director of the Human/Companion Animal Therapy Program at the Blueberry Treatment Center for Children in Brooklyn, New York, a center for autistic children. After a distinguished career that spanned four decades, Dr. Levinson died in 1984.

PET-ORIENTED CHILD PSYCHOTHERAPY

Second Edition

By

BORIS M. LEVINSON, PH.D.

Revised and Updated by

GERALD P. MALLON, D.S.W.

CHARLES C THOMAS • PUBLISHER, LTD.
Springfield • Illinois • U.S.A.

Published and Distributed Throughout the World by

CHARLES C THOMAS • PUBLISHER, LTD.
2600 South First Street
Springfield, Illinois 62794-9265

ISBN 0-398-06673-6 (cloth)
ISBN 0-398-06674-4 (paper)

Library of Congress Catalog Card Number: 96-8968

First Edition, 1969
Second Edition, 1997

With THOMAS BOOKS *careful attention is given to all details of manufacturing and design. It is the Publisher's desire to present books that are satisfactory as to their physical qualities and artistic possibilities and appropriate for their particular use.* THOMAS BOOKS *will be true to those laws of quality that assure a good name and good will.*

Printed in the United States of America
SC-R-3

Library of Congress Cataloging-in-Publication Data

Levinson, Boris M. (Boris Mayer), 1907–
Pet-oriented child psychotherapy / by Boris M. Levinson ; revised and updated by Gerald P. Mallon. — 2nd ed.
p. cm.
Includes bibliographical references and index.
ISBN 0-398-06673-6 (cloth). — ISBN 0-398-06674-4 (pbk.)
1. Child psychotherapy. 2. Pets—Therapeutic use. I. Mallon, Gerald P. II. Title.
RJ505.P47L48 1997
618.92'8914—dc20 96-8968
CIP

This book is dedicated to Jingles, my co-therapist,
To whom I owe more than he owes me;
Who taught me more than I taught him;
Who unveiled a new world of experience for me;
Who doesn't care whether this book is dedicated to him or not;
And who will never learn about it.

Original Dedication Made By Boris Levinson in 1969

PREFACE

Boris Levinson was the first professionally trained clinician to formally introduce and document the way that companion-animals could hasten the development of a rapport between therapist and patient thereby increasing the likelihood of patient motivation. Originally ridiculed by his colleagues for presenting such a "preposterous" technique, he continued to pursue his work nonetheless. This book, originally published by Charles C Thomas in 1969, was the first work to document the technique which Levinson originally referred to as "Pet-Oriented Psychotherapy." Although still frequently cited by those conducting research in the field (Rowan, 1995, pp. 130–131), *Pet-Oriented Child Psychotherapy,* has been out of print for many years. It is reproduced here in its original form; not one word has been deleted. However, in an effort to update and revise the text (which Dr. Levinson always wanted to have done), footnotes have been added to identify and illuminate research and practices which have taken place since the original publication. In addition, a list of Resources is included in the Appendix.

Before looking at Levinson's most popular work, it seems fitting that readers have an opportunity to get to know Levinson the man and to review his work and life. During the course of my work as a "Levinson scholar," I met and interviewed many people who knew Dr. Levinson. Each person recalled the respect that they had for him as an innovator, but few knew the man behind the work. Even fewer hypothesized about the motivation for his introduction of the "pet therapy technique". Everyone agreed, however, that he was a generous man. His wife, Aida Levinson, perhaps, said it best:

> My only regret, is that you could not have met him yourself. If he were alive he would have been more than happy to spend time with you, to talk to you about his work. He was a generous, generous man. He was a good friend to many people, a kind, genuine, generous, honest and gentle man (A. Levinson, interview, February 17, 1994).

THE MOTIVATION BEHIND THE MAN

Background

Boris Mayer Levinson was born in Kalvarijah, Lithuania on July 7, 1907. He and his family immigrated to the United States in 1923, when he was a teenager. Friends said he spoke with a heavy accent (Mira Rothenberg, interview, April 19, 1993). The Levinsons settled in the East New York section of Brooklyn, which at the time, was a farming community. Reflecting back on his early days in this country and noting society's estrangement from nature, Levinson recalled, the following in his last published work:

> It reminds me of the time in my youth when I lived in East New York, on the outskirts of New York City. Ours was the last house within the city limits and only a hundred yards away there was a dairy farm where we could purchase milk. When I last visited that old neighborhood, I found that the farm had disappeared and that the entire area, as far as the eye could see, had been built up (1984b, p. 11).

These early influences of nature and animals may have influenced his later development of the "pet therapy technique" and to an awareness that humans were becoming more and more disconnected from their environments (See also Levinson, 1972b).

Graduating from Eastern District High School in Brooklyn, Levinson became a naturalized U.S. citizen in 1930. He married his first wife, Ruth Berkowitz, in 1934; they had two sons, David and Martin. He was educated at the City University of New York, receiving his Bachelor of Science in 1937. One year later, Levinson earned a Master's of Science in Education. In 1947, he was awarded a Ph.D. in clinical psychology from New York University (Leaders in American Science, p. 417). In 1974, he married his second wife, Aida Penaranda, a diplomat from Bolivia. A deeply spiritual man, Levinson was raised in the Jewish faith (the Ashkenazi line) and was a Talmudic scholar. His spirituality was evident in his writings as the following illustrates.

> Unfortunately, the climate of man's spiritual life has become much polluted by fear, insecurity, loneliness, frustration, and anxiety. We are afraid to feel, to experience, to commit ourselves to a goal. We want to love but find that our love is misplaced, misunderstood or that a monetary value is placed upon it. Pets, paradoxical as it may seem, can help to rehumanize society because they meet many needs not fulfilled by the present social structures. Pets upgrade the quality

of life, bring us closer to nature, provide companionship and emphasize the fact that animals must be accepted as desirable participants in society (Levinson, 1972a, p. 5).

One interviewee noted that Levinson's writing had a spiritual bent and suggested that it was this spiritual connection with humans and animals that kept the scientific community from fully accepting his ideas (Linda Hines, Executive Director of the Delta Society, interview, February 4, 1994).

Professionally, Levinson was a psychoanalytically trained child psychologist. His official biography indicates that he was a Professor of Psychology at the Ferkauf Graduate School of Humanities and Social Sciences at Yeshiva University in New York, a Diplomate in Clinical Psychology, and a member of the American Board of Examiners in Professional Psychology. He was remembered by a student as "an austere, very tough, no nonsense professor. Everybody was terrified of him" (M. Rothenberg, interview, April 19, 1993).

In 1972, after his retirement from full-time teaching at Yeshiva University, Levinson was appointed as Professor Emeritus and, additionally, accepted a position as Director of the Human/Companion Animal Therapy program at the Blueberry Treatment Center for Children in Brooklyn, New York—a center for autistic children. In stark contrast to his reputation as a rigorous academician, Levinson was described by the same colleague while at Blueberry, as:

> A wonderful man. He was loving and warm—he loved the children. He came everyday with Jingles, but the children never called the dog Jingles; they all called him—Levinson. They loved Grandpa Boris. He was completely different from that person who taught at Yeshiva (M. Rothenberg, interview, April 19, 1993).

Levinson was a prolific writer, with an active and creative mind who was constantly exploring new techniques and approaches to healing those who were emotionally troubled (Levinson and Mezei, 1973; Levinson, 1975a, 1976, 1979b). In speaking about his work, Mrs. Levinson noted:

> He was first a researcher. He was always working on something—a new idea, a new article. In fact, he kept a small light and paper by his bed at night so that if he had an idea in the middle of the night, he could write it down. He then clipped all of his ideas together and then wrote about them. He wrote so well that some people thought it was easy. He just made it look easy—he worked very hard at it (A. Levinson, interview, February 17, 1994).

Levinson's first published articles were not about animals or children, but about men from the Bowery area of New York City. Levinson's doctoral dissertation, entitled "A Comparative Study of Certain Homeless and Unattached Domiciled Men (Levinson, 1947), established him as a pioneer in the study of homeless men. He continued to study this population throughout his career (1958a, 1963, and 1966),

But he had wide research interests as well. These included: the psychological traits of children of traditional Jewish backgrounds (1959); childhood autism (1980a, Levinson and Osterweil, 1984); mental retardation (1958b, 1959) and, of course, animal-assisted therapy.

"PET THERAPY"

In 1961, Levinson presented a paper to his colleagues at the Annual American Psychological Association Conference in New York City in which he first officially described Pet Therapy, specifically reporting on cases where the success of the treatment "was attributed largely to the function of a dog featured in the therapy constellation" (Levinson, 1962, p. 60). Recalling what he termed "the accidental discovery" of the technique, Levinson, recounted, in his now famous story involving Jingles, how he began to develop insight into the possibility of utilizing a dog as an accessory in the treatment of a severely withdrawn child whom he had treated in 1953. At the time, he "rejected any thought of pursuing the subject further because it seemed much too unorthodox" (p. 60)—but, by 1961, he decided to share his findings at the conference, stating that he was at a stage (of professional security) where he no longer hesitated to modify accepted therapeutic principles if he felt that the patient would benefit. As was his custom in all of his subsequent articles, Levinson concluded his first article, by raising questions and calling for a definite research program into his newly proposed technique.

Talking about companion animals and their role in the therapeutic process, made many clinicians uncomfortable. Perhaps in response to their own discomfort, many professionals ridiculed Levinson and belittled his findings, even making disparaging remarks about his work (Levinson, 1969a). Rogers (1963) identified this response as a general reaction and resistance to new psychotherapeutic techniques. Others, however, (Corson and Corson, 1973; Quaytman, 1963; Weigel, R.G. and Straumfjord, A.A. 1969), were intrigued and began to examine the impact of animals on humans.

In fact, Levinson and colleagues, surveyed a random sample of 435 psychotherapists (50% of the membership) for the Clinical Division of the New York State Psychological Association on the extent to which pets were recommended by psychotherapists, as therapeutic aides. Thirty-three percent of the 319 who replied had utilized pets as therapeutic aides. Of those, 91 percent found them useful (1972a, p. 154).

Levinson's first article is important not only because it was one of the first contributions to the professional literature published in the human-companion animal bond field (Bossard said similar things in a 1944 article, also in *Mental Hygiene*), but because it lays the foundation for future research and ideas. However, it was his second article (Levinson, 1964) that first coined the term "Pet Therapy" (p. 243).

This article further defined Levinson's approach and pointed out that pets are useful in two ways: "first, as psychotherapeutic aides, i.e., as catalytic agents helpful in speeding up therapy in the therapist's office, and second, as aides in psychotherapy, i.e., being placed in the homes of emotionally disturbed children where they tend to restore a healthy communication between members of a family (Levinson, 1964, p.248).

The article was also reprinted as a chapter in a book that addressed issues in Residential Treatment for children and youth (Whittaker and Trieschman, 1972) and was the first apparent recognition of Levinson's pet-therapy by child welfare professionals. Levinson was an advocate for utilizing animals with children in residential treatment and wrote extensively about it (Levinson, 1971; 1979a; 1980a; 1983b). He also surveyed the utilization of pets in residential schools (Levinson, 1968a) and found that most did not permit pets in the schools. He also found that it was not universally acknowledged that children needed love objects and that poor self-concept and depression found in children who reside in residential centers "may stem from the fact that these children do not have someone to love, care for, be protective towards, and have confidence in" (p. 413). Twenty three years later, Mallon (1994a) found that a dog in a children's residential center played an important role as confidant.

In 1968, Levinson contributed a chapter (1968b) to a book which discussed abnormal behavior in animals (Fox, 1968), in which he focused on the interpersonal relationships between pets and human beings. The chapter outlined nine areas for discussion: the historical relationship between man and animal; the symbolic meaning of an animal; the child and his pet; the child and his or her fear of animals; the pet and the family; the pet and the child's bereavement; the role of the pet in old age; the pet in psychodiagnosis and therapy; and once again, he writes about the veterinarian and mental hygiene (see also Levinson, 1965a).

PET–ORIENTED CHILD PSYCHOTHERAPY

In 1969, Charles C Thomas published the first of three books by Levinson (1969a). This book, reproduced here, was the first comprehensive text to discuss methods of utilizing animals in the treatment of emotionally disturbed children. In the introduction, Levinson states:

> The thesis of this book is that contact with the inanimate and particularly the animate world via the pets is most important to a wholesome emotional development (p. xiv).

It was at this point that Levinson stopped calling his technique "pet-therapy" and moved to a broader characterization, renaming it "pet-oriented child psychotherapy." He relied heavily on the concepts of contact comfort (Harlow, 1958; Harlow and Zimmerman, 1959) and on transitional object relations (Winnicott, 1953) to provide a grounding for pet-oriented child psychotherapy, as well as on the work of major figures in child development and attachment (Bender and Rapoport, 1944; Erikson, 1963 and 1968; Piaget and Inhelder, 1952; Searles, 1960; Spitz 1960; and Winnicott, 1965). According to him, the young nonverbal, the inhibited, the autistic, the withdrawn, the obsessive-compulsive, and the culturally disadvantaged child would benefit most from pet-oriented psychotherapy. Nonetheless, Levinson also warns that "using pets is not a magic solution to the 'inner world' of the child" (p. 71).

Throughout the development of his ideas about pet-oriented psychotherapy, Levinson expanded his interests to include a variety of populations. While he maintained a primary focus on its theoretical applicability for children (1965b; 1970c; 1972c; 1978; 1980b) Levinson began to focus more on applications for the aged as he grew older. Levinson's (1969b) article addressed the use of animal-assisted therapy with the elderly and encouraged professionals in the field of aging to explore its applicability. For example, Levinson and his associates (Levinson, 1970a; 1970b) identified possible benefits of the therapy as including: opportunities for touch, alleviation of loneliness; exercise; and companionship.

Levinson's (1972a) second book expands his ideas about the technique of pet-oriented psychotherapy for children to include other populations.

The theme of reconnecting humans to animals and nature in an attempt to rehumanize them and as a means of assisting them in their own developmental processes is also strongly represented in this work. While this theme of human-animal-environment interconnection is found in many of his writings, Levinson, however, also found it necessary to make a cautionary statement about the limits of animal-assisted therapy. In the prologue, he writes:

> It has by no means been the intention of this writer to indicate that pets are a panacea for all the ills of society or for the pain involved in growing up and growing old. However, pets are both an aid to and a sign of the rehumanization of society. They are an aid in that they help to fill needs which are not being met in other, perhaps better ways, because society makes inadequate provision for meeting them. In the meantime, animals can provide some relief, give much pleasure and remind us of our origins (p. 3).

Gaining international recognition for his work, Levinson (1975b) was asked to present a paper entitled, "Pets and Environment" at a conference in London, England. He told colleagues that the English rolled out the red carpet for him and the British press called him "The Freud of Dog Therapy" (M. Rothenberg, interview, April 19, 1993). The paper which he presented later appeared in a book edited by Ronald S. Anderson.

Until 1973, Levinson's development had largely been self-constructed, with little or no contribution from other professionals. However, in the early 1970s, Corson and Corson of Ohio State University, began working with some of Levinson's techniques, conducting one of the earliest pet-facilitated psychotherapy studies using a colony of 20 dogs at Upham Hall Psychiatric Hospital. They reported encouraging results in 28–30 patients who had failed to respond to traditional treatment including electro-shock therapy and psychotropic medications. Corson and Corson continued to work on the development of this technique and made significant contributions to its legitimacy and acceptance in the scientific community (Corson and Corson, 1973, Corson and Corson et al., 1977).

In 1981, at the International Conference on Human/Companion-Animal Bond, held in Philadelphia, Levinson, along with the Corsons, was presented with The Delta Distinguished Service Award recognizing his outstanding contribution to the Human-Animal Bond field. In a letter to the Mrs. Levinson after his death, the founder and the executive director of the Delta Society wrote:

> We recall the happy times we had with both of you at the Philadelphia meeting in 1981, and remember his insightful presentation . . . he was truly a pioneer and made outstanding contributions to our understanding of the human-animal bond. With your permission we would like to establish a Boris Levinson Memorial Research Award (L. Bustad and L. Hines, personal correspondence, April 9, 1984).

In response, Mrs. Levinson granted her permission to establish the award and wrote: "One of his greatest honors was to have been the recipient of the Delta Distinguished Service Award" (A. Levinson, personal correspondence, April 23, 1984).

As a long time proponent for research, Levinson (1982) initiated a discussion concerning the future of research into relationships between people and their animal companions. In a paper presented to the International Conference, he noted that while the field of animal-human relationships had become respected as a legitimate area of scientific investigation, that it was not, as yet, a full-fledged discipline, "having still to develop a name, a theory, and a methodology of its own" (p. 283). While noting that knowledge was not the result of methodology, Levinson called on professionals in the field to examine various methodologies, advocating for the utilization of both intuitive and scientific approaches in an effort to encompass the full richness of the animal-human interaction.

He specifically called for investigation into four areas: the role of animals in various human cultures and ethnic groups over the centuries; the effect on human personality development of association with animals; human-animal communication and the therapeutic use of animals in formal psychotherapy, institutional settings, and residential arrangements for handicapped and aged populations" (p. 283). Throughout the paper, Levinson outlined each area and delineated "fruitful avenues for researchers" to investigate. Levinson continued this discussion in the foreword to a book on animals in the helping professions (Arkow, 1984). (Levinson, 1984b).

Levinson continued to write and speak on the human/companion animal therapy (a term he coined in 1984—Levinson 1984a) until on April 2, 1984, while working with one of his beloved children at the Blueberry Treatment Center for Children, Boris Mayer Levinson suffered a fatal heart attack and died. If it was possible for one to choose where they would spend their last moments on this earth, Levinson would probably have chosen to be with "his children." Levinson (1983a), then 76 years old, called his job as a therapist to severely disturbed, autistic, nonverbal children at Blueberry's Treatment Center "the most fulfilling one I ever had." He noted that the experience had helped him to gain insight into himself and to "discover his repressed feminine qualities of nurturance and protectiveness" (p.253).

> I want to care for, touch, be with my children, I miss them on weekends. They are my children and I love them all. I joyfully join in the barking of one child, rock along with another, make funny noises with a third, I am called Grandpa Boris. I want to help my children and only them (even though I know that the world outside is going to hell!). After all, doesn't the Talmud say that if you save one person it as though you saved the world? (Levinson, 1983, p. 253).

A generous, kind, and gentle man, Boris Levinson is remembered for his valuable scholarly and personal contributions to the human-animal bond movement.

INTRODUCTION

The World Is Too Much With Us
William Wordsworth (1770–1850)

The world is too much with us: late and soon,
Getting and spending, we lay waste our powers:
Little we see in Nature that is ours;
We have given our hearts away, a sordid boon!
This Sea that bares her bosom to the moon;
The winds that will be howling at all hours,
And are up-gathered now like sleeping flowers;
For this, for everything, we are out of tune;
It moves us not—Great God! I'd rather be
A Pagan suckled in a creed outworn;
So might I, standing on this pleasant lea,
Have glimpses that would make me less forlorn;
Have sight of Proteus rising from the sea;
Or hear old Triton blow his wreathed horn.

Long ago, poets foresaw the lonely dilemma that would descend upon a mankind[1] which had divorced itself from the elemental processes of nature. Today, the predictions of Wordsworth have sadly come to be. Alienation is widespread in our society. Man finds that he is a stranger to himself. He surfeits in this largess and cries out in his anxiety. He apparently lost the key to self-understanding. Man's anxiety is partly due to his withdrawal from the healing forces of nature and its foremost representatives, the animal kingdom. No longer able to identify with nature and its representatives, man finds himself in a psychological no-man's land. He may be able to regain some of his emotional harmony by reestablishing his bond with the animate and inanimate world.[2] Through identification, this process proceeds in three stages: first, with inanimate nature; then with the animate nonhuman world; and finally with human beings. "The disharmony of man's existence generates needs which far transcend those of his animal origin. These needs result in an imperative drive to restore a unity and equilibrium between himself and the rest of nature" (Fromm, 1955).

Pets represent a half-way station on the road back to emotional well-being. This is why the possession of a pet is so important for the alienated, and why pets are so helpful in handling childhood behavior disorders.

The thesis of this book is that contact with the inanimate and particularly the animate world via the pet is most important to a wholesome emotional development. We can start tracing this with the infant. The child, to borrow a phrase from William James (1890), is born into "great, blooming, buzzing confusion." At first, the young child feels omnipotent and cannot differentiate between inner sensations and outer reality. Many authorities think (Des Lauriers, 1967; Freud, 1965, Piaget, 1952, Searles, 1960, Werner, 1957) that the infant does not feel the difference between self and nonself or the world at large. The infant lives in an omnipotent state where he and the world are a unity.

As the child begins to explore the world, many authorities believe that the haptic modality is the first sense modality to emerge. Searles (1960) suggests that "the earliest modality of experience is mediated via tactual-kinesthetic sensations" (p.33). The child will try to explore the world using this modality and he will begin to differentiate the inner reality and outer world in terms of haptic manipulation and will tend to learn about the world at first from touch and later from vision. As the infant begins to feed, the mother nourishes him and supplies him with the warmth, cuddling, and softness that the child associates with love and security. He touches his mother. She is soft and seems to be yielding, succorant, and comforting. This reinforces innate feelings. He begins to associate soft touch sensations, sensations pleasing to the haptic senses, as productive of security. As a matter of fact, the desire for "contact comfort" (Harlow, 1958) with a soft mother appears to be unlearned. This is the inference drawn from the studies made by Harlow (1958) of the behavior of very young monkeys in their responses to soft cloth "mothers" and to wire "mothers."

Very young monkeys were reared singly in uncomfortable cages which had two mother figures: a "wire mother" and a "cloth mother." Behind each mother there was a light bulb providing warmth and each mother could be equipped with a nursing bottle attached to its "breast." One group of monkeys had their cloth mothers equipped with nursing bottles and another group of monkeys had their wire mothers similarly equipped... Both groups spent relatively more time with the cloth mother than with the wire mother in spite of the fact that only one group secured its nourishment from the cloth mother (Harlow, 1958).

Needless to say, one must be careful in generalizing from animal behavior to human behavior. However, the preference for the cloth "mother" was quite clear because apparently while "both mothers provided the basic known requirements for adequate nursing, only the cloth mother provided an additional variable of contact comfort" (Harlow and Zimmerman, 1959). We may infer that contact with something soft symbolizes to very young children feelings of comfort, security, and love.

In this connection, it is interesting to note that in a study made of "Cuddlers" and "Non-Cuddlers," i.e., very young children who did and did not actively seek physical contact with their mothers, it was established that it was "not contact per se that is avoided by Non-Cuddlers but only the restrictions of movement that is involved in certain of the contact situations" (Schaffer and Emerson, 1964). Both groups of children avidly sought contact with their mothers.

It need not surprise us, therefore, that most children at the age of four to twelve months acquire "transitional objects" which become the child's most treasured possession (Winnicott, 1953). Interestingly, the "transitional object" is usually something soft, a piece of blanket or a soft toy. Apparently, contacting and touching something soft, warm and cuddly satisfies some of the infant's inner needs, is reassuring and is another reason why a soft cuddly animal is so important. The need for a "transitional object" is normal and indicates that a beginning is being made in reconciling reality and fantasy. As the normal child grows older and develops other interests, his need for the "transitional object" decreases until it disappears. However, in times of crisis or emotional tension, the transitional object may become "a defense against anxiety," which for the child is a safe and innocuous way of lessening anxiety (Stevenson, 1954).

Generally speaking, the warm cuddly pet is usually a "treasured possession" (Stevenson, 1954) which can become the transitional object bridging the development from a state of primary narcissistic omnipotence to that of the beginning of relationship to the real (object) world.

However, if the "transitional object" continues to be a symbol of security, a comforter and a refuge when the pressure of relating and unifying inner fantasy life and other reality experiences into a unified whole become unbearable, it may be considered a regressive manifestation of withdrawal (Stevenson, 1954). This occasionally happens with children and with adults who withdraw from life and spend all their time with a pet. Nevertheless, in this writer's opinion, it is to be preferred to a complete narcissistic withdrawal.

Only because modern man seems to have lost sight of non-man-made natural process, is it necessary to state the obvious truth that man is an integral part of nature. Early in the course of his development, man identified intimately with the living and inanimate elements of his environment. At first, we find man worshiping the inanimate forces of the universe such as trees, streams, and nearby mountains. Later, after developing powers of abstraction, we see him worshiping and endowing with human traits the heavenly constellations and the elementary forces of nature such as wind and fire. With his kinship for nature, primitive man long continued in awe of animate forces such as the animals and the inanimate forces of the forests and neighboring fields. He projected his fears of the unknown onto the animals and he endowed them with the awful and frightening powers that he felt stirring within himself. In order to placate these powers which could destroy as well as heal, man began to worship and offer to animals precious gifts like first-born children and first fruits of his field.

By domesticating an animal, man demonstrated his kinship to nature. This friendship was expressed by adopting various species of animal life as pets even before any economic benefits were evident. Psychologically, this was the beginning of a symbiotic relationship between pets and human beings in which man supplied the material needs of the pet while the pet satisfied the psychological needs of his master.

For as long as man continued in his association with nature, terrified as he may have been, he did not feel alienated either from himself or the universe. Today, however, this **kinship** with nature which encompassed all of man's relationship seems to be vanishing. In this very busy twentieth century, man is a lonely creature. There are too many alienated individuals who lack human companionship. They lack purpose and productivity. A simple addition to these lonely lives can sometimes accomplish major changes. The possession of a pet who eagerly awaits one and responds to one's care and attention may mean the difference between maintaining contact with reality or almost total withdrawal into fantasy. Literally, a pet can occasionally represent the difference between life and death.[3]

> Let us admit this and not lie to ourselves that we need the dog as a protection for our house. We **do** need him, but not as a watchdog. I, at least in my dreary foreign towns, have certainly stood in need of dog's company and I have derived

> from the mere fact of his existence, a great sense of inward security, such as one finds in a childhood memory or in the prospect often scenery of one's home country, for me the Blue Danube, for you the White Cliffs of Dover. In the almost film-like flitting-by of modern life, a man needs something to tell him, from time to time, that he is still himself, and nothing can give him this assurance in so comforting a manner as the "four feet trotting behind" (Lorenz, 1952).

However, the reasons for the adoption of pets need closer analysis. In this connection, we must recall that the most popular pet, the dog, looks at the human being as part of his family, part of a mixed pack. A further fact is very important and that is that most animals, and particularly the dog, retained their juvenile characteristics under domestication (Zeuner, 1963). This enhanced the usefulness of animals to primitive man as it tended to bring forth protective and kind feelings toward the animals in question. Searles (1960) hypothesized that various inanimate objects in our environment may be considered as parts of one's anatomy and separation from objects in our environment is equivalent to the loss of parts of our body. I would like to extend this concept in terms of Winnicott's (1953) concept of the "transitional object" and indicate that our immediate environment may function naturally in this way. This, I believe, can be seen clearly in the feeling of personal loss experienced when visiting an old neighborhood where one has spent childhood years and finds the old district destroyed and new buildings substituted. This also happens, at times, when a family is relocated even if the change is from a slum hovel to a modern apartment. This kind of grief and/or anxiety may last for a long time, according to Fried (1963), and stems from "a longing for the remembered security of the early days." The security may or may not have been real, but a familiar environment often provides feelings of security just because even the dangers were known. In this sense, the familiar environment can also become a transitional object.

Psychologists have not studied extensively the problems arising from man's reactions to his physical environment (Wohlwill, 1953). However, as has been noted, man's conquest of nature has not been accompanied by a similar conquest of his inner self and the inner forces which motivate behavior. This, with other factors, brings about widespread alienation. By destroying nature, man alienates himself from his inner being and in a sense commits suicide. Throughout the ages, nature and particularly its animals have assumed for mankind the role of "transitional objects" which mediate between the known terrors of outer reality and the unknown terrors of the inner world. Unlike the animal, man can adapt himself to all kinds of nonhuman environments. This is at once his virtue and undoing. By removing himself from nature by being independent of nature, man also loses part of his psychological (and physical) strength. Despite man's ever-increasing power over the forces of nature, despite the immeasurable increase in our comfort and wealth for the past fifty years, our feelings of security have not grown commensurably. Paradoxically, the reverse seems to be true. With the increase of man's knowledge and power, there has strangely been a corresponding increase in tensions, fears, anxieties, and lack of ease.

"The world today is sick to its thin blood for lack of elemental things; for fire before the hands, for water welling from the earth, for air, for the dear earth itself underfoot" (Beston, 1928). With the satisfaction of our bodily needs, we discovered that we were chasing after the will-o'-the-wisp and our inward unhappiness has not been assuaged. We learned that what we were striving for was meaningless too. We developed existential despair.

Searles (1960) indicates that when man has the "sense of relatedness" to nature it "helps to assuage man's existential loneliness in the Universe, the loneliness which resides in his knowledge that he, a self-aware, reasoning being, must always stand somewhat apart from the rest of Nature" (p. 122). As a consequence, man began to feel worthless and of no account either to himself or to his fellow human beings or to the universe. It is only by coming back to nature, by developing respect for life in all its manifestations, that man develops respect for himself. During the past few centuries of the development of the modern world, important thinkers have periodically recommended "back to nature" movements. Infinite variations in naturalistic philosophies have been thoroughly propounded. To the Rousseaus, Thoreaus, Bubers and others, the dehumanization and mechanization of the human being with its accompanying illnesses was early apparent. Huxley, (1952) put it succinctly and well when he said: "Only as we discover and assimilate the truth about nature shall we be able to undertake the apparently contradictory but essential task of re-establishing our unity with nature while at the same time maintaining our transcendence over nature" (p. xi).

Further crystallization of the need for a revitalized union with Nature came from Albert Schweitzer, whose overwhelming "reverence for life" brought inspiration to himself and all those around him. Schweitzer felt such intimate identity with all . . . everything on this earth, animate or inanimate, that he respected and revered everything around him, regardless of how strange or different (Joy, 1950).

Since the discovery of fire, instead of cooperating with nature man frequently fought against it. This fight with nature has created an alienation from self. This was due to the fact, as has been pointed out by Henry (1963), that man was primarily interested in providing for his physical needs: food, shelter and clothing. His spiritual needs, his emotional needs which, as we indicated above, depend so much upon our union with nature, were barely considered. This has further increased man's isolation from nature with a consequent increase in his inner emotional turmoil.

SUMMARY

At different levels in the development of the individual, man needs a feeling of communion with all of nature. This seems to be a common experience for everyone regardless of age or maturity. This need expresses itself in many ways. For some it is the intense yearning for a vacation in the wilderness. In others it is evidenced by an intense interest in the conservation of our natural resources including wildlife and fisheries. For some, it is an expedition at dawn to catch a brief, refreshing glimpse of some rare bird. Millions of city dwellers find faith, comfort, and optimism in the flowering of a begonia plant on the dusting window sill.

Authoritative voices from different disciplines seem today to be making two disparately opposite prognoses for mankind. Some claim that man is on the brink of totally destroying himself and the world in which he lives. Others contend that out of the present scientific maelstrom man will fashion a better organized society, free from material wants and surfeited with the goods of the spirit. All, however, are in accord with the estimate of modern man's loneliness. Some even go so far as to claim that modern man's constant fight against nature is breeding not only man's inhumanity to man but the deterioration of any individual tranquility.

Nevertheless, there seems to be a law of relatedness. A human being must relate to the world outside of himself and the world inside of himself; to things know and unknown; to things awesome, incomprehensible and bigger than himself; to things known and equal to himself and to creatures lesser than himself such as pets.

A human being has to remain in contact with all of nature throughout his lifetime if he is to maintain good mental health.

NOTES

[1]Dr. Levinson uses the masculine pronoun to describe the experience of people throughout this text, as was the custom at the time it was written. Today it would be more appropriate to either identify both genders or to use the more inclusive term "human."

[2]Human estrangement from nature and from the healing process which can occur when a healthy relationship exists between humans and the natural environment, was a recurrent and constant theme throughout Levinson's work. Beck (1990), Beck and Katcher (1987); Bustad (1979) have all written about the importance of contact with natural surroundings and companion animals.

Several authors from the field of social work have written extensively about an ecological view of practice which clearly resonates with Dr. Levinson's work. The ecological perspective focuses professional attention to the person-in-environment. It posits that living organisms and environments can be thought of in terms of an adaptive balance or "goodness of fit." To the extent that the "fit" does not meet the individuals needs, one experiences stress between themselves and the "environmental nutrients" (See Germain, 1973, 1978, 1991; Germain and Gitterman, 1980).

[3]There is a growing body of literature which heralds the benefits of companion animals in the lives of people (Allen, 1985; Anderson, Hart, and Hart 1984; Bikales, 1975; Bryant, 1990; Fogel, 1983; Melson, Strimple, and Bustad, 1992; Mugford, 1980; Netting, Wilson, and New, 1987; Rowan, 1988; Yates, 1973). Many of these citations will be identified within the text of this work.

ACKNOWLEDGMENTS

Although writing is a solitary endeavor, no one writes alone. There are several people whom I would like to thank for inspiring me throughout the process of revising and updating this book. In preparing this manuscript, my chief debt is to the late Boris Levinson. His vision and his generosity in sharing his ideas about people and animals makes this book possible. I am proud to have been able to be a part of it.

I thank, also, two teachers. Dr. Sam Ross' enthusiasm about utilizing animals in treatment with children, taught me to approach this work in the same manner. He has truly been my mentor and my guide in this process. Without his wisdom and his sharing of knowledge, I would never have known Boris Levinson's work or known the joy that I have had during these past nine years in working with him at Green Chimneys Children's Services.

I am also grateful to Professor Irwin Epstein, my friend and colleague at the Hunter College School of Social Work in New York, who has always provided me with professional and intellectual encouragement.

Most importantly, my thanks goes to Aida Penaranda Levinson, for trusting me with the work of her beloved husband. Without Mrs. Levinson's trust and permission, this version of Dr. Levinson's book would literally have never been reprinted. To her, I am deeply indebted and most grateful that she has given me this opportunity.

Thanks is also due to Carol Brown, my secretary who dutifully typed every word of Dr. Levinson's original text in preparation for this publication.

G.P.M.

FIRST EDITION ACKNOWLEDGMENTS

The writer wishes to thank the following publishers and authors for their permission to quote from the designated writings:

A B P International: *Man Meets Dog,* By K. Lorenz (Methuen & Co. Ltd., publishers); *King Solomon's Ring,* by K. Lorenz (translated by M. Latzke. Methuen & Co. Ltd., publishers); *The Story of the Dog,* by C. G. Trew (Methuen & Co. Ltd., publishers).

American Journal of Orthopsychiatry: "Territoriality in man—A comparison of behavior in home and hospital," by A. D. Colman; "Animal drawings of children," by L. Bender and J. Rapoport, M.D.; "Some observations on the significance of animal drawings," by A. A. Schwartz and I. H. Rosenberg. "Copyright, the American Orthopsychiatric Association, reproduced by permission."

American Psychological Association: "Introduction and overview," by J. M. Shlien; "Vicissitudes of communication in psychotherapy," by F. Auld; In J. M. Shlien (Ed.) *Research in Psychotherapy,* Vol. III.

Archives of General Psychiatry: "The schizophrenic child," by A. M. Des Lauriers.

Bailliere, Tindall and Cassell Ltd.: *The Behavior of Domestic Animals,* by E. S. Hafez.

Basic Books: *Young Children in Hospitals,* by J. Robertson; "Grieving for a lost home," by M. Fried; In L. J. Duhl (Ed.) *The Urban Condition.*

Beacon Press: *Homo Ludens,* by J. Huizinga.

Brandt & Brandt: *A Park Ave. Vet,* by L. J. Camuti and L. Alexander. Holt, Rinehart and Winston, Copyright (c) by L. J. Camuti and L. Alexander. Reprinted by permission of Brandt & Brandt.

George Braziller, "The Nature of the Symbol" by E. Kahler from *Symbolism in Religion and Literature,* edited by R. May. Copyright (c) 1960 by George Braziller.

Edmund R. Brill: The material on p. 9 is from the *Basic Writings of Sigmund Freud,* trans. and ed. by A. A. Brill, Copyright 1938 by Random House. Copyright renewed 1965 by G. Bernheim and E. Brill. Reprinted by permission.

Christy & Moore Ltd.: *Cult of the Cat,* by P. Dale-Green.

Clarendon Press: *Witchcraft, Oracles, and Magic Among the Azande,* by E. E. Evans-Pritchard.

Columbia University Press: *The Professional Houseparent,* by E. Burmeister; *Tough Times and Tender Moments in Child Care Work,* by E. Burmeister.

Thomas Y. Crowell: K. Z. Lorenz: *King Solomon's Ring.* Copyright 1952 by Thomas Y. Crowell Company, New York, publishers.

Dodd, Mead: *Dogs Against Darkness,* by D. Hartwell.

Doubleday: *Animals and Men,* by N. H. Dembeck; *The Heathens. Primitive Man and His Religion,* by W. Howells.

E. P. Dutton: *Sorcerers of Dobu,* by R. F. Fortune.

Faber & Faber, Ltd.: *Insight and Responsibility,* by E. H. Erikson.

Frederick Fell: *A Letter to the Man Who Killed My Dog,* by A. Joseph.

Victor Gollancz: *Children in Homes,* by M. Brill and B. Thomas.

Harper & Row: *Patterns of Sexual Behavior,* by C. S. Ford and F. A. Beach; *A History of Domesticated Animals,* by F. E. Zeuner; *Religion in Primitive Culture,* by E. B. Tylor.

Hebrew Publishing Company: *Sephath Emeth. Order of Prayers for the Entire Year.*

Hogarth Press: *Collected Papers on Schizophrenia and Related Subjects,* by H. F. Searles.

Holt, Rinehart and Winston: *The Sane Society,* by E. Fromm; *The Outermost House,* by H. Beston.

Humanities Press: *Lunacy, Law and Conscience,* by K. Jones.

International Universities Press: *War and Children,* by A. Freud and D. T. Burlingham; *The Nonhuman Environment,* by H. F. Searles; *The Image and Appearance of the Human Body,* by P. Schilder; K. A. Menninger, "Totemic Aspects of Contemporary Attitudes Toward Animals," In *Psychoanalysis and Culture,* G. B. Wilbur and W. Muensterberger (Eds.); "The Universality of Symbols," by A. A. Brill In *Yearbook of Psychoanalysis; The Experience of Reality in Childhood Schizophrenia,* by A. M. Des Lauriers; The Selection from "The Analysis of an Eight-Year-Old Girl With Epilepsy," by S. Fraiberg, In E. Geleerd (Ed.) *The Child Analyst at Work.* Copyright 1967 by International Universities Press.

Journal of Child Psychology and Psychiatry: "Patterns of Response to Physical Contact in Early Human Development," by A. R. Schaffer and P. F. Emerson.

Journal of Projective Techniques and Personality Assessment, "The Animal Symbol in the Rorschach Test, and an Animal Association Test," by W. Goldfarb.

The Journal Press: "The Cat and the Child" by G. S. Hall and C. E. Browne, In the *Pedagogical Seminary.*

P. J. Kenedy & Sons: *A Priest and His Dog,* by J. Gautier. Reprinted with permission of P. J. Kenedy & Sons.

KTAV Publishing Company: "Animals," by S. Cohen, In the *Universal Jewish Encyclopedia.*

Little, Brown: *The Adolescent in Psychotherapy,* by D. J. Holmes.

Liveright Publishing Corporation: *Patterns of Psychosexual Infantilism,* by W. Stekel, Permission of Liveright Publishers, New York. Copyright 1952 by Liveright Publishing Corporation.

L. Cole Lowie: *Cats and People.*

McGraw-Hill: *The Naked Ape,* by D. Morris.

C. V. Mosby: "Some Interview Techniques in Child Psychiatry," by H. Caplan, In *Journal of Pediatrics.*

The National Association for Mental Health: "I Wrote about Dogs," by J. H. S. Bossard; "The Dog as a 'Co-Therapist' ", "Pets: a Special Technique in Child Psychotherapy," by B. M. Levinson; In *Mental Hygiene.*

National Council on Family Relations: "A Neglected Member of the Family," by N. N. Foote in *Marriage and Family Living.*

The National Humane Review: "The National Humane Review Attends a Pet Show for Handicapped Youngsters,"; "Editorial."

Thomas Nelson and Sons Ltd.: *Animals and Men,* by N. H. Dembeck.

W. W. Norton: Reprinted from *Insight and Responsibility* by E. H. Erikson by permission of W. W. Norton. Copyright (c) 1964 by E. H. Erikson.

Oxford University Press: *The Dialogues of Plato,* translated by B. Jowett.

Parents Magazine: "Baby Meets Dog," by J. Chapman.

Pediatrics Digest: "Some Observations on the Use of Pets in Psychodiagnosis," by B. M. Levinson.

Pet Fair: "Children Need Pets," "When Children Fear Animals," by B. M. Levinson.

Pet Shop Management: "The Child and His Pet," by B. M. Levinson.

Psychoanalytic Quarterly: "On the Role of Animals," by M. Heiman.

The Psychoanalytic Review: "The Role of Animals in the Unconscious," by S. E. Jelliffe and L. Brink. Reprinted by the *Psychoanalytic Review,* Volume 4, through the courtesy of the editors and the publisher, National Psychological Association for Psychoanalysis, New York, N.Y.

Psychological Reports: "Pet Psychotherapy: The Use of Household Pets in the Treatment of Behavior Disorders in Childhood," by B. M. Levinson.

G. P. Putnam's Sons: *In the Beginnings. Early Man and His Gods,* by H. R. Hays.

Random House: *Key Concepts in Psychotherapy,* by E. Singer.

Routledge & Kegan Paul: *Homo Ludens,* by J. Huizinga; *Lunacy, Law and Conscience,* by K. Jones.

Rutgers University Press: *God Had a Dog,* by N. Leach.

W. B. Saunders Company: *Behavior Problems of Children,* by E. Verville; "Interpersonal Relationships Between Pet and Human Being," by B. M. Levinson, In *Abnormal Behavior in Animals,* M. W. Fox (Ed.).

Science: "Affectional Responses in Infant Monkeys," by H. F. Harlow and R. R. Zimmerman.

Charles Scribner's Sons: "Animals," by N. W. Thomas, In *Encyclopedia of Religion and Ethics,* Vol. I.

Sidgwick and Jackson, Ltd.: *Working Dogs of the World,* by L. B. C. Hubbard.

Simon & Schuster: *Journey to the Far Amazon,* by A. Gheerbrant.

Slingerland-Comstock: *Animal Pets: A Study in Nature Education,* by B. C. Cady.

Smith Ely Jelliffe Trust: "Therapy at the Zoo," by N. E. Berl, In the *Quarterly Journal of Child Behavior.*

South Atlantic Quarterly: "Greek and Roman Pets," by A. M. Gates.

Springer Publishing: *Psychotherapy for the Whole Family,* by A. S. Friedman et al.

This Week: "Someone Besides People," by L. Lieber. Reprinted from *This Week Magazine.* Copyrighted 1963 by United Newspapers Magazine Corporation.

University of Pennsylvania Law Review: "The Prosecution and Punishment of Animals and Lifeless Things in the Middle Ages and Modern Times," by W. W. Hyde.

Veterinary Medicine/Small Animal Clinician: "Objectionable Behavior in Pet Animals," by J. Antelyes.

A. T. Watts & Sons: *Just So Stories for Little Children,* by R. Kipling. Permission of Mrs. George Bambridge, the owner of the Kipling copyrights.

Yale University Press: *The Healing Gods of Ancient Civilizations,* by A. W. Jayne.

CONTENTS

PET-ORIENTED CHILD PSYCHOTHERAPY

Chapter 1

HISTORICAL BACKGROUND

Although the exact date when man began to domesticate animals and use them as pets is not known, there is little doubt that animals have played a most significant role in the development and psychological economy of the human organism. It is not an accident that man's earliest art expressions were portrayals of animals. The black and red paintings of leaping bison and galloping horses done by Paleolithic man in the caves of Altamira are ranked by some art critics among the most expressive artistic statements ever made by man (Lewinsohn, 1954).[1]

To capture animals in paintings was indeed a remarkable accomplishment, but to make wild animals captives must have been, in its own way, an equally monumental achievement. Early man must have met many failures in his first efforts to retain or imprison wild animals in outdoor pens. And the rearing and domestication of these animals undoubtedly demanded a new and special kind of human patience.

When man no longer constantly needed to hunt wild animals, he, too, left the wilderness and became domesticated. As a matter of fact, Zeuner (1963) states that the adoption of pets seems to have coincided with the beginning of the permanent settlement of people and the change of "natural environment into a man-made one" (p. 40). Lorenz (1952) remarks as follows: "The pleasure which I derive from my dog is closely akin to the joy accorded me by the raven, the greylag goose, or other wild animals that enliven my walks through the countryside; it seems like a reestablishment of the immediate bond with that unconscious omniscience we call nature. The price which man had to pay for his culture and civilization was the severing of this bond which had to be torn to give him specific freedom of will" (p. 126). Because of the close relationship between the pet and the human being, some writers have gone so far as to posit the "theory" that the pet domesticated the human being. It could very well have been that when man first began to modify his environment and hence to lose contact with it, he felt a great need to strengthen his contact with nature through the adoption of pets.

During the Ice Age, about ten thousand years ago, man actually began to interfere with his material environment and to destroy it. Significantly, the people who were then most advanced in the modification of their environment, the Natufians of Palestine, who lived at what is the present site of Jericho (Zeuner, 1963), had domesticated the dog and possibly the goat at approximately 6300 B.C. Also, "it thus appears probable that the Arabian wolf had been taken into domestication by the ninth millennium B.C." (p. 64). Throwing food to wild dogs that invaded human campsites is considered one of the factors in the domestication of dogs. These acts may seen as "elementary manifestations of the solidarity of life." Many higher animals that have developed a social medium of some sort behave in such manner unless enemies. "Animal friendships between cats and dogs, or, stranger still, between cats and tame birds," are examples of this solidarity. Man's desire to keep all sorts of pets is manifested at its peak by the naturalist who finds supreme satisfaction in being in harmony with living creatures (p. 39).

DOMESTICATION OF ANIMALS

"In the subjugation of the dog, the primeval man forged one of the links in the chain of his own civilization" (Hubbard, 1947, p. 125). Of the various theoretical reconstructions of the origin of domestic animals, any or all may be valid. For instance, Reed (1959) feels that the domestication of animals resulted from man's desire to use pets as decoys. Sauer (1952) indicates that some animals, such as the mummified cats that were buried in Egypt, were domesticated for religious reasons. Proverbially and in fact, the cat has many traits which do not lend themselves to submission or friendliness. In human-cat relationships, the cat rather than man is usually the master. Even to this day, the cat tends to "walk alone" and retain indomitable characteristics which make man consider the cat wild. This is not at all true of dogs. Dogs like to live in packs like wolves or perhaps like men. The dog is generally more sociable, trainable, and submissive. Perhaps the dog was too man-like and docile to be deified.

The reasons for adoration of animals may also be symbiotic. Morris (1967), for example, thinks that the "most ancient symbiont in our history is undoubtedly the dog" (p.218). The dog may have made it possible for the man to herd and to dominate the ungulates (goat, sheep, reindeer). Undoubtedly, hundreds of species of animals were available to primitive man for domestication. Early man must have experimented with the young of different species for adaptability and suitability for "pethood." Those eventually chosen were social animals that even under natural or wild conditions formed "elaborately organized groups" (Scott, 1962, p. 3). Animals have generally played a great role in human ecological adjustment. Just as credible a reason as any for the domestication of animals is their use as pets. In other words, there is as much reason to believe that man's psychological needs were the primary cause for the domestication of animals as that man needed to use animals for such material purposes as the saving of human labor and the satisfaction of a hunger for food.

"It cannot surprise, therefore, that several authorities believe that the habit of keeping young animals as pets is at the root of domestication in general. In this form it is certainly an overstatement, but it is conceivable, and even probable, that pet-keeping provided one of the bases on which domestication on an economic scale developed later on. The mothering instinct of the human female may well have played a part in this process, too" (Zeuner, 1963, p. 39).

It is to be noted that in the process of domestication and due to the fact that we keep our animals as perpetual juveniles (Zeuner, 1963), they lose some of their desirable attributes. Thus we find that wild rodents learn much more rapidly than their domesticated cousins (Kavanau, 1961; Lockard, 1968).

Although the domestication of animals for food and labor may have and probably did coincide with their adoption as pets, the two roles must not be confused or equated. The domesticated animal was strictly a "servant" of man. His cousin, the animal pet, became in short order man's master. The different functions obviously developed to satisfy different human needs. The former catered to man's soma—the latter to man's psyche. That occasionally animals had dual or overlapping roles was as inevitable as the human confusion between the roles of a wife and a mistress. It undoubtedly came to pass that one lamb in a flock responded affectionately to his master, possibly followed him, lay at his feet, licked his hand, nestled up to him when it was cold, and offered many contactual comforts. What pleasure! How satisfying to the ego! How soothing and cheering when loneliness attacked. Did the master, the shepherd, also send this lamb to slaughter? Literature is full of stories that reveal man's favors and devotion to special members of a herd or flock.

There seems to have been a universal need and affection for pets which took different forms in different cultures and ages. Nevertheless, man in every generation found reaffirmation of his unity with nature and with the elemental forces of nature which maybe symbolized by God. It gives man a point of reference and support, and to some people, an assuagement of existential anxiety. It appears that the possession of pets symbolizes this unity with nature and thus satisfies some deep human needs. Human beings always had an affection for pets as indicated by the quotation from Darwin (as cited by Sloan and Farquhar, 1925): "It is certain that associated animals have a feeling of love for each other" (p.206). Pets have been part of human history from primitive societies through ancient and medieval worlds and finally up to our modern times.

PETS AND NONLITERATE PEOPLE

Primitive man, with his precarious hold on life, looked to the animal kingdom for support and treasured his pets as providing him with some modicum of security. The Dobus legends stress the solidarity between man and his dog. The importance of a dog to the Dobus is illustrated in the following (Fortune, 1937):

Among the Dobu Islanders of the Western Pacific

> a man normally cares more for his dog than for mere acquaintances. Also cases of a man spearing his wife out of affection for his dog, which she had treated shabbily over food, have come before the white courts. Not that a dog is not eaten in the last resort-that is always the case. There is a relationship term in Dobu to express the particular relationship between a man and his dog, a term that cannot be used in any other connection. I do not mean that wife-spearing is frequent. But it will be apparent that the man-dog relationship is socially important. In one aspect it has the point of helping to maintain his social value against woman's power in a matrilineal society. Women do not own dogs. The unfortunate animals have become involved in marital disagreements. In quarrels the man may break his wife's cooking pots; she may be unkind to his dog" (p. 267).

Among the most primitive tribes that have discovered fire but have no other amenities, the difference between animal young and human young seems to be minimal. The Australian aborigine women as well as New Guinea women suckle puppies at their breasts (Menninger, 1952). A recent expedition to the Amazon found the Guaharabi women, one of the most primitive tribes in the Amazon forests, indiscriminately suckling animal puppies and human infants (Gheerbrant, 1954).

A counterpart of this practice may be found in the legend of Romulus and Remus who were suckled by a wolf. Even the scientific mind of the twentieth century was eager to accept such legends as partly factual and uncritically accepted stories of feral children who were brought up by animals (Gessel, 1941). Even though these studies of feral children are today viewed as a hoax, nevertheless the existence of such stories and their acceptance as verity emphasized the deep-seated yearning of an individual for a confirmation of the benevolence of the animal world as man's ally in his struggle against the elemental forces of nature.

PETS IN THE ANCIENT WORLD

Pets were popular in the ancient world; just like today, the wealthy owners of pets spent untold sums of money on their favorite pets. The sacred dogs of China had a special place in the Emperor's Court. They also helped to form the Emperor's bodyguard. They slept with him and ate food prepared for the Emperor (Trew, 1940). Nero's wife had her mules shod with gold. Other favorite pets, like deer, were decorated with flowers and precious jewelry, their horns gilded. They were bathed and combed and permitted free access to their owners homes (Gates, 1931). Children could ride doe and he-goats. Sheep and goats were also occasionally hitched to children's wagons. In certain Roman households, bears, lions, and tigers roamed freely in their masters' courtyards and in the street. Sometimes this would lead to lawsuits (Freud, 1960). To make them harmless the animals frequently were overfed and occasionally declawed and detoothed.

In ancient Egypt, household cats were held in great esteem. They were very well taken care of, frequently ate from the same plate as their masters, were often bedecked with jewelry, and when ill were medicated. Even stray cats were gently cared for and fed with specially prepared tidbits (Dale-Green, 1963).

Since it was believed that the cat was immortal, a special effort was made to preserve the body so that she would have a place to return to. The cat was embalmed, placed in a coffin and buried in a sacred vault in a stretch of land along the banks of the Nile preserved as the burial places for cats. Food was placed in the tombs so that the cat's soul would have nourishment on its way to the nether world. The cat's family would shave their eyebrows as a sign of mourning (Dale-Green, 1963).

Gates mentions that next to the dog the horse was second in popularity. Because of the fondness of ancients for certain animals, some were very expensive. The horse Bucephalus cost approximately $16,000 (Gates, 1931). Geese played a role in ancient Greece and Rome similar to that of cats today. Snakes were popular, followed their masters around, and were even permitted to eat at the table. In ancient Thrace and Macedonia, women nourished snakes at their breasts (Gates, 1931). In Greece, dogs were used to guard certain temples and were sacrificial animals. Mice, birds, quail, sparrows, magpies, thrush, partridge, and parrots were also very popular. Cranes were tamed and trained not only to move mechanical devices but to engage in formal fights like cocks (Gates, 1931). Gates (1931) remarks that in ancient Greece and Rome, there was a much closer relationship between "man and many of the lower animals" (p. 419). Yet this closeness to animals did not seem to inhibit or prevent social relationships among humans. As a matter of fact, "the prevalence of animals as companions or servants of the Greeks and Romans seems not to have contributed appreciably to the lack of participation in sports" (Gates, 1931, p. 419). However, some writers, philosophers and statesmen vigorously objected to this practice. While Ovid wrote poetry in praise of his mistress' parrot (Halliday, 1952), a Greek poet, Eubulus (fourth century B.C.) complained that too much love was shown to monkeys, sparrows, and geese. Plutarc reports that Caesar once saw some wealthy strangers in Rome carrying puppy dogs and monkeys up and down with them in their arms and embracing and making much of them. Not unnaturally he wanted to know whether the women were unaccustomed to bearing children. It was subtle reprimand gravely reflecting upon persons who lavish the affection and kindness which nature has implanted in us to be bestowed on those of our own kind upon brutes.

Socrates stated: "... I have a passion for friends; and I would rather have a good friend than the best cock or quail in the world. I would even go further, and say the best horse or dog" (Jowett, 1937, p. 40). However, the sorrow of the masters upon the death of their pets was sometimes very pronounced even in the ancient world which was ordinarily callous to human suffering and death. Poets felt called upon to ridicule what to them appeared to be an unbecoming grief.[2] Thus, Theophrastus (372–278 B.C.) described the man of petty ambition who on the death of his

"Little Melitean dog" would erect a tablet with the inscription, "A Scion of Melita" (Jowett, 1937).

THE USE OF ANIMALS IN RELIGIOUS PRACTICES

Primitive man, in his attempt to be close to nature and to propitiate its hostile forces, evolved many beliefs about animals as well as ceremonials to indicate his unity with them. Some primitive people believed and still believe that humans descended from animals. In these tribes, the animal ancestor generally became the totem.

A totem is "an animal, either edible or harmless, or dangerous and feared; more rarely the totem is a plant or a force of nature (rain, water) which stands in a peculiar relation to the whole clan. The totem is first of all the tribal ancestor of the clan, as well as its tutelary spirit and protector; it sends oracles and, though otherwise dangerous, the totem knows and spares its children. The members of the totem are therefore under a sacred obligation not to kill (destroy) their totem, to abstain from its meat or from any other enjoyment of it" (Freud, 1938, p. 808). Totemism may also be defined as "a relation between a group of human beings and a species of animals characterized by three main features: (a) the assumption by the totem kin of the name of the animal; (b) the prohibition of the intermarriage of persons of the same totem name, and (c) respect paid by every member of the totem kin to the totem animal" (Thomas, 1940, p. 500). There have been different interpretations more recently that incorporate some of the psychological dynamics of this practice. According to Lewinsohn (1954), the totem, representing as it does the cumulative spirit and experience of animal and human ancestors, functions as the conscience of the tribal community, symbolizing the animal revenge to which humans may be subjected, perhaps because of the evils of the past.

Zulus (Howells, 1948) considered certain harmless snakes as their ancestors and snakes became important totems in their spiritual rituals. Zulus also believed that dead men can become snakes. Not only do these people offer food to snakes, but when a snake which is a totem animal is slain, it may not be eaten.

The Australian aborigines, on the other hand, developed totemism as their only recourse in an effort to come close to a niggardly and an inimical nature. As pointed out by Howells (1948): "So the Australians, who can in no wise control nature, take the second course and surrender to it, align themselves with it and make themselves part of it, and not a separate, embattled species of creature" (p. 201).

When we consider totemism or the worshiping of animals, we must remember that it implies that the psychic development of man had retained quite a bit of the psyche of the animal from which he descended. Animals have become the outer symbols and projections of man's inner semiconscious and unconscious drives and desires. Thus, when we study the worship of animals, we must realize that animals per se were not worshipped. However dimly it may have been perceived by the worshipers, the focus of worship was primarily on what the animals symbolized.

In the Amazon region, Guaharibos believe themselves to be descendants of monkeys and the Piaros consider the lamentins, whale-like animal creatures of the Amazon River, to be their grandmothers (Gheerbrant, 1954, p. 111). Animal worship, which was widely spread in the ancient world was another method evolved by primitive man in his effort to be on friendly terms with nature. There are, of course, many theories to explain why animals were regarded as sacred. As was pointed out previously, in the eyes of the primitive man, a certain totem animal was considered an ancestor. Since the spirits of the deceased parents were held in awe, it was only a natural step to try to propitiate these spirits with sacrifices and to begin to deify them. Thus we have the beginning of the worship of animals (Jones, 1955). Some savage tribes had great fear of the animals they were surrounded by and were forced to kill these animals in order to survive. They tried to make amends to the spirits of these animals, and to the great spirit of the animal species killed, by offering sacrifices and by deifying these animals (Tylor, 1958).

At first, human beings were sacrificed to the gods. Later on, animals were sacrificed as substitutes for human beings (Lewis, N.D.C, 1963–64). This transition is vividly illustrated in the biblical story of Abraham and Isaac where a ram was substituted for Isaac. Later on, with the spread of civilization, different gods began to symbolize different ethical, physical, and social attributes and certain animals that were considered more important were worshiped more extensively than others.

In ancient Egypt, the worship of cats was part of the cult of the Goddess Bastet. The cat was "her animal incarnation." Pictures and sculptures of cats of all kinds and shapes, made of all kinds of materials ranging from gold to mud, were very popular (Dale-Green, 1963). "A story is told of how a Persian army once won a victory over Egyptians by taking advantage of their reverence for cats. The Persians were besieging an Egyptian fort when their king had the brilliant idea of ordering his soldiers to throw live cats over the walls. The defending troops apparently allowed the city to be captured rather than risk injuring the animals they knew to be sacred, and which they half suspected to be divine" (p. 7).

Cats' eyes glow in the dark as the pupils of the eyes expand and contract. They have come to be associated with the moon. The moon waxes and wanes at night, like the cats' eyes, hence the cat became a moon goddess determining the destiny of human beings and even in control of the weather and the ties of the sea (Dale-Green, 1963, p. 142). In Japan, certain sects still believe that a cat with a black patch on its back is housing the soul of an ancestor. In Siam, cats play important roles in the burial of the king, in his coronation, and in many religious ceremonies (Dale-Green, 1963). Dog worship in ancient Egypt was associated with Syrius, the dog star. Syrius was worshipped in ancient Egypt as his rising was the beginning of the New Year and a presager of the flooding of the Nile valley upon which the livelihood of the people depended (Sloan and Farquhar, 1925). The god Anubis had the head of a dog and the body of a man and was responsible for the protection of the soul of the dead on their voyage to the underworld (Sloan and Farquhar, 1925).

Some animals are beneficent and others are to be avoided because they are harmful. The Dobus, for example, believe that: "A monstrous dog called Weniogwegwe, that dates from the Creation still roams in the forest at night, and many men have seen his great red eyes; one, I met, had even given his flank a resounding whack with a paddle. He is as big as a house and his eyes are like fires" (Fortune, 1963, p. 59).

Many nonliterate people ascribed the eclipse of the sun or the moon to its being swallowed up or attacked or in some other way molested by dogs. Beating dogs to make them howl, these people believe, would serve to relax the hold the dogs in the sky have on either the moon or the sun (Leach, 1961). In Nepal, "dogs are worshipped and garlanded with flowers at a festival called the Khicha Puja. Among the Bhotiyas, a Himalayan tribe, once every year a dog is made drunk with bhang and stoned to death in the belief that no diseases can fall upon the village for a year thereafter, because the dog as a scapegoat, has taken them away" (Leach, 1961, p. 176).

In the primitive Indo-Iranian beliefs, the dog is the property of Ahura Mazda, the chief god, and is thus a sacred animal. The dog could purify a corpse (a most unclean thing) by merely looking at it. The *Venidadad,* the Bible of the Zorostrians, has two books discussing in great detail the care, treatm and protection of the dog. Severe penalties are imposed on any one who in any manner mistreats or kills a dog. To dogs, as well as birds, is assigned the task of devouring the dead (Leach, 1961).

Pythagoras believed in memepsychosis, that is the rebirth of the individual either in animal or human form. He preached the transmigration of human souls into animals and whenever a favorite disciple would die, he would hold a dog to his mouth to catch his spirit (Papashvuilly and Papashvuilly, 1954). The Egyptians believed that immediately after the death the human soul entered into an animal where it remained for 3,000 years before returning to the human body.

The variety of sacred animals has been so extensive that, in the course of man's history, almost every species has gloried in a godly or reigning day. The snake, as such, was worshiped in many different countries and to him were ascribed many human virtues. For example, the Bible mentions the cult of the Brazen serpent. In some districts of India, cobras are venerated and are not killed even when they bite human beings. The person bitten do not look for remedies as they are considered to have been justly punished for some crime or transgression committed (Hopley, 1956). In sixteenth century Sweden, snakes were household deities, and in certain remote areas of India and in Japan, the snake is still worshiped.

The Parsees of India venerate the cock as the symbol of the sun (Dembeck, 1965). The Gauls used the cock for their symbol of virility and pride. Horses came in for their fair share of attention, too. Riding horses was first mentioned in the time of Hammurabi, about 2,000 B.C. in Mesopotamia. Earlier, the horse had been a draught animal used for military purposes. However, to the Greeks the horse was a heroic figure recognized for his beauty which appealed to them more than his utility. Many legends presented the horse as godly in origin. The first horse was called Arion and supposedly sprang from the union of Poseidon and Demeter. In Greek myth, horses symbolize foaming waves. Pegasus, the flying horse sprang from the head of Medusa and bore the poets up into the realm of fantasy. In the *Theogony* by Hesiod, Pegasus is described as a spirited war horse that brought thunder and lightning to Zeus (Lewinsohn, 1954).

Then, of course, there is the Phoenix, the wonder bird which, according to Herodotus, flew every 500 years from Arabia to the temple of the sun at Heliopolis to sit beside its father's remains. The Phoenix was a splendid heron with feathers of glittering gold (Lewinsohn, 1954).

THE PROPHETIC POWERS OF ANIMALS

Ancient legends and myths are steeped in man's belief that animals have prophetic powers. Not only did these long-ago people look to the animal kingdom for predictions of the future, but ancient man further interpreted animal symbols as signs of the will of god. Thus, according to the ancient Greek myth, "Cadmus had to follow a cow for a long time before she settled down to show him where to found a town." Similarly, "the ancient Aztecs wandered until they saw an eagle sitting on a cactus" with serpent in its mouth before the location for Mexico City was chosen (Howells, 1954, p. 71).

"Cynomancy is divination from the action of dogs. The belief that the howling of a dog indicates coming death is so widespread" that even modern man is a bit frightened when he hears a dog howl in the night. "In Formosa, when the dog howls, the family sends for a priest, anticipating the death of someone in the family" (Leach, 1961, 9. 316). The ancient Chaldeans, who were master soothsayers, also interpreted with great care the actions of dogs. The color of a dog entering the temple could signify whether the gods would desert it, remain in it, and even whether the temple would be robbed (Leach, 1961). The Bible also states, "Dogs howling predict death" (Leach, 1961). In Greece, the howling of dogs was considered a bad omen. "When the Angel of Death comes into a town, all the dogs know it and freeze in their tracks! Sometimes a man will push his dog forward to it, thus causing the dog's death and saving his own life" (Leach, 1961). In Ethiopia, the inhabitants would elect a dog for their king. By growling or wagging its tail, the dog would indicate whether a favorable decision was to be made (Trew, 1940). "Quaint indeed are the omens drawn from the behavior of dogs. When a white dog pisses on anyone, poverty will overtake him; if a black dog does the same, sickness will seize the man; if a brown dog does the same, that man will be joyful" (Hays, 1963, p. 68).

In biblical times, "animals were frequently used in divination; the weasel, bird and fish being especially mentioned" (Cohen, 1939, p. 325). And even today, a species of divination exists in the form of popular superstition and folklore regarding the meaning and the behavior of certain animals. If a cat washes herself, guests may be expected to arrive according to Jewish folklore. " 'Thrice the brindle cat has mewed' is a significant of evil to befall the household" (Hall, 1904, p. 13). If a cat jumps over a coffin, she must immediately be killed or a great misfortune will follow. Similarly, it was believed that "if a cat sneezed on a wedding day, she brought good luck to the bride" (Hall, 1904, p. 14). If a kitten comes to a house in the morning, it is lucky; if in the evening, it portends evil of some kind, unless it stays to prevent it (Hall, 1904, p. 14). In Lapland, black cats are thought to be reincarnated relatives and their opinion is asked for when family affairs are decided. The cat's advice is always sought regarding the weather before an important trip is begun (Gay, 1950, p. 257). The position of the cat's tail was believed, a few centuries ago in England, to be a good indicator of the weather. If it was towards the fire in the hearth, a cold spell could be expected. If the cat licked its tail, rain would follow (Gay, 1950). Even today, many Japanese and Chinese think that black cats can predict weather conditions (Gay, 1950). If the cat licked its left eye a few times, expect guests (Gay, 1950). If the cat sneezed a few times, members of the family would have colds (Gay, 1950).

Ornithomancy was also well developed among the ancients. If the message conveyed to the augurs by the flight of birds was unfavorable, the scheduled event would be canceled. This, as a matter of fact, was also a true to the denizens of Borneo who would not built a house unless the birds agreed, and continued to show their approval throughout the construction (Howells, 1948).

Chickens also served as oracles in ancient times. "When the time came to take the auspices, the priest would draw a circle on the ground, write the letters of the alphabet about the edge, and place a grain of wheat in each letter. The sacred hen would then be released from its cage. As it pecked the grain, the letters would be carefully noted and the answer construed from them. The pulli were always consulted about the outcome of a forthcoming battle" (Dembeck, 1965, p. 200).

THE HEALING POWERS OF ANIMALS

The idea that animals were ordained to be man's servants is presented in Genesis (1:26): "And God said: Let us make man in our image after our likeness: and let them have dominion over the fish of the sea, and over the fowl of the Heaven, and over the cattle, and over all the earth, and over every creeping thing that creeps upon the earth." The Bible thus, in a sense, confirms the pre-Biblical primitive semitic custom of seeing animals as servant sand helpers and possibly as healers.

The pharmacopoeia of almost every nation has some reference to the medicinal powers of the various bodily parts of certain animals. Frequently, the animal and its particular organ were selected because of the symbolic meaning and the supernatural powers construed to that animal in a particular culture. The cat, for instance, has wide-spread medicinal use in ancient cultures. "The imaginary uses of the cat have been far greater than the actual especially in medicine-medieval literature furnishing abundant evidence of the superstitions in this respect. Some of these cures are very curious and evidently connected with a belief in the supernatural powers of a cat. A cure for erysipelas was to cut off a cat's ear and let the blood drip on the affected part. A recipe for preserving the eyesight was to burn the head of a black cat to ashes and have a little dust blow into the eyes three times a day. A whitlow could be cured by placing the affected finger a quarter of an hour each day in a cat's ear; and the fat of the wild cat was considered a remedy for epilepsy and lameness" (Hall, 1904, p. 4). In the Middle Ages, certain European farmers who believed in the magic powers of the cat, in order to ensure the future fertility of their fields would put a cat in the last harvested bundle of corn, thrash the bundle until the cat was dead, cook and eat the cat (Rice, 1968).

In Babylonia and Assyria, Gula, the healing deity whose emblem was a dog, was worshipped by physicians (Siegrist, 1951). Dogs were also used for healing at the great shrine dedicated to Asclepius at Epidaurus in Greece. Tablets at the shrine indicated that the healing occurred through the dogs licking the patients. Furthermore, to promote the healing, the Athenians would offer sacrifices to the sacred dogs and to "dogs leaders" who were apparently some kind of a deity (Halliday, W.R., 1922). "If a man thought he was in danger of going insane, he carried a dog about with him in the belief that it would keep the Evil at bay" (Trew, 1940, p.46).

Almost every part of the ox was used for medicinal purposes in ancient Egypt. The pig's brain, the gall of tortoises, blood, and excrement of animals were also used (Lewis, 1964). In ancient Rome, women in labor were medicated with the feces of eagles, hawks, and vultures to assist in expelling the child from the womb (Lewis, 1964). According to Pliny, stomach pains could be healed by transmitting them to a puppy or a duck. Sometimes the disease could be transferred to a fowl which was then set free (Tylor, 1958).

There was also a widespread belief that eating certain animals could make one handsome. Thus the ancients believed that through eating the hare's flesh one acquired charm for nine days and that eating the hare induced sleep (Hall, 1904). Ancient legends describe many medicines from animal substances. One such potion, highly prized at royal courts, was made from the horn of the unicorn. It was considered a panacea against murder plots, since it was supposed to protect one against poisons. Snakes were also thought to be healing agents and the association with the snakes was considered conducive to good health.[3] "And the Lord said unto Moses: make thee a fiery serpent, and set it upon a pole; and it shall come to pass, that everyone that is bitten, when he see it, shall live" (Numbers, XXI:8). During an epidemic, snakes were introduced in Rome (Gates, 1931).

"The serpent was a familiar animal in Greek religion and mythology as a sacred and mystic being having magic powers which were associated with prophecy, dreams, and healing. Helenos, Kassandra, and Melampous acquired their supernatural understanding and mantic powers after their ears had been cleansed by the tongue of a serpent. The serpent always had a chthonic significance. It was used as a symbol of the Underworld deities and heroes, and was frequently associated with the healing cults. The oracles of Trophonios at Lebadeia were delivered by a serpent (Jayne, 1962, pp. 222–223).

In Greece, divine healing power was transmitted through sacred serpents and dogs. A man's foot that had been badly lacerated by the bite of a wild beast was promptly cured after the wound was licked by one of the cult reptiles. Thyson of Hermione was blind but immediately recovered the sight of both eyes after they had been licked by a sacred dog. It is also told about Proklos, the philosopher, who was probably suffering from arthritis, that he had covered the part with a cloth when a sparrow scared to Asclepius plucked the cloth away and the disease vanished (Jayne, 1962).

According to legends, the sacred serpents were responsible for the selection of several places in Greece where shrines were located and the serpent as the incarnation of the chthonian hero or god was transferred when a sanctuary was established. In the temple, while the sick ones were sleeping, the priests would enter, followed by the sacred dogs and serpents. They would in certain instances direct the attention of the dogs to the diseased part. The serpents would creep over the patient and whisper the remedy for the illness. The dogs would lick the diseased part (Jayne, 1962).

"Both serpents and dogs were used in the Asklepian cultic practice as ministers of healing, usually by the use of the tongue, but it is asserted that the disciples of Asklepios sometimes recommended that the flesh of the sacred dogs be given to patients as medicine. . . . The serpent was the emblem of life and healing, and was used in the cult as a ritualistic symbol, being sacred and revered as the incarnation of the god" (Jayne, 1962, p. 284).

Women who were sterile would sleep in the temples and would have dreams of being visited by serpents. The children born thereafter were believed to have been sired by a snake-god (Jayne, 1962).

THE EVIL POWERS OF ANIMALS

It need not surprise us, therefore, that in many nonliterate societies physical illness was ascribed to the machinations of the devil who in many cases assumed the guise of an animal. Howells (1948, p. 94) reports the complete cure of such a self-deluded individual when "the doctor put a bat in a bag and took the man into a bog; then he made a small cut in the patient and set the bat free; he pointed to it as it flew away and said: 'Behold, there, the devil is gone.' "

Evil spirits seems to be highly migratory in their nature and throughout history have had the power to find domicile in various forms, from stones to trees to animals to man. "An identical mode of thinking is contained in the idea of the **versipellis,** known the world over, meaning the man who can change his skin and temporarily take on the form of an animal—the werewolf, for instance" (Huizinga, 1960, p. 141). Man spent centuries devising methods, usually part of religious rituals, for driving these evil spirits away even though this was frequently just a temporary respite.

"Under certain circumstances, it was customary to offer the demons a substitute victim for the sick person, generally a kid or a suckling pig, the sacrificial animal being killed, and the carcass being laid beside the invalid while the exorcist transferred the evil spirit to it. In the following text, Ea, the supreme healer and lord of incantation shows the method of treatment and placing the victim before Marduk, he says:"

The kid is the substitute for mankind
He giveth the kid for his life,
He giveth the head of the kid for the head of the man,
He giveth the neck of the kid for the neck of the man,
He giveth the breast of the kid for the breast of the man
(Jayne, 1962).

With the advent of Christianity, a spirit of withdrawal from the world, its pleasures and temptations began to manifest itself. Man's overt acknowledgement of his debt and dependence on nature was frowned upon. Vigorous opposition developed the worship of animals, which to the early Christians personified man's lust and subjugation to man's animal nature. This in turn created an opposition to certain popular and easily obtainable domestic pets that at one time were deities. They were transformed to their opposites: devils and witches.

During the Middle Ages, the conviction that some animals were in league with witches or possessed by witches was almost universal. Since cats are predatory night creatures, the medieval mind began to conceive particularly of cats as night prowling demons or witches or as animals in league with witches and demanding sacrificial offerings of human beings (Dale-Green, 1963). The belief that the cat was the devil's symbol (Zeuner, 1963) was particularly prevalent during the sixteenth century in France, Germany, Spain, Italy, and Scotland. Under the law, anyone who was either a witch or a lycanthrope was to be executed.

Boguet, one of the chief magistrates in 16th century France, wrote as follows: "Ugliness and depravity are shown by Satan in his carnal knowledge of the sorceresses. To some he appeared in the form of a **black man;** to others, as some beast or other—dog, cat, he-goat, or ram. Francoise Secretain has confessed that her demon sometimes appeared as a cat, sometimes as a cock when he wished to know her carnally" (Stone, 1937, p. 138).

A crowing hen called a cockatrice (a hen which developed secondary male characteristics) was considered to be a witch. Popular belief had it that a person or animal viewed by the cockatrice was doomed to death. Treated as a person, this hen was tried in court and condemned to death (Edgar, 1960). The Azande even today consider some animals as witches. "The dog has a malicious way of looking at people and is so greedy that it resembles human beings, and on account of these and other deficiencies, Azande think that dogs are often witches" (Evans-Pritchard, 1937, p.

50). This is held to be particularly true of nocturnal animals such as bats and owls.

Superstition attributed to witches the ability to "transform themselves into all kinds of animals for the performance of their diverse nefarious business." The range was broad and included "various birds, ravens, geese, ducks, owls, magpies and seagulls, rats and mice, sheep, horses, cats, toads, snakes, and hares as well as dogs and wolves and even flies and butterflies." Wherever belief in witches and their practices prevailed, there was belief that injury or death caused to the animal housing the devil or witch would inevitably bring an identical or similar "injury or even death to the witch." A Northumbrian witch testified in 1673 that "Ann Baites transformed herself in rapid succession into a cat, a hare and a greyhound merely to show off and with the applause of the Devil" (Leach, 1961, p. 160). During the famous Salem witch trials in Massachusetts (1692–1693), a dog was condemned and hanged for being ridden by a witch even though invisible (Leach, 1961).

OBJECTS AND ANIMALS ON TRIAL

Primitive man endowed everything in nature with a "spirit." From this animistic premise it was an easy step to assume that inanimate objects have a will of their own and are responsible for their acts. Even today nonliterate people punish objects considered instrumental in bringing death or any calamity to a member of the tribe. North American Indians, for example, destroy the arrow which wounded them and aboriginal tribes of Australia burn any weapon that killed a member of the tribe (Hyde, 1956). In ancient Greece, the notion that objects carry full responsibility was further advanced and legislated on. Inanimate objects such as tones, tools, beams, etc., which were instrumental in causing the death of an individual, were put on trial at the Prytaneum (Veper, 1954).

The belief that animals, because they are rational and know the difference between right and wrong, could be held accountable for their acts was prevalent in the ancient world. Among the Hebrews, an ox which killed a human being was subject to the death penalty by stoning (Exodus XXI:28–32). This belief brought about the enactment of laws for the formal court trial of animals. The ancient codes of Lycurgus and Draco provided for the trial of animals (Hall and Browne, 1904), and was based upon the ancient Greek belief that regardless of who committed the murder, whether it was committed by an animate or an inanimate object or whether the murder was inadvertent or intentional, the crime had to be expiated for otherwise great calamities would befall the people. The trials which were carried on with due process of law were further based upon the principle that "the community had been disturbed by the murder and that somebody or something must be punished" (Hyde, 1956, p. 698).

In the Middle Ages people continued to believe in the accountability of animals for their misdeeds (Veper, 1954). Animals were personified and were entitled to the same legal protection as human beings (Hyde, 1956). A distinction, however, was made between domestic animals which were tried in the ordinary criminal courts and wild noxious animals such as rats which were tried by the ecclesiastical courts. Animals were sometimes admitted as court witnesses (Hyde, 1956). The legal basis for church trials for animals was the fact that animals were considered "diabolical incarnations" (Hyde, 1956, p. 217). Both courts could impose the death penalty. The ecclesiastical court also had the power to ex-communicate animals. A duly appointed clerk would go to the places known to be frequented by the animals and thrice summon them to appear in court. If they did not appear, judgment would be entered against them by default (Hyde, 1956). Incidentally, the same treatment was accorded to very young children.

In 1457 there was an interesting trial of a sow that murdered and devoured her piglet. She was found guilty and was hanged (Hyde, 1956). In another case in 1474, a cock which had laid an egg, was burned at the stake (Hyde, 1956). Occasionally, an animal was imprisoned prior to execution. As a matter of fact, as late as the seventeenth century, books were written tending to prove that animals could reason and had free will. As late as 1906, a dog was sentenced to death in Switzerland (Hyde, 1956).

Even today, in certain nonliterate tribes, animals are considered responsible and are put to death if they transgress the law. As a matter of fact, in certain remote parts of Kentucky and Tennessee, the mountaineers try to punish animals (Hyde, 1956).

ANIMAL SYMBOLISM

Throughout man's evelopment, historical records clearly demonstrate that he has been surrounded by and connected with various animals, some of which he has made into food, others into servants, and still others into companions. One must assume that these animals have influenced man's behavior and become part of his psyche (Lewinsohn, 1954).

It is impressive to note how frequently the most significant human experiences are portrayed in the unconscious by such nonhuman symbols as plants and animals (Searles, 1960 p. 264). There must be a deep affinity between the human being and his nonhuman environment. And it is generally agreed that the symbol is more powerful in expressing ideas than ordinary words. It brings together the various levels of one's thinking into a unified whole. The symbol also indicates the conative drives in the individual, even though the meaning of the symbol changes from time to time according to the circumstances of one's life (May, 1960).

"The symbol originates in the split of existence, the confrontation and communication of an inner with an outer reality whereby meaning detaches itself from sheer existence" (Kahler, 1960, p. 53). Our speech is replete with animal symbolism. In our fables, dreams, myths, and fairly tales, the animals assume significant roles (Fortune, 1937). The varying shapes of animals, their extraordinary appearance and swiftness, their ability to fly about, provided the primitive mind with a storehouse of symbols (Freud, 1960).

Psychoanalysts see animals as symbolizing the lower nature of man, his base passions. This can be seen in the "universality of animal fantasy" (Freud, 1937) and in the fact that animals may easily be made to represent "crude and unbridged wishes" (Jones, 1959).

As was pointed out by Levinson (1968), there are few psychological studies of the meaning of animal symbols to children and adults. These have come mostly from the study of projective techniques. However, we do have a plethora of anthropological research regarding the meaning of an animal to nonliterate people and to primitive man. This symbolism will be dependent upon the level of the cultural development of the people, their religious ceremonials, and the meaning of the animal, from a social, psychological, religious, and an economic point of view.

In early German mythology, certain animals such as wolves were considered devils (Lewis, N.D.C., 1964). Birds were seen as phallic symbols, the dove as the symbol of Venus. In discussing the characteristics of the guardians of the city, who ere warriors, Plato felt that they should be like dogs who "are perfectly gentle to their familiar and acquaintances, and the reverse to strangers" (Jowett, 1937, p. 639). Argos, the Odysseus, is usually cited as an example of a dog's underlying loyalty to his master. Argos, who was a puppy when Odysseus left for the Trojan War, recognized his master after twenty years of absence (Gates, 1931)

Generally speaking, animals in everyday life symbolize "good" and "bad" drives within the human being. Quite a bit has been written about the symbolic meaning of the snake. He is seen both as a healer and a deadly killer, an animal that is extremely wise and yet treacherous (Hassall, 1919; Oldfield, 1956; Aymar, 1956). Snakes have also been considered by many people as a symbol of "resurrection and immortality" (Tylor, 1958). In ancient Greece, apes symbolized "gross wickedness, hypocrisy, and base flattery" (Gates, 1931). "The hare was sacred to Venus and often served as a love gift" (p. 415).

The **Talmud** even derived moral principles from the behavior of animals. A Talmudic passage states that, "if man had not been taught the laws of propriety he might have learned them from the animals; honesty from them, which doesn't steal from the stores of other ants; decency from the cat, which covers its excrement; manners from the cock, which courts the hen by promises and duly apologizes when he is not able to fulfill; cheerfulness from the grasshopper, which sings although it knows it is fated to die; piety from the stork, which guards the purity of its family and is kind to its fellows; chastity from the dove." In another statement, all animals are described as worshipping God (Cohen, 1939, p. 326).

The role of the animal as a scapegoat, the carrier of the guilt of the group, as illustrated in the Bible, has great mental hygiene significance. Even today, among certain sections of orthodox Jews, poultry is used as a symbolic substitution for forgiveness when the High Holy days come around. Some orthodox Jews practice the ritual of whirling a chicken around their head and then throwing the chicken on the ground as an atonement substitute for their sins on the eve of the Yom Kippur. The following prayer, which has been part of their service for many centuries, is generally said by the male (a slightly different form is used by the female) in accompaniment to the ritual described: "This is my change, this is my compensation. This cock is going to be killed and I shall enter upon a happy and peaceful life" (Sephath Emeth, p. 301).

Animal symbolism has not only pervaded our dreams and our literature but has been incorporated into the art of the East as well as the West throughout the centuries. The meaning of animal symbolism in biblical times and in Christianity can be charged, as it is below (Allen, 1967; Cohen, 1939) showing some of the similarities and differences between the New and Old Testament.

The Meaning of Animal Symbolism

Animal	*Old Testament*	*New Testament*
Ant	economy, industry, thrift	
Ass	peace	self-will
Bull		strength
Camel (female)	lust	
Cattle	wealth	
Chameleon		hypocrisy
Deer		longing for Christian salvation
Dog	evil-doers	fidelity
Dove	innocence	The Holy Spirit; the soul
Fish		Baptism
Fox		cunning
Hyena		impurity
Horse	war	
Lamb	household pet	Christ; believer; meekness of
Lark		Christians singing praises of the Lord
Lion	royalty, power, strength	courage
Owl	loneliness	darkness
Pelican		redemption
Peacock		immortality
Phoenix	immortality	immortality
Pig	unworthiness	
Ram	oppression	
Snake, serpent	treachery, craftiness	caution; prudence; the Devil
Stag	speed, grace	
Swallow	innocence	

NEW DIRECTIONS

It seems that we are now going thorough a pet revolution. Whereas in the ancient world the pet was worshipped and thus, in a sense, removed from the experiences of everyday life, we in modern times have elevated the pet to a being on a par with man. The affection of civilized man of his pets seems to have no bounds, as may be inferred from the excellent veterinary care now available. Witness also the a mammoth industry that has grown up around the various grooming, clothing, and feeding needs of pets.

A tremendous literature is extant, devoted primarily to the history, care, value, and relationship between man and his pet. Summarily, the historic highlights of the domestication of animals and the development of pets have been presented in this chapter.[4] Although this information is highly significant it only points toward the main focus of this book which is an exploration of some of the diverse psychotherapeutic uses of pets and some of the techniques that have and can be developed in the systematic and structured employment of pets in psychotherapy; a field that is completely new, relatively undeveloped and a highly promising adjunct in the mental health field.

What knowledge of pets and their many functions in relationship to man has become apparent in modern times is covered in great detail in the following chapters. It is merely mentioned here to foreshadow what is ahead for the reader. However, the historic admiration man has shown for his domesticated animal friends is epitomized in Walt Whitman's poem which it seems particularly fitting to quote at this point (Whitman, 1963).

Animals

I think I could turn and live with animals,
They are so placid and self-contained.
I stand and look at them long, and long.
They do not sweat and whine about their condition,
They do not lie awake in the dark and weep for their sins
They do not make me sick discussing their duty to God,
No one is dissatisfied, not one is demented with the
mania of owning things;
No one kneels to another, nor to his kind that lived
thousands of years ago,
Not one is respectable and unhappy over the whole earth.

NOTES

[1]Cave paintings discovered in December of 1994, in the Ardeche region of southeastern France, have been verified to be at least 30,340 years old, making them the world's oldest known paintings. The Chauvet cave, named for Jean-Marie Chauvet, who uncovered the paintings, contains more than 300 animal images. More than half of the images are of dangerous animals like lions, rhinos and mammoths, rather than horses and bisons which appeared in cave paintings which were previously uncovered. Such distinctions suggest that the beliefs, the attitudes toward animals of earlier people have changed over time. One scientist noted that such a change may point to an evolution of earlier humans myths about animals (See Cronin, 1995; Simons 1995).

[2]Twelve years later, Levinson (1981) wrote again about the issue of grief and

loss of a companion animal. Other contemporary examples of human grief responses to the loss of an animal can be found in the edited works of: Cohen and Fudin, (1991) and Kay, Cohen, Fudin, Kutcher, Nieberg, Grey, and Osman, (1988). Nieberg (1981) has also written and conducted extensive research in this area. His guide, co-authored with Fischer (Nieberg and Fischer, 1982), is the definitive work on pet loss. Quackenbush has also written extensively in this area (1981, 1983a, 1983b). Harris (1989) wrote specifically about children and pet loss.

[3]It is interesting to note that historically animals were thought to have curative powers. It is also interesting to note that the medical profession only began to take this issue seriously when it was proven to be so, first by Friedmann and her colleagues (1980) and subsequently by many others (Beck and Katcher, 1983; Friedmann, Katcher, and Meislich, 1983; Jenkins, 1986; Katcher, 1987; Katcher and Friedmann, 1980, Katcher, Segal, & Beck, 1984; Siegal, 1993; Serpell, 1991) who have also made major research contributions and did much to elevate the esteem of this novel and neonate intervention. See Friedmann (1995) for an overview of the physiological effects of pets.

[4]Connections between humans and animals have been occurring since prehistoric times. Offering support that an affectionate relationship existed between humans and companion animals, Davis and Valla (1978) reported that a human skeleton from 12,000 years ago was found holding a skeleton of a puppy. Additional insights into historical perspectives on human-animal bond connections can be found in the works of: Bustad and Hines, (1983); Clark, (1977); Fox, (1976); Messent and Serpell, (1980); and ten Bensel, (1984). Walshaw (1984) provides the reader with a contemporary perspective on the relationship between pets and people. A recent issue of the *Unte Reader* (Glenn, 1996) not only featured several articles about the relationship between people and their animals, but provided a very informative timeline (Scheib, 1996, pp. 51–61) tracing the relationship between people and animals from 12,000 B.C. to the present.

Additionally, Rowan (1987) identified several articles (Gould, 1979; Leach, 1964) which are not often cited but important to note. Similarly, contributions by (Herzog and Galvin, 1992; Ludwig and Jamieson, 1981) should also be of interest.

Chapter 2

THE PET AND MENTAL HYGIENE

At the bedrock level of human problems, it becomes apparent that no aspect of public welfare is more crucial than the maintenance of physical and mental health. This, in the last analysis, is at the core of human survival. Tremendous studies have been made to help man avoid or cure physical illness. The prevention and treatment of mental disorders, on the other hand, is a situation that can be compared with a caravan traveling through a desert of ignorance and stopping at one little oasis of knowledge after another. "The activity of psychotherapy remains no science at all . . . but a practical art . . . Even with the American genius for technology, the attention to behavior and the massive public demand for a psychiatric industry or what may be a form of sociotherapy, psychotherapy is still, as Jessie Taft put it, an intensely personal affair with intensely personal feelings.' Our research still circles around those meanings and struggles to encompass them in a scientific framework" (Shlien, 1968, p. xi). There is an ever-increasing volume of psychiatric literature while the amount of available incontestable knowledge is small indeed.

Throughout history, man has had important insights which were subsequently put to scientific use. Europeans, for instance, learned about quinine as a successful cure for malaria long after the Indians had been using the bark of the Cinchona tree for the same purpose. The witch doctors in England used the leaves of foxglove for herb tea long before Dr. Withering was able to pry the secret from a witch doctor and put it to medicinal use for digitalis. The very recent history of tranquilizers, or the use of snake venom or curare, further illustrate this. Such discoveries as the force of gravity and the fact that we need oxygen to live waited for someone who was willing to examine the obvious as well as the esoteric. This was done in spite of the objection of the skeptic who already had a "scientific" explanation for the phenomenon and therefore saw no further need for exploration. It is to be recalled that many of the major methods by which the presence of physical disease was reduced in the population were worked out on the basis of "plausible" hunches many years before the science of epidemiology had validated these measures.

Since the problem of mental disorders in children is so vast (Caplan, 1961; Kessler, 1966; Verville, 1967),[1] any plausible measure that promises diminution deserves investigation and testing. Even with the enormous escalation of scientific research, little is known concerning what brings about improvement. Some authorities in the field question whether therapy of any kind is effective (Eysenck, 1960). Furthermore, the current methods of treatment, assuming their effectiveness, are very lengthy and costly, therefore, there is a need to develop new ways of cutting down on cost and length of success treatment.[2]

One such method is through the use of an animal pet. Pets of all kinds can play an important role in helping to maintain emotional stability. Frequently, a pet is the only remaining link with reality, albeit a tenuous and sporadic connector. There have been cases of psychotics who maintained some degree of equilibrium and were able to continue to function only because some animal reinforced a fragile defense structure. A psychotic breakdown can and sometimes does occur when an animal "friend" is removed (Searles, 1960).

In all probability, the acquisition and training of pets was a defense used by man ever since he climbed out of the primeval slime, in his struggle to preserve his emotional well-being (Searles, 1960; Levinson, 1968). Searles (1960) remarks: "It is my conviction that there is within the human individual a sense, whether at a conscious or unconscious level of relatedness to his nonhuman environment, that this relatedness is one of the transcendentally important facts of human living, that—as with other very important circumstances in human existence—it is a source of ambivalent feelings to him, and that, finally, if he tries to ignore its importance to himself, he does so at peril to his psychological well-being" (p. 6).

If one has ever observed men and women feeding pigeons in the parks, it becomes quickly obvious that most of these are lonely people. Try to strike up a conversation with some of them and they withdraw with a suspicious look. Should one be successful in establishing some communication with these "pigeon-feeders," one would more likely discover that these people live alone, isolate themselves, and feel unwanted. Animals perform a singular service for them. Animals bind them to life and make them feel important.[3]

Apparently, these men and women can make contact with reality only on the basis of dispensing favors to animals who neither threaten them, intrude upon them, nor betray them. A concentrated example is visible at the zoo, any day of the week. Unconsciously, what these people are trying to do is to compare themselves with animals because they are dimly aware of the fact that many human traits are actually animal in origin and possessed by animals to the supreme degree. Lorenz (1952) indicates that "what we are wont to call human weakness is, in reality, nearly always a pre-human factor and one which we have in common with the higher animals. Believe me, I am not mistaken in assigning human properties to animals: on the contrary, I am showing you what an enormous animal inheritance remains in man, to this day" (p. 152).

In a sense, our relationship with pets crystallizes our relationship with our children. Children have been viewed as anything from burdens to blessings. Some adults have felt that the more children you have, the more workers you have. Sometimes children were considered burdens to be exposed and killed. Sometimes children were sold as slaves to the highest bidder (Bossard, 1966). It is only in the twentieth century that children have been accepted for their own worth or contribution to the family and it was only when we began to speak of childhood as worthwhile in itself, rather than as a preparation for adolescence and adulthood, that the pet came into his own.

THE ANIMAL AND INSTINCTUAL DRIVES

When confrontation with reality is too painful to face, animals may gratify indirectly instinctualness which cannot be met otherwise. For instance, there is a "sexually tinged" pleasure in the ordinary sensation brought about by petting an animal. There is ample, authoritative evidence to show that cats are preeminently capable of arousing sexual sensations (Stekel, 1959). Schwartz and Rosenberg (1955, p. 732) indicate that the cat represents a "formalized and safe expression of the phallic wish in narcissistic women." Therefore, "animals are at first libido objects, then become libido symbols" (Jelliffe, 1917, p. 271). Morris (1967, p. 206) thinks that our stroking an animal's fur gives the individual an outlet for his "ancient primate grooming urges." Menninger (1951) maintains that our attitudes toward animals are similar to those we have for people. Some of us love both animals and people; others love only animals and some neither. However, it is known that most animal lovers in cities are adults (Foote, 1956, p. 215) who apparently either do not have or cannot have or do not care to obtain a human love object.

Unfortunately, psychological problems prevent many people from fulfillment in life because they cannot satisfy their love for human beings. Some of these people, consequently, prefer animals. This, from a letter written to Joseph (1956, pp. 67–68): "I guess some people think that it is silly to love a dog so much but a dog is easier to love than some people I know." This sentiment is not as rare as one might imagine. For fifteen years of my life, I heard it expressed by a dog-walking neighbor, a lady in her late sixties when I last saw her. As I observed her over a period of more than fifteen years, her style of life never failed to intrigue me. Even before I ventured out each morning, I knew when Mrs. "X" was about to emerge from her domicile. A large bevy of birds, mostly pigeons, who inhabited the trees across the street would suddenly, **en masse**, come flying toward our houses. Within seconds, Mrs. "X" would appear with two very large bags full of bird food. An enormous ornithological retinue crowded behind her, some practically at her heels—others gently touching down on her shoulders as she moved, vigorously scattering food along the way, to her appointed feeding rounds. Weather never deterred her; nor can I remember any absence over the extended number of years. She must have enjoyed extremely good health. Little did I really know about her other than that I sometimes, later in the afternoon or early evening, would see her leaving her house with a man who was obviously a contemporary and who I assumed to be her husband. After the bird feeding, he would go back home, soon to reappear with about a dozen paper dishes of fresh beef liver for her cat friends in stores around the corner. On her third trip, she would bring out her dog. Each day she greeted me, but her remark never varied in intonation or number of words spoken. Each day as she passed me with her dog, Mrs. "X" would say, "You can trust a dog." There was usually a wry smile on her face as she spoke these words. I am, however, much indebted to her. In those thousands of repetitions, my imagination was launched by her remark. Had I written the hundreds of stories my mind contrived to explain her words, I probably would have become the most prolific writer of the twentieth century. It is just as well that none of these pathetic tales ever saw a printed page.

Menninger (1951), indicates that the animals to which we are attached usually represent "totemic" figures, a father, a mother, or some other authority figure. He recalls that in his childhood he had many pets such as pet cows, pet trees, but that the pet horses were the most important ones. He only rode the pet horse to whom he gave most of his attention. But he considers these attachments as "definite romantic and somewhat consciously erotic" (p. 13). He indicates that our attachment to particular animals is due to an unconscious transfer of feelings for a human being to whom they may not be shown. We may find many persons engaging in sexual activities with animals (Stekel, 1959), especially those who in the course of their daily activities take care of animals, like shepherds, hostlers, grooms. Such sexual behavior is considered normal by Stekel (1959).[4]

"Something between 40 and 50 percent of all farm boys have had some sort of animal contact, either with or without orgasm, in their preadolescent, adolescent and/or later histories" (Kinsey, 1948, p. 671). As a matter of fact, it is pointed out that in some Western communities where children live with animals, there may be as high as 65 percent contact. However, as soon as these young men establish relationships with girls, for whom the animals have been a substitute, animal sex contacts are usually discontinued. Many boys and girls are fascinated and sexually aroused when they observe copulation by animals (Stekel, p. 72).

As late as 1750, a man was executed for having sex relations with a she-ass. The she-ass was acquitted because, according to the sworn statements of the prior of the convent and representative citizens of the community, the animal was of exemplary behavior and was forced against its will to submit to this nefarious practice (Ford, 1951).

The ancient denizens of Mesopotamia believed that women could give birth to various kinds of animals (Siegrist, 1951). Since the equation between man and animal was made so easily, sexual relationships with animals were common. To put a stop to what the ancient Hebrews must have thought to be an idolatrous practice, the death penalty was prescribed for this activity (Leviticus 20: 15–16). The myths of the American Indians included beliefs that women had animal spouses (Alexander, 1916).

In certain primitive societies, bestiality is a capital offense; in others, it is merely considered a disgusting and inferior sex practice; and in a few others, it is accepted as a matter of course when a human outlet is not available (Ford 1951). Cases are reported of women having sex relations with dogs and of being severely injured when the dog could not free himself because of the "tie" (Stekel, 1959). Pet dogs have also been taught to participate in cunnilingus. The following story by Rasmussen (as cited in Ford and Beach, 1951) is told by a Copper Eskimo among whom intercourse between man and animal is accepted: "There was once a woman who would not have a husband. Her family let dogs copulate with her. They took her out to an island, where the dogs made her pregnant. After that she gave birth to white men. Before that there had been no white men" (p. 240).

Generally, other than the above myth, sexual relations with animals is reported to be much rarer among females than among males. Only 1.5 percent of preadolescent girls and 3.6 percent of adult females have sexual contact with animals. However, "in only 1.2 percent of the total sample (5,940) had there been repeated genital contacts which aroused the female erotically, or mouth-genital relations or actual coitus" (p. 505). Interestingly enough, the Talmud prohibits a widow from owning a pet dog, lest there be any suspicion of sexual activities (Epstein, 1935).

Occasionally an individual has so completely identified with a particular animal that he has to go through animal-like love-making before he can have a successful sex act with a human being. Stekel (1959, p. 277) illustrates the psychogenesis of this in the following case of "psychosexual infantilism":

> The younger of two boys, I grew up on a farm, in the country. Very early in life I developed a great interest in animals, especially in birds. My first toy was a little metal cock, actually a sort of whistle. My brother and I played animals for hours. Animal figures were our favorite playthings. Some of them we associated with fairy tale figures such as enchanted princes. I still preserve a little cloth monkey, and were I not afraid of being laughed at, I would even now take it with me to bed, as I used to when I was a little boy.
>
> I got my knowledge of the facts of life watching mating animals. Once I tried to abuse a hen, but the fowl raised such a ruckus that I became frightened and gave up at a very tender age, and always visualized myself as an animal in the act. It did not matter which animal; I was every one of them in turn. Besides fairy tales, it was Kipling's *The Jungle Book* which strongly spurred my imagination. I read the book a hundred times if I read it once, and I wished I had grown up among wolves.
>
> When I was in high school, I was constantly puzzled by the "strange" propensity of my classmates to run after girls. I thought of dogs and horses, and dreamed of getting rich and having a corral filled with animals. My first introduction to sexual intercourse at the time, although successful, was a disappointment as compared with masturbation accompanied by visions of animals. But I soon came across one prostitute with a bird's face, and I became her frequent guest. I had begun to notice animal features on human faces at an earlier period.
>
> A performance of Rostand's *Chanticleer* gave me an opportunity to acquire a

> discarded rooster-costume, and an "ad" in the paper brought me the acquaintance of a girl as confused as I, and the two of us enjoyed a glorious imitation of a poultry-yard romance. Unfortunately, the girl soon left for Vienna, and I was stranded again. My attempts to play the rooster with prostitutes brought only humiliation and mockery.
>
> My unhappy state became acutely tragic when, at the age of twenty seven, I became engaged to a very nice girl. I was impotent on the wedding night, and with tears in my eyes confessed everything to her. She was willing to "debase" herself—and our love—with animal personifications.

While people may become dimly or even consciously aware of the exciting sexual element in handling their pets, few realize, unless they have been psychoanalyzed, that the pet may represent father or mother or sibling. Similarly, when an individual exhibits cruelty or sadistic behavior toward animals, he may be aware of the fact that he is cruel, but not conscious of the fact that in reality he wants to harm human beings (Menninger, 1951). It is contended that an occasional man, when he comes face to face with an animal, becomes afraid of what he is trying to valiantly to forget, namely his animal nature. Such a man may be repelled by sexual activities and think that they are low and degrading (Menninger, 1951).

Occasionally, sexual relationships with animals may become so intense that an individual may develop a feeling of guilt because of betraying the animal when engaging in normal sex relations. Menninger (1951) reports the case of a salesman who, after he got married, felt guilty whenever he had sex relations with his wife, for he felt that he was betraying the mare with whom he had had a liaison.

HUMAN IDENTIFICATION WITH ANIMALS

Because animals helped preserve man's life and sanity, they sometimes became substitutes for human companions. Symbolically, they began to stand for father, mother, husband, wife, and child. It was (Menninger, 1951) natural for human beings to project onto animals, with whom they so readily identified, their own characteristics or to assume that humans possessed the characteristics of animals. This is one of the factors that makes animals so important in the treatment of human beings.

In the Biblical story of Adam and Eve, the snake symbolizes the animal nature of man, and precipitates a situation which strips man of his primordial innocence, thus pushing him into the world of reality.

Man learned that he was mortal (something animals are apparently not aware of), that he was weak, that he was afraid, and finally that he was human. Possibly then man began to look to the animal kingdom for pets with whom he could closely identify and who could protect and support him in his struggle against ferocious predatory animals.

Furthermore, it is difficult for us to "face directly with ourselves and our children the negative, mutilating, destructive impulses in us as humans and our consequent tendency to project these impulses onto animal figures who thereby become quasi-human. Our primary need is thus to cast the evil and the bad out of ourselves onto the fantasy figures of malevolent stereotypes" (Goldfarb, 1956, p. 10).

This need may have given rise to the belief prevalent in the ancient and medieval world that a human being can become an animal (lycanthropy) and that an animal can become a human being. Nebuchadnezzar, the King of Babylon, thought that he was a wild animal (Coleman, 1964). The Aztecs believed that pregnant women could be changed into animals and give birth to mice. Some primitive tribes believe that their medicine men can transmute people into beasts (Lewis, 1963).

There are many recorded instances in ancient and medieval times of mentally ill persons believing that they had been transformed into wild animals. Bucknill (as cited in Lewis, 1963–1964, p. 12), quotes a report of epidemics of belief in such transformation:

> Those suffering under wolf madness and dog madness, abandoned their homes to resort to the forests, allowing their nails, hair and beard to grow, and carrying their ferocity so far as to mutilate and sometimes to kill and devour children. In the year 1591, Peter Burgot, Michael Verdun and another were tried for this strange affliction and pleaded guilty. Peter Burgot avowed that he had killed a youth with his wolf-paws and teeth, and would have eaten him, if the peasants had not given him chase. Michael Verdun admitted that he had killed a little girl gathering peas in a garden, and that he and Burgot had killed and eaten four other girls. These three unfortunate persons were all burned alive.

In the religious dances of primitive man, the distinction between man and animal disappear in the eyes of the participants (Werner, 1957). Schilder (1950, pp. 204–205) notes: "The body-image changes continually and we triumph over the limitations of the body by adding masks of primitive peoples which actually identify the wearer with the animal."

"Savages talk quite seriously to beasts alive or dead as they would to men alive or dead, offer them homage, ask pardon when it is their painful duty to hunt and kill them (Tylor, 1958, p. 317). Many primitive tribes believed that animals have souls and therefore when a person would die they would kill animals to accompany him to the nether world where he could lead a similar but a happier existence than the one he had on earth. We find that some Eskimo tribes would slay a dog and put his head in the child's grave so that the dog could lead the child's soul to the land of the dead (Tylor, 1958, p. 56).

There was also current a belief in the transmigration of human souls into animals which is still prevalent over a large part of the globe. "The Cabbalists and their successors, the Hasidim, believed in metempsychosis and that the souls of men after death frequently passed into animals. Their stories are full of this theme" (Cohen, 1939, p. 326).

We further learn that some primitive people (the Maravi) think that the souls of bad men become jackals and of good men snakes (Tylor, 1958). Some primitive people also believed that one animal species may be transformed into another (Gates, 1931).

Because of the equation between man and animal, man has also endowed the animal with human characteristics. The animal thus acquires a soul and man prays for the animal just as he prays for himself. The thought that pet has no soul horrifies man and the very idea that the pet will leave no trace when it dies is unbearable. Meller (1951) therefore brings in theological arguments to prove that the animals are immortal. Cock (1937) looks forward to a "future life" for the animals when they die; Jean Gautier (1957), a Roman Catholic priest, while not going so far as stating that pets (dogs) have souls, implies that they do have what he calls a "vital principle." "If there is an animal heaven (to use a term currently employed in secular circles), it can only be a place, supposing that it actually exists, where the animal enjoys those gratifications appropriate to his limited sentiment nature" (Gautier, 1957, pp. 110–111).

Prayers have been and are still offered for animals. Bishop (1927, p. 64) cites the following prayer from the Russian Church Liturgy.

A Prayer for Animals

And for those, also, O Lord, the humble beasts,
who with us bear the burden and heat of the day,
and offer their guileless lives for the well-being
of their countries, we supplicate Thy great tenderness of heart,
for Thou hast promised to save both
man and beast, and great is Thy loving-kindness, O
Master, Savior of the world. Lord have mercy.

Both normal and sick people identify with animals for a wide variety of reasons. An unpublished study by the author indicates that a normal child is likely to want to become a favorite, loved animal, while a disturbed child would rather be an animal, whether favored or disliked, that can protect itself against enemies or be safe from predatory attacks. This is explained by Money-Kyrle (as cited by Bender and Rapoport, 1944, p. 521) in the following manner: "In discussing the relationship between animal phobia in children and totemism, says, 'Many children develop not only a great respect and dread of certain animals but also a marked tendency to identify themselves with the very animals they are afraid of. In other words, they invent themselves like a private system of totemism; they are spontaneous.' " Sometimes people seek animal form and behavior to escape from agonizing sex conflicts (Searles, 1960). Occasionally, when a person expresses a wish to be an animal, it indicates a desire to overcome profound feelings of helplessness through identification with an all-powerful creature that can achieve the impossible and change into anything it desires at will (Searles, 1960).

There is the further possibility that because of the stresses under which we live, we may desire to resign from the human race, thus escaping from all responsibilities. We may wish to live freely and fearlessly, or we may wish to be loved and overprotected without any guilt since by not being human we no longer carry the human burdens and responsibilities.

ATTEMPTS AT PET PSYCHOTHERAPY

A relatively new aspect of mental health that has so far been all but absent in psychological literature is the use of pets as psychotherapeutic aides or aids in psychotherapy.[5] The meaning and effect of a pet is rarely discussed in child psychology texts. There are occasional scattered references, infrequent and inconclusive. One full chapter on this subject appears in a book by Bossard and Boll (1966) on the sociology of child development. On the other hand, popular literature is replete with stories about the relationship of pets to children. Inevitably the question that follows from these circumstances is: Do professionals consider this subject too humdrum, too lowbrow or "unscientific" to warrant serious consideration and investigation?[6]

In this connection, it is important to remember that Searles (1960, p. 120) maintains that "personality development in the healthy and the emotionally ill is not solely the product of man s relationship to man, but is much influenced by his relatedness to the animate and inanimate nonhuman world about him." With unconscious awareness of his reasons, man has used animals to satisfy his mental health needs for many years. More recently, however, man has begun to use the animal in a conscious manner to help him adjust.

In the middle of the eighteenth century a new kind of mental hospital, "The York Retreat," was established in England where new and then revolutionary approaches were applied to the handling of the mentally ill. Among the unusual techniques employed in this institution was the carefully planned introduction of the care of pets by the patients. This experiment is described by Jones (1955, p. 61) in the following way: "There was an airing-court in the grounds for each class of patients and each court was supplied with a number of small animals—rabbits, poultry and others—so that the patients might learn self-control by having dependent upon them creatures weaker than themselves." "These creatures are generally very familiar with the patients, and it is believed that they are not only the means of innocent pleasure, but that the intercourse with them sometimes tends to awaken the social and benevolent feelings," commented Samuel Tuke (Jones, 1955). "Every attempt was made to occupy the patient suitably. Some cared for the animals, some helped in the garden, the women knitted or sewed" (Jones, 1955).

There seems to have been no further reference to the employment of pets until some two hundred years later, despite the fact that there is every indication that "The York Retreat" found some success with their method. This type of hiatus is not uncommon in history and there are many examples of historic "rediscoveries" which have represented the loss of hundreds of years to the welfare of mankind.

One finds an experiment in the use of dogs in the AAF Convalescent Center, Pawling, New York by the American Red Cross during 1944–45 (American National Red Cross, 1962). From the report it appears that there is "little doubt that the undertaking was worthwhile and that it has met with unusual success. While the dogs offer an outlet for recreation primarily, they have been therapeutic for some patients in distracting an individual's attention from himself and presenting a responsibility for care and training which could be assumed, affording in some instances normal entry to a group."

The American National Red Cross reports further that their project for securing dogs "started with a special request from one of the officer patients. One of the lieutenants had received a serious leg injury and was scheduled to remain at the Center for some time. The lieutenant publicized among the Junior Hostess Groups that visited the Center his great desire for securing a dog as a pet. He was so urgent and enthusiastic that various groups became interested and almost simultaneously three puppies were available. The one with a slight time priority was a beautiful full-bred German shepherd puppy and he was immediately accepted. He was christened "Fritz" by his new owner and did wonders for the officer patient. The lieutenant developed increased security, ambition, and interest through his feeling of responsibility in having a dog to care for and through the dog's immediate devotion to his new master. We were fortunate, too, that the sergeant in charge of the stables at the Center had previously been in the Air Corps Canines and knew how to train dogs. He helped the lieutenant constantly in caring and training the dog."

"The success of this initial enterprise was bound to have repercussions, particularly in the Officer Patient Cottages where the dog was very much in evidence." This "produced an avalanche of similar requests from both officers and enlisted patients as well as from detachment. . . . A request form was setup. . . . The signee agrees that no accepted dog be given away or sold; that if the owner cannot keep the dog, he is to be returned to the Red Cross for redistribution." Consequently, a two-hour dog training class became a regular daily part of the rehabilitation program.

The two instances quoted above provide a record of the meager, planned use of pets in psychotherapy. Even these haphazard attempts were not known to me when the whole subject became the focus of my attention. My first insight into the use of a dog as an "accessory" in the treatment of disturbed children came about inadvertently. And it was my own dog, Jingles, who played the leading role in what proved to be a most startling drama.

Early one morning, Jingles was lying at my feet while I was busily writing at my desk when the door bell rang. Jingles was never permitted in my office when I expected patients, but this day no one was due until several hours later. Jingles followed to the door where we were greeted by a very distraught parent and child—several hours early for their appointment. This child had already been exposed to a long stretch of unsuccessful therapy. Hospitalization had been recommended. The appointment with me had been set up for a diagnostic interview, at which time I would decide whether or not to take on as a patient this boy who showed increasing symptoms of withdrawal.

While I greeted the mother, Jingles ran right up to the child and began to lick him. Much to my surprise, the child showed no fright but instead cuddled up to the dog and began to pet him. When the mother wanted to separate the boy and dog, I signaled her to leave them alone. Before the end of the interview with the parent, the child expressed the desire to return and play with the dog. With such auspicious beginnings, the treatment of Johnny commenced. For several subsequent sessions he played with the dog, seemingly unaware of my presence. However, we held many conversations during which he was so intent upon the dog that he seemed not to be listening to me although his replies were coherent. Eventually, some of the affection elicited by the dog spilled over onto me and I was consciously included in the play. Slowly, we came to the establishment of a sound rapport which made it possible to work out Johnny's problems. Some of the credit for the eventual rehabilitation of Johnny must go to Jingles who was most willing co-therapist.[7]

When presented at the Annual Convention of the American Psychological Association in 1961 (Levinson, 1961), my findings met with a mixed reception. While most of the auditors were enthusiastic, some guffawed and a few others asked whether my dog shared in the fees. This reaction was commented on by Carl Rogers (1963) who felt that it was symptomatic resistance to new psychotherapeutic techniques. I feel, however, that the reason some therapists objected to the use of the dog in a psychotherapeutic relationship was because of the anxiety which clinicians "possess along with other human beings, generally, concerning our relatedness with the nonhuman environment" (Searles, 1960, p. 25).[8]

Subsequently, many child psychiatrists and child psychologists indicated that they had similar experiences with pets, and outstanding child therapy centers offered to cooperate in further investigations. However, to indicate some of the opposition I met even in this quarter, I am citing the reply of a center whose cooperation was solicited in an experimental study of the therapeutic use of dogs (Anonymous, 1962). "Some members of our staff have expressed concern over the statement in your letter to the effect that the dog may be used as a vehicle on which quite a bit of family's aggression, resentment, sibling rivalry, etc., may be projected. Their feeling is that placing a dog in the home of an emotionally disturbed boy may not only at times not help the child, but may be positively injurious to the dog. Some members of our staff are very fond of their own dogs, and they even suggested that perhaps the project should be cleared with the ASPCA." I would like to note, in passing, that in the case where I prescribed dogs, the families were carefully chosen to make sure that no harm occurred either to the dog or to the child.

The public response in the form of radio and televisions commentaries, cartoons, newspaper editorials, featured magazine articles and a heavy volume of mail to the idea of using pets in therapy was rather overwhelming.[9] However, the general tone of the commentaries made by therapists who used pets was that the pets use is similar to that which the therapist makes of his tape recorder, dolls, puppets, finger paints, and microscope. These are useful but not crucial factors in treatment. Quaytman (1963) summarizes this point of view. Siegel (1962) advocates the use of pets as psychotherapeutic aides with children. Among those who used pets in their work with children and adults are the following: Jean Hodgin (1962), Harold L. Trigg (1962), A. Quaytman (1963), Mira Rothenberg (1960), Nise de Silveira (1966), H. Aschaffenburg (1966), Mollie Schildkrout (1967), Jon Geis (1967).

Dr. Mollie Schildkrout (1967) views pet therapy as "another variant to play therapy." She makes the follow observations:

> 1. I use my cocker spaniel, a very gentle dog with great affection for children, as a transitional object in Winnicott's sense. This is especially relevant in the case of children who collect stuffed toys as imaginary and bed companions until well into their latency years. 2. I find the dog useful as a means of desensitization in children with dog phobias. This does not exclude the use of concurrent, appropriate dynamic interpretations. 3. As a "safe barrier" in untrusting children, who, for good reason, prefer animals to humans. This is similar to your use of pets with autistic children, but I also find it applies at times in the case of neurotic children. The three of us often take walks. 4. As an area of mutual affect investment. In these cases verbalization of feeling often plays a grater role than activity. This is a modus operandi used by many therapists, with the spectrum of interest ranging anywhere from goldfish to elephants. 5. As an area for the safe exercise of rituals seen especially in obsessive-compulsive children. These patients gratify a need to say hello, goodbye and feed the dog a sweet (identification with the self) repetitively.

Most psychoanalysts have approached the problem from a different angle. They have discussed the role of the dog in dreams and symbols. They were rarely interested in finding out how the course of therapy is affected if a dog is adopted by their patient. Rather, they were concerned with the dog who was already a patient's pet and what he symbolized to the patient. Generally speaking, they felt that the animals gave the neurotic a chance "to maintain a partial sublimation" (Jelliffe & Brink, 1917, p. 271).

Dr. Jon Geis, "who practices rational-emotive psychotherapy, which treats the therapy session not as an experience per se but as a situation where the therapist is an expert teacher and the patient is helped to learn about himself and solve his problem in a rational, highly cognitive way," finds that cats are very useful as therapy aides. He reports as follows (Geis, 1967):

> I have had my cat Charlie in the room when I work with people. Charlie is an alley cat now seven years old. His colleague, Gunther, has been present for over one thousand of these hours. Gunther is also an alley cat, now under one year old. Charlie is multicolored with a mantle of white all down his front and Gunther is sleek and cream colored. Most patients have commented that the cats are quite beautiful. Sometimes they fight and hiss playfully, tearing around the room (only occasionally must they be removed because they are distracting); often they nuzzle against the patient and jump in his lap or walk over him. Charlie has a fondness for sitting on the patient's coat and both cats love to inquire into his bag or briefcase. Often the cats will be sleeping peacefully alongside the therapist or in some favorite resting place within the patient's sight. In short, both cats are friendly and frequently active.
>
> Some of the dimensions important in my use of my cats with patients include the following:
>
> 1. ***Use of the patient's reaction.*** If a patient reacts negatively, especially fearfully, to my cats, I generally find an opportunity within the session to use this as an example of irrationality of being fearful in general. "Why be afraid?" "What is there to be afraid of?" "How could he really hurt you?" "This is just like your being afraid in those other situations (specifying one)—there is nothing to be afraid of." I then go on to show the patient how he can overcome his fear by persistent self-questioning in the presence of the stimulus. That is, he can learn not to fear, or to tolerate, something (like my cats) even though he may never find it his preference.
>
> 2. ***Use of pets as ice-breakers.*** I have found pets to be useful sometimes as objects for a patient to focus on when he is anxious during the opening moments of an initial interview. Especially is this true of children and highly disturbed adults. With adults especially, I don't let them linger too long with the cats but move directly into why they have come to see me. Some patients who are nervous in such an interview will seek to distract the therapist's attention from themselves by engaging in discussion of the cats, but I have found that one can quite easily get back to business with such remark as, "Yes, but let's get back to *you*." One woman came in the door and stopped in her tracks when she saw the cats. Obviously she was very afraid. I stopped too. I waited her out to see whether she would literally require that the cats be removed, but my silently forcing her to confront her fear, while after a moment reassuring her that "they won't hurt you,"

helped her continue into the room to begin the session. Later she told me that this was the first time in her life of forty-eight years that she had ever remained in a room with cats. Always before that she had yielded to her phobic impulses, but the therapist's confrontation had helped her overcome this.

3. ***Holding imaginary conversations with pets.*** I have sometimes found it useful with children, but also with highly disturbed adults who find themselves blocked or refuse to talk, to hold conversations with my cats, which is a technique used to expose the patient to important content. Examples: "Let's suppose, Billy, that Gunther there could talk. What do you think he'd say about you? Probably he'd say that you're a friendly boy who is scaring himself when really there is nothing to be scared of. He'd say, 'Now how come Billy is so scared of talking when Charlie and I know there's really nothing that could hurt him, nothing at all. Dr. Geis is really here to help him!' " This kind of therapist response seems to be more acceptable to the patient because it is not a direct confrontation by the therapist and also is novel and interesting. Another use of this technique is to address the cats directly, telling them about the patient and his dynamics. Example: "Fellahs, Jo Anne here seems, in my view, to be on a sit down strike against her parents . . . Though she hasn't said this, that seems to be my guess. Now, if she *were* rebelling against them she'd probably . . . ."

4. ***Using pets as at-hand examples of Being.*** Most patient problems quickly get down to what the patient believes about himself. Within this therapist's personality theory it is useful to distinguish between such self-evaluative orientations as (a) extrinsic or contingent personal worth (I am worthwhile or worthless to the extent that I perform well in school), (b) intrinsic or non-contingent worth (I am worthwhile *whether or not* I do well in school, am pretty, etc.), and (c) nonevaluation (I just go ahead and go to school, be whatever I am, etc., without placing a value upon myself for being it). Regarding the non-evaluation orientation, I use the cats to illustrate and make more real this Being aspect. Example: "Now Charlie here doesn't give a good———about how much value he is to himself. He hasn't got the self-reflecting capacity that humans have. He just goes ahead and is what he is. He's more focused on *being* than on being *something*." I have found that this example often goes along way toward helping patients reorient their thinking in less negatively self-valuing ways.

IMPLICATIONS

Weigel and Straumfjord (1969) report:

The use of a dog as a therapeutic adjunct in an eighteen-hour marathon treatment group of seven male and two female college students with emotional problems. The human therapists were a psychiatrist and a psychologist: the dog co-therapist was a friendly five-year-old mongrel hound ("Blue"). The dog was present throughout the eighteen hours of the group session, and demonstrated a unique ability for equal time-sharing with each of the group members.

The introduction of the dog is shown as having a similar effect in group treatment with adults as Levinson (1961, 1968) reports with children themselves, and also between members and therapists: most members formed an early positive relationship with the dog, and later shared this mutual relationship with other group members and the therapists. In addition, interactions were generated around the "safe" topic of the dog and his behavior which had important therapeutic implications. Interestingly, three members who initially expressed fear of dogs reported that such fears had disappeared by the end of the group session.

NOTES

[1]Obviously, there are many other theorists who have addressed the mental health needs of children since Levinson first wrote this.

[2]Levinson was again ahead of his time in suggesting that there was a need for therapists to maintain and to be conscious of cost effectiveness in treatment.

[3]Several studies have been conducted with respect to people and their dogs in public places. Rossbeck and Wilson (1992) studied the issue of whether or not the presence of a dog makes people appear more likable. Sanders, Robins, and Cahill (1991) from an ethnographic perspective, also examined the experience of dogs and their owners in public places.

[4]Sexuality was a theme that Levinson frequently discussed in his work. Calling it the "dark side of the force" Rowan (1993) called for researchers and practitioners to examine the taboo issues of sexuality between animals and humans. Beck and Katcher (1983, pp. 73–77 and 216–219) also engaged in a lengthy discussion about "using an animal as a collaborator in sexual activity" (p.73).

[5]Due in large part to Levinson's contribution, there is now a growing body of literature which addresses the utilization of pets as psychotherapeutic aides or aides in psychotherapy. Prior to Levinson's work, there were few references (with the exception of Bossard and Boll's work, 1966) which discussed the utilization of animals in therapeutic situations with children. The research literature on the human-animal bond experience, methodologically flawed as it was portended by some to be, began in the 1970s with a paper by Mugford and M'Comisky (1975) and reports by the Corsons (Corson et al., 1977).

[6]This question continues to be debated among academics, human-animal bond professionals, and researchers. Levinson, himself a serious researcher, was committed, in almost all of his publications to calling for further research into the human-animal bonding experience. In a paper published in 1982, Levinson furnished an extensive analysis of his views on the future of research into this area.

Odendaal (1993, p. 2), in an *Anthrozoos* editorial, identified three important articles which he noted helped give further direction to the human-animal bond movement. "The first was a review of the value of the research studies and reports that were published up until the early eighties (Beck and Katcher, 1984). The second was the discussion of an all-inclusive theory on human-animal interaction (Kidd and Kidd, 1987) and the third related to the ethics involved in animal-assisted therapies (Iannuzzi and Rowan, 1991).

[7]The story of Jingles and Levinson is one of the most famous stories for those interested in the human-animal bond field. Although Levinson worked with other dogs in his career, none of the others were ever identified by name, except Jingles. In recognition of the contributions made by this first co-therapist, the Delta Society sponsors the "Jingles" Award at their annual conference which honors therapy and service animals who are recognized for dispensing exceptional service to people in need.

[8]Therapist's apparent uneasiness in utilizing animals in practice situations and the general anxiety of those in the helping professions with respect to discussing the utilization of animals in therapeutic situation is addressed in Mallon's (1994c) article which reviews the work of Dr. Levinson.

[9]See also Bossard's (1950) article entitled, "I Wrote About Dogs" in which he speaks about the overwhelming positive response he received when he published an earlier article (Bossard, 1944) about the mental health effects of dog ownership.

Chapter 3

THE USE OF PETS IN PSYCHOLOGICAL ASSESSMENT

Clinical assessment is much more difficult with children than with adults because children lack a stable personality structure of which there is either explicit or implicit normative data. The circularity and fluidity in their development is reflected in their test protocols; therefore, the tests tell (somewhat inaccurately) what the child's intelligence scholastic abilities, and personality traits may be, but they quite frequently fail to show how these traits and abilities are used in day-to-day situations or what roles the child plays in the family constellation.

It is a clinical truism that in a diagnostic workup, one must try to evaluate the total personality: the child's strengths and weaknesses. In psychodiagnosis, one would like to expose the child (without the latter being aware of it) to everyday life stresses in which the child's behavior and defense mechanisms are clearly delineated. Frequently, it is important to know whether the difficulty the parents are complaining about has become internalized or not. With very young children, in particular, the pet can give us valuable clues.

When he is seen professionally, the child frequently fails to reveal the reputedly deviant behavior described by anxious relatives. Even the most skilled examiner is hard put to detect and examine this behavior for tests alone. The child patient is on guard, often expecting the worst from his encounter with a psychologist. Carefully, he avoids displaying the behavior for which he knows he is being studied. In most cases, he has been threatened by his parents or other authority figures that unless he changes his behavior, he will be taken to the clinic. The child sometimes thinks that the psychologist can read his mind so he feels he must be careful. Therefore, frequently and unconsciously, the examiner reads data obtained from the case history into the test protocols.

In borderline cases[1], it is sometimes very difficult to tell from the child's projective records and other test data whether questionable behavior is a healthy attempt to cope with an impossible home situation, or whether neurotic or psychotic distortions have already affected the child's defense processes and he therefore needs psychotherapeutic interventions.

Child therapists have demonstrated that psychotherapeutic methods used with adults have to be drastically modified when used with children (Freud, 1951). For a variety of reasons, play has been shown to be the best means of communication with the child (Axline, 1947; Murphy and Krall, 1960). When a child's attention is captured by a play object he temporarily forgets his fears of the therapist and relaxes. The child is less likely to censor his replies or disguise his feelings. In addition, the way in which the child relates to and treats the play object can provide important clues for the observer.

The clinical psychologist should make provision for a play session during his study to permit the child to engage in nonverbal communication. This is an area in which a young child excels. A "must" in child psychodiagnosis is the opportunity for participant play observation. Busy clinicians generally agree with this, but claim they have no time for it; yet play sessions can easily be more telling than the CAT (Haworth, 1966; Rabin, 1968) or the Rorschach test (Klopper and Davidson, 1962; Rabin, 1968). An extra hour spent in play may avert serious diagnostic errors and save many hours in therapy.

Invaluable as the play session may be, however, its success is problematic to the degree that the child shows interest in and becomes involved with the toy or craft. Almost sure and even more revealing is the response of a child to the living toy-playmate, a pet. The use of pets gives the diagnostician an almost ideal way of observing the child in action, off-guard. On the basis of clinical experience, pets are useful in psychodiagnosis and in the play session interview.[2]

There are certain obvious advantages to the use of pets in diagnostic procedures. The pet becomes part of a standard procedure and informal norms can evolve as to what behavior is to be expected. The child's reaction becomes idiosyncratic.

Reliable indicators, not only of the child's thinking but also of his pattern of behavior and the roles he plays in the family constellation, may be obtained in this fashion. Children of all ages find playing with the dog or cat reassuring and relaxing since the psychologist seems to have brought in the animal just for "the pleasure of it." The threatening fact that he is under "examination" is forgotten by the child and the tensions are dispelled. The presence of a pet is particularly helpful when the child is not cooperative either because he is afraid of the interviewer or because he is carrying out a behavior pattern learned at home.

Through the "playing with a pet" interview, the psychologist can expect to find answers to such basic questions as: Can the child relate to the therapist? On what level? What seems to be the underlying conflicts that the child observed at home? Are there firm ego boundaries? What is the child's frustration tolerance? Does he erupt in a sudden rage at the pet or at his own inability to master the pet? Does he tend to withdraw into sullen almost autistic silence? Does the play itself have neurotic or psychotic overtones? How does the child handle his instinctual drives?

Some clues concerning the role aggression and passivity play in the economy of the child's organism can be obtained from observing the kind of activities in which the child chooses to engage with the animal. A child who perceives my dog Jingles as an aggressive animal or one who misperceives the dog's stance as threatening, may do so because the child feels aggressive tendencies stirring within himself which he finds difficult to control. It may also indicate that the child perceives the world as a dangerous place.

How the child perceives and acts to the dog's untidiness, loss of hair, and shedding all over the room, is highly significant. Does the child like to observe it or is he revolted by it? One child whose mother had difficulties in his toilet training was afraid of dirt and was overly clean. This child, in particular, liked to feed the dog little tidbits in his dish, played with the dog's shed hair, and then would repeatedly wash the dishes.

USING PETS IN THE CLINICAL ASSESSMENT OF YOUNG CHILDREN

Young children, especially at the "fantasying" age of three or four, love to be "interviewed" by a dog and very readily enter into the spirit of the game, forgetting that they are being examined. Important information is received in this manner which might not otherwise have been obtainable. Generally speaking, the more passive the examiner, the more spontaneous will be the reaction of the child. If the clinician has to interfere and becomes active, it will alter "the psychodynamics of the situation and consequently alter the play" (Murphy and Krall, 1960, p. 294).

A technique for successfully employing a dog as an interview "tool" with preschool children generally begins by sitting in a casual threesome around a table. A flexible "ritual" is followed. First, the dog "shakes hands" with the child in introduction. Then the dog "whispers" in the clinician's ear that most children have secrets which they usually share with him (the dog). Guilt over the disclosure of family secrets may thus be averted. The psychologist tells the child what the dog wishes to know, and the child tells the dog the information requested. In each case, the therapist acts only as agent or intermediary, relaying the message to the dog or the child, carefully stating that "Jingles says" or "Johnny says."

Many questions can be asked the child in this manner. I would generally begin with asking the child whether he has a pet. If so, what kind? Who wanted it? How was it obtained? Who cares for it? How do members of family, and particularly the child, feel about it? If the child does not have a pet, he should be asked whether he had one and, if so, what happened to it? If the child never had a pet, he should be asked what kind of a pet he would like to have.

Putting together the facts obtained from this questioning the therapist can profitably introduce at this point the "story completion" game (Lansky, 1968). The therapist should advise Johnny that he is going to hear a story and should proceed to tell Johnny a story based as much as possible on the case situation. If the facts obtained or thus far known about Johnny are scant, the clinician will have to invent them "intuitively." At some point the therapist should stop and ask Johnny to complete the story. Most children enter into this game willingly and consider it fun. From the endings they provide, one can often reconstruct an important family relationship situations well as gauge the child's expectations. More often than not, Johnny will complete the story with details from an incident or incidents in his own life.[3]

One such particularly revealing occasion comes to mind. It was the second visit to my office of a five-year-old boy whom I shall call Edward. This boy was so frightened of cats that my cat had to be removed from the office on his first visit and before Edward would come into my office on this day he wanted to know whether the cat was present and if so, would I please take the cat away. I reassured Edward the cat was not only not in my office but had left the house to go for a long walk in the woods. That afternoon I tried the story completion exercise with Edward. I told him a story about a little boy who was an only child and wanted very much to have a kitten as a pet, but his father wouldn't permit it. (Edward had said in the previous interview that his parents would permit him to have a pet, but he didn't want one). "One day David (the little boy in the story) was visiting with some friends in the neighborhood who had a big, beautiful brown and white cat (just like Dr. Levinson's cat, I interjected.) This big mother cat had a litter of five little butterball kittens who all looked just like their mother. They wandered all over the house, played with almost anything they found on the floor, licked your hand, stumbled all over themselves, and usually found their way back to their mother where they purred softly, drank some milk, and fell sound asleep. David fell in love with the littlest one of the kittens. Eager to find homes for the kittens, this friend offered David the kitten if David would promise to take good care of it. David was so excited he forgot that he should ask his mother's permission. He took the kitten, carrying it under his jacket gently and warmly. When he arrived at home with the kitten, his mother was waiting anxiously for him because he was a little late and it was almost dark . . . "

At this point I stopped. Edward had been fully engrossed. I asked if he would finish the story and tell me what happened when David's mother found out about the kitten. Edward picked up the thread and wove a tale that was quite remarkable. He said: "David's mother was very angry when she saw the kitten and said he would have to take it back. David cried very hard. He asked his mother over and over why he couldn't keep the kitten; it was so cute, and so sweet, and it wouldn't hurt anything, and he would take care of it. David's mother told him that he could keep the kitten overnight, but he would have to take it back in the morning because kittens are very dirty and they have fleas. When David asked his mother what fleas were, she said they were bugs—like the bugs they sometimes saw in the kitchen and that everyone could get sick from having bugs around." Edward paused at this point, but when I asked him whether the kitten was returned the next morning, he said very sadly, "No! No! No!" Edward began to cry. I asked him why he was crying and he said, "Because David killed the kitten; David killed the kitten." Edward explained that "David decided to get rid of the kitten's fleas so that his mother would let him keep it. David took the can of spray that his mother used to kill the bugs in the kitchen. David sprayed and sprayed the kitten because he wanted to make sure that it was very clean and had no more bugs. Then the kitten stopped moving. He couldn't get it to move any more. It was dead. David killed the kitten."

I asked Edward what David did then. Edward filled in the remaining details. "David went to his mother to get a doctor, but David's mother said it was just as well the kitten had died; it was dirty and it would probably have died of some disease it picked up from digging in garbage cans anyway."

Needless to say, it turned out that Edward had been relating to me most accurately an event from his own experience and one that had shocked this little boy and left him with tremendous feelings of guilt. It also revealed the depth of his mother's "dirt" phobia and her insensitivity to Edward's urgent needs.

Separation experiences from the pet may also be diagnostic. Is the child free to express his feeling of aggression toward the animal? How does he do it?

The story-completion technique should not be limited only to young children. Changing the content and the presentation, of course, it can be used with almost any age group. Adults may not participate in the "game" quite as readily as very young children but a patient with whom the therapist has established a sound relationship will generally cooperate. A college-student patient once provided some invaluable clues to her relationship with her mother through the completion of a story dealing with the acquisition of a pet.

THE USE OF PETS IN THE PSYCHOLOGICAL ASSESSMENT OF OLDER CHILDREN

The range of diagnostic techniques involving pets increase rapidly with the advancing age of the patient. The age limits indicated in this chapter are by no means fixed, however. What can be done with a very precocious five-year-old can sometimes not be used with a rather slow eight-year-old. The applications must depend, as they always do, upon the estimate and judgement of the therapist. The classifications are merely organizational conveniences into which the majority of cases I have handled fall. There have been numerous exceptions.

It is frequently important to discover a child's dominant fantasy themes. Both my dog and cat have provided amazing shortcuts toward this end. By asking my young patients what Jingles dreams about, I have been inundated with stories of dreams, usually the patient's. (There have been noncooperators, too.) From the dream material, however, much has become apparent. Are the dreams aggressive? Is the death theme dominant? One can inquire about the frequency or recurrence of the same dream?

One can learn, also, about the occurrence of nightmares and the disturbance of rest and sleep.

Of course, we are more interested in how a child feels about his parents and the role they play in his fantasies than whether what he says is true in reality. What does the child think about his parents? Does he feel that his mother is a kind person? Does the child believe that he has been adopted? Does he have the foster-child fantasy?

One of the most unusual aspects of the use of pets in psychotherapy, is the development of the "peripatetic" therapy session. Weather permitting, I like to go on dog walks with my patients as soon as the situation and the rapport indicates. Innumerable aspects of personality are revealed on dog walks.[4] The first situation that presents itself, generally, is "Who shall hold the dog's leash?" Jingles is so well trained that I can safely acquiesce when a child asks to hold the leash. How does the child accept this responsibility? Does he retain and maintain it? How quickly does he tire? Does he just drop the leash? What maturities and immaturities show up in this role? How does he react to the dog's urinating? Defecating? How does the child react to the swift approach of another dog?

In our work with children we often use food as a potent way of approaching children and developing relationships with them (the parents' consent is always obtained in advance). In a nearby refrigerator I keep an adequate supply of candy, cake, milk, and eggs. There are various kinds of dog food, also, on a nearby shelf. Occasionally food is introduced even in working with dependent adults. When a child or adult refuses to accept food, it may be a pathognomonic sign of undue suspiciousness. With a child, the refusal may stem from a fear of being harmed or a parental prohibition not to take food from strangers. What an asset Jingles has been here too! Children who would not themselves take food are often happy to become involved in feeding the dog. Some understanding of the child's family role may be obtained from observing the child's behavior during the preparation of the meal, the meal itself, and the clean-up period. During the meal, if it is for the child, we can test whether or not he is willing to share—with the therapist or with the dog or cat. We can see, also, if the child cleans things up, whether he feels guilty if he makes a mess, and possibly whether he projects this upon the dog. Does the child like to regress and play the role of the infant who has to be fed and cannot assist in the preparation of the meal? Does he eat food that he obviously does not relish and impose the same discipline on the dog (asking him to eat unpleasant food). Very often this projective material gives more reliable clues to the child's problems and defense structures than the C.A.T. ((Haworth, 1966) or the Rorschach (Klopper & Davidson, 1962).

How very revealing such techniques can be is indicated in the following excerpt from my records of a session with a seven-year-old patient.

> B. was glad to be introduced to the dog; she shook hands with him and began to play. B. seemed pleased to have an admiring, noncompetitive audience, very readily entered into the spirit of the game and gave the dog the information asked for. She was delighted to share her lunch with the dog who was presiding over the luncheon at the head of the table. Still, throughout the session she gave the distinct impression that it was the novelty of the situation that brought about her favorable response, rather than the fact that she was relating on a lasting level to the writer as a person. In an unobtrusive way, she was demanding. She had a big lunch and did not volunteer to help. She even expected the clinician to shell her egg, and did not offer to assist with the dishes. She accepted whatever was done for her as if it were her due, thus apparently repeating a pattern she was exhibiting at home. In a sense, she viewed the psychologist as an extension of her self.

Projective questions may be introduced at this point (David, 1955; David and Leach, 1957; Freed, 1965; Kaplan, 1967). Make believe that everyone had to be an animal for twenty-four hours, that you are an animal. Which animal would the child most want to be? Which animal would he least want to be? What are the three best things about this animal? What are the three worst things about this animal? This may give us additional clues concerning the kind of world the child lives in. One must know what the child's previous experiences with pets have been to be able to appreciate the meaning and all the nuances that transpire in a pet session.

The type of animal a child chooses to identify with will vary depending, among other variables, upon the child's defensive structure and his problem. However, it frequently helps to clarify the psychodynamics of the core problem. We find that when a child selects a domestic animal like a cat, dog, or horse, he is likely to have a mild behavior disorder. However, identification with ferocious and powerful predators is indicative of severe emotional and social disturbance. This is similar to Hammer's (1958) findings.

Pathognomonic Signs

The pet play session will give the psychodiagnostician a chance to observe the child in a natural situation; thus, he can make a more valid judgment as to how the child functions and what his ego defenses may be. Some children are insecure and ask for permission to play with the pet. Others take the situation in their stride and seem to accept it naturally. It is also important to notice how rapidly the child adjusts to the pets used in an interview and to observe whether he acts differently to different animals.

Does the child get "on all fours," imitating the dog in a deadpan (not playful) fashion. (This is not unusual behavior in a very young child who often pretends to be an animal in his play, speaks to his pets and regards them as of equal status with himself). In an older child such posturing could point to emotional conflicts and disorientation.

Whether the child does or does not touch the animal and which parts of the pet's body the child touches can be highly significant. Does the child reach for or touch the dog's phallus? Clues to the child's conflicts may be shown by the child's avoidance of the dog. Not touching Jingles may indicate not only the fear of an unknown animal, but also the worry that his hands may become aggressive instruments which could hurt the dog. Sometimes a sudden cessation of play, when the child is unable to continue the game or involvement, points to diagnostic factors. Did the child unwittingly express aggression toward the pet or the therapist? Did he feel guilty? What has he done to undo the situation? On the other hand, overt aggression towards pets also spells pathology. A child who insists on kicking the dog or pulling the cat's tail or trying unobtrusively to kill some of the fish in the aquarium presents an aberrant picture. Sometimes pathognomonic signs of severe maladjustment and even childhood psychosis become evident.

Sometimes the writer's cat sneaks surreptitiously into the office and jumps on the desk while the examination is proceeding. When the cat snuggles next to the patient, stretches her neck out, languidly lies on her back and is obviously asking to be petted, the child's response or lack of response may be symptomatic of a personality disorder.

Prognostic Clues

The child's behavior when he sees a pet and his response to a pet's friendly overtures may give early clues about his recoverability and the likelihood of success in treatment. Generally speaking, children who identify with the dog, even though they may be afraid of him, are better therapy risks. A child who does not hesitate to pet the dog may indicate his need for affection and thus often presents a more promising therapy subject. On the other hand, withdrawal from an obviously inoffensive, friendly animal indicates, in a sense, a withdrawal from environmental stimulation, portraying the child's view of the world as being inimical. Such behavior generally presages poor or long, drawn out therapeutic results.

Animal Pets in the Home

Pets may play an important role in the diagnosis of family relationships. "The presence of animal pets in the home is often advantageous in forming a relationship with a withdrawn, psychotic family member, or diagnostically in understanding the family relationships. Pets display behavioral reactions that are extensions of the behavioral reactions of the family members. Pets are very sensitive to emotionally charged affective states within the family" (Friedman, 1965).

Children who own pets should be permitted, if they ask or encouraged if they do not suggest it themselves, to bring their pets to the therapy sessions. The pet should always be welcomed and made part of the session. Often additional diagnostic material may be elicited. Pearson (1968), reports the case of an enuretic child patient who thought urine was poisonous. Nevertheless, the pet bird which he brought to the therapy sessions hade been named "Pee Wee", the term the child used for urine.

Examples of Use with Adults

From a symposium reported in the *Psychoanalytic Quarterly* (Heiman, 1953), one learns of the limited[5] but telling experiences others in the field have had:

> Dr. Lewin opened the discussion with a description of three adult patients who brought their dogs with them to the analytic hour. The dogs vomited on the floor, jumped on the couch, and acted in various ways reminiscent of the behavior of some children in analysis. Dr. Lewin then presented the case of an agoraphobic woman in her second marriage who was preoccupied with her difficulties in mating her two dogs. She complained that they did not love each other. This obsession was accompanied by an obsession to have a baby. It turned out that the male dog was what was left over from her first husband. In the analysis, this dog's love stood for the love of the lost husband to whom she was very much attached. The wish for a baby was related to the frustration of this wish in her first marriage which had been sterile.
>
> Lewin described a second patient who had several dogs, each of which was unmistakably the replacement for a lost love object and was involved by this

> patient in her depressive mechanism . . . Dr. Lewin also pointed out that many adults in their relationships with dogs find an opportunity for repeating infantile attitudes toward objects. Sometimes they relive actively, through the dogs, incidents which they had previously experienced passively.

Another doctor described "a woman who had become interested in the sex life of her cat whenever her own sexual desires were unfulfilled. Although unaware of her own castrating impulses, she had named her cat Medusa."

The role of animals in psychodiagnosis is further illustrated by a case presented to the same symposium.

> A thirty-five year old woman started analysis because of in tolerable anxiety in anticipation of her forthcoming marriage—her second. She had had three years of treatment with two other analysts prior to his analysis. She could only have four interviews prior to the marriage, shortly after which she became pregnant and terminated her treatment just prior to delivery.
>
> Two weeks after she returned from her honeymoon, she first spoke of her dog which had been in the bedroom on an occasion when she and her husband were having intercourse. This recalled primal scene memories. Her identification with the dog became quite clear, particularly in a series of incidents relating to bowel movements (her own and the dog's). She talked of how bad her dog was, that he was a nuisance to everyone, that he was noisy, and filthy in his soiling. The patient indicated that she derived vicarious satisfaction from the dog's uninhibited behavior. After the patient became pregnant, she identified the unborn child with the dog. Hostile impulses toward the child were projected as hostile impulses to the dog. On another occasion, following an outburst of rage against her mother, she beat the dog. As the treatment progressed, there was a striking improvement in the dog's behavior which preceded that in the patient. One time the dog was taken by the patient's mother. In the dog's absence, the patient soiled, and in the analysis recalled the childhood experiences of soiling in the presence of her father. As the patient came to accept her femininity more willingly, she referred to her dog as "she" for the first time.

The cases cited above indicate how the skilled analyst can make use of the man-animal relationship in obtaining swifter and keener insights into patients. References to pets must be treated as having great import. Eventually, it is to be hoped, a more systematic knowledge and understanding of the symbolism involved in man-animal relationships will make all those who work in the mental hygiene field much more alert and sensitive to this. In fact, as reported in the past case, the patient involved had already experienced three years of treatment with two different analysts prior to her visits to Dr. Heiman. Whether or not the previous therapists had also obtained critical clues from the woman's description of her dog, or whether the material had been presented by the patient at all in their previous treatment is not indicated in the record. Suffice it so say that the reporting analyst was greatly assisted in understanding and helping to resolve some of the complexities of this case through his perceptions of the role of the pet.

It has been found by clinicians that many adults, in their relationships with dogs, find an opportunity for repeating infantile attitudes toward authority figures. Sometimes they relive actively, through the dogs, incidents which they had previously experienced passively. Frequently there is an underlying phallic significance in the animal . . . Dreams and fantasies involving horses and dogs reveal penis envy in women. In addition to serving as repositories of id material, animals also relate strongly to anal fantasies. This may result from the soiling proclivity of domestic animals, particularly dogs, and the ambivalent pleasures with which humans observe animals performing these functions (Ellis, 1937; Heiman, 1953; Stekel, 1959).

One of my patients wrote a report of her therapeutic progress which she volunteered to let me use in this book because the contents were so salient to the role of animals in psychodiagnosis and psychotherapy. Although extremely relevant, he material was too lengthy to reproduce *in toto*. Consequently, I have selected excerpts which will, I hope, indicate the role that animals played in revealing and solving this girl's problems.

> In her middle twenties and unmarried, this girl had been brought up in a home characterized by "plastic covers and an anti-live attitude." When she began treatment, she was unaware of her feelings about or attitudes toward animals and cats in particular. "The awareness of cats began to come into focus as the result of my therapist owning a cat," she says. "At that time I had a vague fear of all cats and dogs. I recoiled if his cat got close to me and I frequently requested that the cat be placed in another room during our session. I feared a strange cat initiating action toward me; I wanted to decide if I wanted such an interaction. The only thing I decided, after a while, was that I enjoyed watching him (the cat). He was so graceful, aloof, independent, strong, and handsome.
>
> Gradually, my therapist began to incorporate the cat in our discussions. The cat was sometimes used to make points more graphically. After quite some time, I became interested in stroking the cat and periodically liked him very much. At moments I believe I was jealous of the affections that were given to the cat and wished they were given to me instead. At this point I sometimes began to initiate stroking or reaching out to the cat.
>
> My doctor and I frequently discussed the possibility of my getting a kitten. At first the idea was appalling to me and I experienced real anxiety when I contemplated such a prospect. My thoughts and feelings about getting a kitten

didn't change for about a year and a half. At this time I had returned to school, had a part-time job, was committed to several other activities but felt extremely lonely through it all.

I began to seek a kitten and a friend put me in touch with someone who had a kitten to give away. I made all arrangements to go over and get it, but at the last minute I copped out. I was too scared. However, the thought and desire kept recurring and eventually I found, at work, someone who was looking for a home for three kittens. She was very involved and in love with these kittens and very encouraging about how wonderful it would be to have kittens around. I decided to take two kittens because I didn't want either one to feel alone during the day.

Pepper and Tunkel were very different kittens. Pepper was very bright, and he was rather affectionate. Tunkel, on the other hand, was not attractive to me (she had small hazel eyes and a spotted coat of dull black and off white). Her personality was also unattractive; she was high-strung, extremely sensitive to noises, was a "picky" eater and cried frequently. I found myself getting irritable with Tunkel merely because she was herself—playful, curious and heedless of her activities. I didn't like it when my flowers were eaten, my furniture was scratched, when my sleep was interrupted, when my reading was interrupted, when my ash trays were broken, when I found the phone off hook. I wanted to get rid of Tunkel, but I felt guilty about it. Eventually I decided that Tunkel deserved a home in which she was loved and gave her away.

My relationship to Pepper has grown into a very strong friendship. I like Pepper and he has helped me in many ways. Through Pepper I have become much more realistically aware of people's reactions to me. I believe that people frequently react to my kitten, verbally and non-verbally, in a way that is dictated by the way they feel about me. I had not seen people's reactions clearly before. I can give several examples of what I mean.

I was amazed at the reaction of one friend to Pepper. Because this gentleman has three cats that he is very attached to, I had expected him to react in a friendly, affectionate, positive way to mine. Nothing of the sort happened. He gave Pepper only a token stroke of concern. Verbally, however, he expressed intense con-concern for Pepper's welfare, making me promise that I would first consult with him if anything happened. It struck me that he behaved toward me in the same way he did toward the kitten; he is verbally very concerned about my welfare and always asks to be consulted if I need help, but when he touches me it is in the same removed, controlled, tight, and possibly patronizing manner that he hastily stroked Pepper. We are solely platonic friends and recently are enjoying each other's company less and less.

My reactions to another man, whom I have recently met, were clarified through Pepper. At the slightest provocation or frustration, this man brusquely pushes the kitten away saying, "Get away, Cat." He also refers to me as girl, or woman, or honey (when he is angry) and most infrequently by name. He says that his mother loved cats and that he therefore knows how to handle them although there is no evidence to substantiate this. He has urged me to get rid of Pepper. At times I think I'm such a source of conflict for him that he would like to get rid of me. In all probability our friendship will be short-lived.

> An artist acquaintance with two cats of his own loves playing with, watching, handling and talking to Pepper. Likewise, we have a ball. Recently he held Pepper up high above his head and said, "If I could take you home with me, I'd show you a couple of tricks." I'm sure he would, too.

CONCLUSION

Psychodiagnosis is an ongoing procedure which becomes fused with treatment. As I have indicated throughout this chapter, and as the various cases cited have shown, psychological assessment is never complete and is continually evolving. This is just as true where the pet is used as an assessment tool as it is where pets are not introduced. However, the more one is able to observe the patient interacting with a pet, the sharper one's conclusions can become. Later observations provide one with data that often compel a modification of earlier assessments and conclusions. This is true regardless of whether the therapist has the pet in his office or the patient brings his own pet to interviews or relates experiences which describe interactions with a pet at home.

Pets do and can provide for the therapist who has become alerted to and sophisticated with the value of these tools, a vital source of clues and insights into personality disturbances. What is even more startling is the way in which the changes in a patient's relationship to a pet generally coincide with an increasing ability to handle his other problems.

NOTES

[1]In this statement, Levinson is not speaking about Borderline Personality Disorder, but the child who is straddling the border between health and some form of psychosocial stress which is impairing his/her everyday functioning.

[2]Levinson often referred to play therapy as a means of making his case for the utilization of animals as adjuncts in the treatment of children.

[3]Burch, Bustad, Duncan, Fredrickson, and Tebay (1995) provide an excellent overview of the role of pets in a therapeutic program. The section by Burch is particularly insightful in its description of utilizing animals in clinical settings.

[4]Utilizing animals outside of the therapy office can be a liberating experience for both the professional and the client. Children, who are so constantly "parented" by adults, have little opportunity to practice being a parent themselves. Pets provide such opportunities (see Savishinsky, 1974, for an insightful article about the child as the father of the dog).

[5]There is a growing body of literature on utilization of animals with various adult populations, but due to space limitations, these are not cited here.

Chapter 4

ANIMAL AIDES IN PSYCHOTHERAPY

The use of pets in the treatment of children's emotional difficulties is a comparatively new development in psychotherapy. It is founded not only on the premise that it is easier for a child to project his unacceptable feelings on a pet, but also on the pet's faculty for supplying some of a child's need of cuddling, companionship, and unconditional acceptance. Added to the therapy setting, the pet supplies the child with an opportunity to feel "the master of the situation" while in treatment.

Although pet adjuncts in psychotherapy are invaluable aides with all children, children who have been culturally disadvantaged respond even more positively and actively. To these children who have lived in substandard conditions, generally in broken homes[1] with little intellectual stimulation, being treated by a therapist with different standards can be terrifying. Even the therapist's "neutrality" can be exceedingly threatening to the ghetto child, who more than anything else, wants someone to care about him.

How fortuitous and efficient in such circumstances is the introduction of a pet into the therapy situation. Whether it is a dog, cat, lizard or mouse—how classless and acceptant is the animal world. Pets do not react to the color of a child's skin, his uncombed hair, dirty clothes, bad report card, or substandard speech. The pet's approach to life is elemental. Basically, the pet cares nothing at all for societal values, but responds primarily to love and kindness. Therefore, there is generally an immediate affinity between child and pet. Even the angry, hurting child learns quickly to be gentle with the pet that eagerly demonstrates a desire "to be friends."

When the child plays with the dog, he establishes his own world, the boundaries of which he himself prescribes. The therapist, therefore, participates in common adventure by entering into a corner of the child's world where the child feels secure. This is where the therapist and the child find an equal footing; this is where the doors of communication are likely to open early between child and therapist.

The child's need for cuddling should be met by selecting a pet which is cuddly, is not threatening, does not scold and does not expect the child to be on his best behavior. A greater understanding of the child's need for cuddling, love, and affection by animals and human beings would lead, quite frequently, to more rapid recovery in many children. It also appears that all children have an intense need to master someone or something that does not talk back, that accepts one regardless of what one is. This is overwhelmingly prevalent among disturbed children who especially do not want to be judged. They want to be accepted, admired, and permitted to regress as far as possible without being berated by someone or something loved and without the consequent guilt.

In relating to a dog, the child has the enriching experience of complete mutual "acceptance." In identifying with the loved dog, the child is bound to make comparisons and ask why, even though the dog urinates, defecates, masturbates, and has public and almost indiscriminate sex relations, he is loved and accepted. If the dog does not feel guilty, the child wonders why he should, and if the dog is permitted to enjoy his body, the child wonders why he cannot.

In one case, a mother felt guilty over her son's masturbation and punished him for continuing with this practice. This mother felt that her son was a degenerate and since he was her own small child, he should be "innocent" and should not enjoy sex play. The child continued to masturbate in secret, but he felt guilty about it. When this child saw our open acceptance of the dog even though the other relished licking his penis, it helped him to accept his own sexuality. It is to be recalled that the child, and particularly the boy for whom our culture does not tolerate regression (Harrington, 1960) and who has fewer opportunities to get vicarious gratification from regressive behavior, now has a socially and therapist's accepted and approved means of regression. The child can therefore permit himself to regress gleefully and joyfully.

Disturbed children have a strong need for physical contact but are afraid of human contacts because they have been hurt so much and so often by people. Since the hurt is not associated with the dog, this conflict resolves itself. They will permit a dog to approach them, and they will pet the animal while telling him all about their difficulties. A dog apparently poses less of a threat because he can satisfy the child's need for physical contact without the painfully embroiling emotional entanglements that the child already knows accompany emotional involvement with humans.[2]

STRUCTURE AND FUNCTION

The structured use of the pet in the therapeutic process has many applications dependent upon the psychodynamics of the specific case. Just a few of the possible functions of the pet are as follows:

1. Use of the pet as a "transitional object" (Winnicott, 1953).
2. Use of the pet where cuddling, affection, and unconditional acceptance are indicated.
3. Provision of a setting where the child can be the master of the situation. For the child to be able to profit from treatment, he must not feel challenged; the pet usually presents no such threat.

AUTISTIC CHILDREN

Pet therapy is specifically useful for the nonverbal, severely ego-disturbed child.[3] It is well known that most children learn about the world and the differences between the self and nonself through the medium of their bodies. Particularly is this true for the autistic child whose contact with reality is most tenuous (Des Lauriers, 1967).

These children are internally disorganized, have a short attention span and sometimes think in solipsistic terms. Distrustful of their therapists, their confidence is hard and long won. For them, the world never existed, is dead or no longer exists. They are the only ones left alive. As a result, they frequently create an imaginary world with imaginary companions. When there is a cherished pet nearby, it may help to bring a ray of reality into this child's world. No longer need this severely disturbed child fill his world with imaginary loving playmates when there is a real, tangible, fun-loving playmate at his side.

The therapist then intrudes himself upon the child via the pet. The child reacts to the pet and much later to the therapist. While working with these children, it is necessary to permit them to go at their own pace and give them support throughout the therapeutic interaction. Much of this support can come from the pet and most importantly is of a physical contact nature. As was indicated by Des Lauriers (1967), "The communication must be full of sensory stimulation."

Most emotionally disturbed children need to touch as if by this act they can affirm their existence as independent entities. They discover themselves, their own bodies, and through this discovery they learn about the outside world. Through the sense of touch these children begin to master the pet and through the pet the world.

Some of these children must learn fundamental facts about their bodies. The child is asked to imagine he is just like the dog he is playing with. The child then rolls, walks on all fours and even barks like a dog. Through this activity the child learns about his body, gets some intimations of where the sensations he is puzzled about originate and discovers that his body has an orientation.

"Reality, for the schizophrenic patient, is found the presence of the therapist, in the physical contact with the therapist, in the sensuous bodily experience of that presence, in the inescapable nearness of that presence" (Des Lauriers, 1967, p. 95).

The role of pets becomes particularly important in the case of autistic children where "adult control and direction of the child's behavior are mandatory" (Verville, 1967, p. 180) if this behavior is to change. The autistic child needs constant stimulation; he should not be left alone to engage endlessly in his alienated autistic preoccupations. Active intervention and stimulation by a well-trained pet should at first bring about groping, then tentative and finally purposive efforts to engage with human companions.

The autistic child appears at ease only with his material environment. He treats people as objects and aspects of nature. He cannot, by himself, advance from his relationship with the nonliving world to that of living things, whether animals or human.

We know that one of the characteristics of infantile autism is autistic aloneness. Unlike other child psychotics, these children never establish these ties and it seems to this writer that using pets in the way indicated would accomplish this, particularly since these children are fascinated by objects which they try to manipulate. A well-trained dog can lend itself to such practices. Again, I wish to point out that so far no psychotherapeutic methods seem to be effective with these children. Let us then try pets![4]

One must repeat again and again that a severely disturbed child, because of the almost complete a lack of reality-oriented object relationships, lives in a state of omnipotence where the self and nonself are barely differentiated. It is thus necessary to provide the child with experiences that will help him to develop a self concept in which there is a definite distinction between self and nonself. When this is done, as the primitive ego tentatively gropes for the opportunity of reestablishing contact with reality, it begins to reach out to its nonliving environment in space which surrounds it. First, it gropes its way to nonliving objects, then plants large and small, then animal, and finally people. The animal or pet is one of the links in the golden chain leading to good mental health. Or as has been pointed out by Searles (1960), "relationship with nonhuman, rather than the human, elements of their environment may be the initial development in their slow struggle back to reality" (Searles, 1960, p. 413).

We should remember that using a pet is not an open sesame to the "inner world" of the child and particularly with very much disturbed children the progress is at best very slow. However, clinical experience indicates that having a pet does speed up therapy and a relationship is established much sooner. Some therapists, after they have made a valiant effort and find no response from a child (even therapists are human beings and look for some gratification from their patients!), may feel that the child is hopeless. They cannot, however, fail to notice that the child does eventually respond to the pet, which shows that the child has some potential for recovery.

A pet can serve to strengthen such a child's cathexis and help him become aware of the cause and effect relationships. The schizophrenic child, just like any other child, needs to love and be loved. When he develops the ability to do this fully, he will become a happier human being.

It seems to me that if we trained pets to give bodily comfort to the autistic child in his crib or while he is still a toddler and thus provided constant stimulation throughout his waking hours, it would assuage the autistic child's all-consuming anxiety and help him to establish a firmer grip on reality. A child may be in therapy only twice a week, but the pet can exert his healing influence on the child twenty-four hours a day, every day of the week.

Some schizophrenic children are afraid to get physically close to the therapist. Possibly, they are afraid that the hostility they emanate will alienate the only person who cares about them unconditionally and nonjudgmentally. They may also be afraid of getting close to the therapist because they sense that they have very loose ego boundaries and that their egos may be swallowed up by the stronger ego of the therapist. A dog presents no such threat. (Other schizophrenic children are also preoccupied with "introjected bad me." It is much easier for them to find a "bad me" in the dog that is tolerated, accepted, and loved, than in themselves.)

One of the manifest differences between the psychotherapeutic treatment of children and adults is the lack of continuity of theme in children. The use of a pet frequently provides a unifying thread which helps to unravel more quickly the basic elements in the child's nuclear neurosis.

INDICATIONS FOR PET PSYCHOTHERAPY

Pet psychotherapy is indicated for the following children: the young nonverbal, the inhibited, the autistic, the withdrawn, the obsessive compulsive, and the culturally disadvantaged. It is not too effective with organic, acting out, character disorders, and extremely bright children who can verbalize well.

Pet therapy can meet the needs of a variety of severely disturbed children. For the child who is disorganized and fears that he may lose control over his own impulses and do something which he may later regret, pet therapy provides limits which help protect the child against his own impulses. Having to work with the pet, having to accept certain rules, makes it easier for the child to bring some organization into his thinking and conduct.

On the other hand, for children who are submissive, withdrawn, and fearful, the association with a pet who accepts everything they do, will help these children loosen up and enable them to eventually venture unafraid into certain uncharted areas.

Pet therapy is indicated for the very young child because these children tend to act out rather than verbalize their experiences. For children who are fixated at early developmental levels, gratification of their needs will help them regress, get satisfaction at this level from associating with the pet, and then go on to satisfaction in other life situations.

Our clinical experience has indicated the effectiveness of the use of pets with culturally disadvantaged, emotionally disturbed children. A child who finds it most difficult to verbalize and to tell us how he feels about things and about his dreams, relationships, etc., "finds his tongue" when he has to discuss his problems with the dog.

While it may be easy to get introspective observations from middle class children who are consistently asked how they feel (so that these children develop some ability at introspection), this is not true for lower class Puerto Rican and African American children. These children's feelings and thoughts are not very often considered, and hence, they have little need or ability to think in that direction.

We tell the child that the dog is "unhappy"; and therefore the dog cannot relate to the child. These children can verbalize quite well when they are talking to the animal, but not the therapist. They particularly enjoy playing with the cat, when the cat is trying to grab the string and they pull it away from her. They make believe that the dog is the teacher and they make uncomplimentary remarks about him and classroom procedures.

Pet therapy will affect the substratum of the child's emotions and his unconscious concept of self as a desirable person. In pet therapy the therapist no longer has to handle *in toto* the basic affectional needs, and therefore, he could work on higher conceptual level.

PSYCHOTHERAPEUTIC IMPLICATIONS

The use of a pet as a tool brings new dimensions to child psychotherapy and of necessity helps to crystallize new concepts. To begin with, a completely different relationship is required when a therapeutic situation is structured to include a pet. It is no longer the "one-to-one" relationship of ordinary play therapy but comes closer to working in a group situation. It is an advantage both for the therapist who can observe the child's behavior with the pet and for the child who has a relaxed opportunity to identify, project, empathize, and patronize. How the use of a pet can accelerate the therapeutic process is discussed later in the chapter.

As long as childhood behavior disorders were considered specific disease entities, emphasis on the use of pets in psychotherapy appeared esoteric and far-fetched. However, as soon as such disorders are looked upon as a maladaptive response patterns, using pets to modify these patterns and aid children in reorganizing their "style of life" by shedding maladaptive patterns of behavior can appear reasonable.

In an article, Quaytman (1963) reports on the use of animals in child therapy and makes the following points: "Their use is not advocated as a general procedure, but rather to encourage play therapists to venture and use whatever potentialities exist among their life experiences, interests, and hobbies, to enrich the play therapy experience, and as aids in reaching the withdraw child (p. 35). I believe that Quaytman is in error, for pets should not be placed in the same category as other "experiences, interests and hobbies." For maximum effectiveness, pets must be planfully introduced into the therapy hours, and in certain cases they must become part of the treatment plan. Furthermore, pets must be trained for the part they will take in the treatment, and therapists should be oriented to the use of pets.

Another implication of the use of pets, since they are so active, is that the main locus of therapy need no longer be in the playroom, but it can be in the wider world, in the street or playground or wherever the child's and his pet's fancy takes them. The pet can literally lead the child into a larger world in which the child can eventually function. Therefore, to refer to the use of pets in therapy as play therapy is a misnomer. The word "play" connotes a self-chosen activity which is largely absent in the structured setting of a clinic or a private therapist's office where the purpose of the activities is predetermined or the time set beforehand. What we are actually doing in play therapy is engaging in directed make-believe. It is well known that through play a child may rehearse and try to resolve some of his life's problems. Therefore, it is more accurate to call therapy that involves the planned use of pets—pet therapy.[5]

Adults ascribe human attributes to animals; children reverse the process and attribute animal qualities to human beings. Contrary to the widely held impression (Bellak and Adelman, 1960; Blum and Hunt, 1952; Boyd and Mandler, 1955), it is easier for a child to identify with a human being than with an animal. However, it is even more difficult for the child to project life into and identify with an inanimate object. The great virtue of pet therapy is that it permits this identification with a living object as a transitional or intermediate level. Experienced child therapists know that dolls, clay, finger paints, and other appurtenances of the playroom cannot be truly loved. They are not alive; they do not grow, digest, and respond. The child intuitively knows that they cannot share his feelings with him. As was pointed out by Bender and Rapoport (1944, p. 521), "Animals have certain attributes which furnish the human mind with an excellent medium for displacement of the repressed drives." Unlike his reaction to a doll, a child can conceive of the pet as being part of himself and his family and sharing his experiences.

Further, "emotionally disturbed children who have experienced difficulty in their relations with people relate more easily or quickly to animals" (Berl, 1952, p. 207). There are many examples of the unique value of the pet. An adopted child, for instance, is often resistant in therapy and does not want to confide in the therapist. The child thinks he is bad, otherwise he would not have been surrendered for adoption. With the aid of the pet, it is possible to shortcut this process and the child can develop a good relationship with the therapist.

It is often necessary for infantilized children with behavior disorders to gratify some of their elementary needs before any attempt can be made to approach their nuclear conflicts. A child who has been sadly deprived of love may find it most difficult to accept the affection of an adult, but he capable to receiving it from a pet.

Thus the way a child handles his pet is much more expressive and revealing of his problem and attitude toward the world than his finger paintings or his play with puppets. The child creates his own fantasies and fairy tales revolving around the pet. The pet provides him with an outlet for his emotions and a way of abreacting to them. The job of the therapist consists in penetrating into this life and trying to help the child use his imaginary resource in self-healing.

A sensitive therapist can utilize the child's play with the pet to understand the child. Understanding what the child is trying to convey strengthens the therapeutic relationship with the child. The pet can also solve the problem of sharing, separation, and formulation of self-image.

Pet therapy could also be called ambulatory therapy. Special dimensions are called to the therapeutic situation by taking walks with the child and the dog. As we walk with a child and the dog, the child inevitably notices that the dog stops in many spots, smells, and in certain spots, urinates. The child wonders why the dog has to "go the bathroom" so many times within such a short interval. The child's and therapist's common experiences of having to go to the bathroom, of constipation and diarrhea are mentioned. The child is startled. Somehow or other he did not conceive of the therapist as a human being with all the frailties that the flesh is subject to. So the therapist is human after all! The child unconsciously begins to dethrone the therapist and to rise in his own self-estimation. In following the dog's lead and favorite spots which the dog finds only through clues known to him alone, the child begins to discover a new world; former two-dimensional objects assume three dimensions, new ways of experiencing, of sensing, of relating seem to arise. It appears as if the pet acts as a catalyst in reawakening and reanimating the child's awareness.

Not only does the walk provide motor release for some children, but the therapist is enabled to increase the scope of mutual experiences shared with the patient. These experiences also make possible observation of the child's reactions to adults and children, to noisy traffic, to flowers, to store windows, to a blind or crippled child and most importantly, to the responsibility of taking a dog for a walk. Beecher (1957) has said that if he could observe a child for a full twenty-four hours, he would know almost everything he needed to know, as a therapist, about the child's "style of life." Every therapist knows how much time is consumed by trying to unsheathe the verbal disguises of both parents and children. Observations accelerate the therapist's insights. Dog walks, which broaden the scope of observed experiences involving all three—the dog, the child, and the therapist—are an important catalyst in the therapeutic process. (The author cannot resist the impulse to state the obvious that such walks are highly recommended also for the health of the therapist.)

However, it bears repeating again and again. Merely assigning pets to emotionally disturbed children without at the same time making a provision for psychotherapeutic intervention may not only not be useful, but even harmful. A child's playing alone with a pet may reinforce his regressive withdrawal patterns, make him dependent for companionship solely on the pet, and remove him from competitive and therapeutically useful social anxiety produced by interactions with his peers.

CREATION OF A PSYCHOTHERAPEUTIC RELATIONSHIP

It is sometimes forgotten that the same techniques cannot be used with children as with adults. Children ordinarily do not admit there is anything wrong with them or that they need treatment (Freud, 1951). They usually do not feel an inner urge or need to come for help. They are not aware that whatever discomfort their anxiety causes them can be alleviated by the therapist. By and large, parents initiate the therapy. We need the parents' cooperation in order to continue. Since the child did not initiate the referral, the child feels that the therapist is his parents' ally and not his. This means that there is an extra responsibility placed upon the therapist, which is usually nonexistent with the grown-up, to create a beginning in a therapeutic relationship. The therapist must prove his usefulness to the child (Freud, 1951).

This is one of the special problems in child therapy. Since the child did not seek out the therapist, the child is unlikely to recognize his need for help. Generally he claims that his classmates or his teacher or even his parents are at fault, but not he. Adults are also prone to this point of view except that in "seeking help" the adult makes implicit admissions of his own responsibility for his problems.

In this connection, it is worthwhile to remember that although the child may tell us that he does not know what it is all about, actually he is aware, whether consciously or unconsciously, that there is something wrong with him and that he is not like others. The mere fact of his being discussed at home, of parents being unduly concerned about him, of his being brought in to a psychologist for an evaluation, brings about a qualitative change in the child's self-evaluation and feeling of being atypical, unusual, or odd.

Something reassuring must be done in the first interview to make the child feel that the therapist will make living more comfortable, that the therapist understands him and is ready to help. A dog brought in at this point may "break the ice" and be of assistance in developing a relationship with some children. In fact, the therapist who has pet assistance may, through his handling of a pet, elicit the young patient's admiration and lead more quickly to patient-therapist rapport.[6]

In my practice, the procedure for introducing Jingles to the child, or the child to Jingles, automatically standardized itself. Generally, the child plays with the dog, asks Jingles to shake hands and dance. A cookie may be offered to the dog as an incentive. One child said to me, "I am also Jingles—I also want to dance." This child got down on his knees, started to bark like a dog, and asked me to give him a cookie. In great joy and glee, he then picked up the wastebasket, scattered its contents, put it on his head and started howling like a wolf. This apparently relieved him and he went on with his play as usual. He then said to me, "Why can't you have two dogs, and why can't you take me as one of them."

Interspersed with his requests were questions about me. Did I have a wife? How many children did I have and how big were they? It was clear that the child wanted to become part of my family. If the human complement was full, perhaps the dog complement was not, and he would like to be considered, if a vacancy existed.

Other therapists have noted that the desire to become a nonhuman may be seen as regression in the service of the ego, as a satisfaction of a need to rest by the roadway before further progress is made. From this point of view, such a regression can be a significant step toward recovery (Searles, 1960). However, in the situation mentioned above, the child playing with the dog; while the child acts like an animal, he is aware of the difference between himself and an animal. He is not going through a lycanthropic phase and does not believe that he was transformed into a dog.

SETTING LIMITS

In pet therapy, children frequently fantasize verbally about the pet's behavior. In spite of the fact that these stories are very often aggressive and involve the destruction of the therapist, the parent or the child himself, nevertheless finds these stories acceptable to the pet, to the therapist, and hence also to himself. This gives the child a chance to ventilate his aggressive drives and to secure a catharsis.

This will meet some of the child's needs for self-expression and will provide experiences which will increase feelings of self worth. These children cannot accept too many limits. A very minimum should be applied. Sometimes testing the limits is also testing the therapist's attitudes. Is he really strong or weak? Does he mean what he says? It is difficult for such a child to get along in a group.

It is easier, however, for the child to displace his repressed impulses, aggression, anger, and hostility from the therapist onto the pet. He may claim the pet is bad and should be punished. This helps the child to free himself even further from guilt. It is then, usually, that the child confides that he has nightmares about aggressive and fear-inspiring animals such as lions, tigers, or crocodiles and he identifies the pet he plays with as being somewhat similar to them. The child sometimes expresses a desire to hurt or to kill my dog Jingles. We must understand what happens in the sequence of play therapy to bring out the hostility of the child at this point. While we do not wish to restrain the child from expressing himself, it is obvious that we cannot permit the child to hurt the dog or the cat or even the fish. "In therapy, the patient may say whatever he pleases; he is not free, however, to *do* whatever he pleases" (Auld, 1968, p. 170). Limits must be set. Without such limits, the child would experience severe guilt feelings as well as fear and anxiety. The child would expect the animal to retaliate and therefore he would develop feelings of persecution. The child, knowing that he is engaging in the desire for socially unacceptable activities which he cannot control himself, is usually in intense conflict. Unconsciously aware of the dire results of his desires, he ambivalently wants others to stop him.

I am able to interpret to the child that maybe there was something about Jingle's behavior that he did not like and that he wished to kill that part of him which was responsible. (I would greatly hesitate to make the same interpretation to the children who tell me, and this happens so frequently, that they hate me and wish to kill me.) I can then gently lead into the topic of our not liking something in ourselves, looking and finding it in others, and then wishing to destroy it.

Furthermore, setting limits also indicates to the child that he is not omnipotent and cannot engage in activities in the therapist's office which he could not do elsewhere. It makes him face reality. As was indicated by Singer (1962, p. 156): "contrary to the often voiced and popular belief—prevalent even among the psychologically sophisticated—the feeling of omnipotence is one of the most disturbing and troublesome human experiences imaginable, because it entails feelings of unreality and paradoxically a sense of nothingness or nonexistence." A child learns that one cannot transgress with impunity against a living creature. The child develops a respect for life in all of its manifestations. This he may later translate in his dealings with his peers and authority figures. He begins to realize how living things react, feel, think. From this understanding of the limits of reaction and behavior for him in the therapeutic situation, he is further led to see that limits exist elsewhere and for everyone. Therefore, when we enforce limits, we convey acceptance of the child in treating him as we do everyone else.

Occasionally, the child becomes so involved with the dog and generally with what is going on outdoors that he begins to "doodle" so as to exceed the allotted time. It occasionally becomes necessary, therefore, to take the child firmly by the hand and lead him back to the office. In this situation, the child's feeling of possible rejection has been handled as follows: It is pointed out that the therapist understands and is quite sympathetic with the child's desire to spend more time outdoors with the pet but that neither the therapist nor the child can control time, and no matter what they may wish, time will run out regardless. Besides, there must be other children waiting at the office who, too, must be concerned with the passage of time.

The feeling of hurt and deviancy that a child feels because he has been "picked" for treatment thus may be dissipated. Further, we indicate to him that he was different in terms of the fact that he has some recognition of his problems which in our eyes indicate that he has strengths rather than weaknesses. We believe that setting limits tends to counteract "feelings of worthlessness and insignificance."

VARIETY OF SUITABLE PETS

Although I have thus far mentioned only cats and dogs in the therapeutic process, there is an almost limitless choice for the clinician who can then have one or many in his office. Children usually respond to any "living toy."

In my waiting room there is an aquarium. This is where the children spend their time while waiting for their therapy session. Occasionally, some children furtively reach out and try to touch a fish or a plant. When their fingers get wet, they are startled, possibly because of guilt. Others watch the antics of the fish and weave many a fantasy which later may be played out in the therapy session. For others, the aquarium is a potent projective device. Looking at the fish is like looking at a fire on the hearth. Possibly the reason why some children benefit from observing the aquarium is because it personifies some feared fantasy object. The aquarium permits to child to bridge the land of his imagination (unconscious) with that of reality.

Richard, aged nine, a new patient, was sitting in the waiting room with his back towards his mother and the aquarium and was alternately opening and closing his mouth as if imitating the oral play of the fish. I took some fish food and motioned to Richard to help me. Like any other child therapist, I try to establish contact with a child whenever and wherever I can reach him. Richard reluctantly accepted this assignment. I put the food in his hand and let him drop it in the aquarium. (Generally speaking, feeding time is an enjoyable time for most children.) The child seemed concerned and perplexed when he noticed the lively competition for food among the fish. I casually remarked that the big fish do not devour the small fish but that they all live amicably in the aquarium although they compete for the available food. The next few sessions were devoted to the observation of the fish and a discussion of their names and habits. Richard's primitive fear of being devoured was thus assuaged, and some boundaries were established between what the fish seemed to be and the reality of their existence. Later Richard wanted me to show him how to start an aquarium of his own. This was the crucial point in my relationship with him, and was reached much more quickly with the help of the aquarium.

Some children are afraid to grow, to develop, and to mature since growth symbolizes leaving the dependent childish state and becoming responsible for one's self and one's actions. They engage in magic rites and develop neurotic symptoms to delay as long as possible this inevitable process.

Observations of the fish in the aquarium and discussion of their growth and development may help a child to see his own misgivings in their true light. The child observes the fish as their entire life cycle unfolds before him. He notices some fish are small, others big, and notices live bearers giving birth to small fish. While wondering whether all these belong to the same species, he begins to muse about growth. At this time it is possible to discuss sex differences in fish, impregnation, and birth.[7] The inevitability of growth may be stressed along with the idea that size is a relative concept, for a big fish in the aquarium may be very small indeed if compared with the fish in the river.

Thinking about his changing body, the child may turn suddenly to his parent, as David did on one occasion and ask for his baby pictures. When the pictures were given to David by his mother, he proceeded to look at himself and compare his present bodily size with his appearance as a baby. This usually helps to develop a more adequate concept of what the child is like and what his body is like. This will enable him to look without trepidation to the future when he will be fully grown.

CASE HISTORIES

The cases that follow are merely suggestive of the use of pets in psychotherapy. The discussion of therapy sessions has of necessity been telescoped, and case data had to be changed to avoid any possibility of identification.

Miriam Lev, aged eight, was referred for treatment by her day school (Yeshiva), because she was a regular "tomboy," her work was below her potential, and she was abusive to teachers. Frequently she started fights with boys, and yet she would very easily burst into tears. Mr. Lev was very reluctant to follow up on the school's recommendations since he thought that Miriam was merely lazy and too noisy. However, he had no alternative since the school threatened to expel his child. On the other hand, Mrs. Lev felt that the school was justified in the referral for she thought that Miriam, who had frequent nightmares, was stupid, constantly fought with other children, was disobedient, had no friends.

Mr. Lev was an extremely pious man who arrived in this country penniless. By dint of very hard work and clever business deals, he had managed to become moderately wealthy. Mr. Lev lost his entire family in the concentration camps, and at age fifty, he remarried. He was unhappy over the fact that his wife was "too young looking," refused to wear a wig (required by the Orthodox Jewish women), was "too attractive and sexy," was a poor housewife, and was unable to manage Miriam. He was always comparing Miriam unfavorably with his sons who had perished. Mrs. Lev admired and loved her husband, but she was most unhappy that she could not produce what her husband wanted most, a boy (Miriam was a "Caesarian baby" and Mrs. Lev could not have any more children). Since Mrs. Lev felt inadequate both as a wife and mother, she did not support Miriam for the sake of family peace.

At the office, Miriam visibly brightened up when she saw my dog. She confided that she had nightmares in which ghosts tried to kidnap and kill her because of her "sins." Her imaginary companion, David, tried to help her to chase the ghosts away but to no avail. Much to her father's displeasure, she would then run to her parents' bedroom. Miriam further told me that she had always wanted to have a dog, but her parents would not hear of it. It later transpired that Mr. Lev felt that it was not proper for an Orthodox Jewish child to play with a dog. At the office, Miriam played with the dog and took him for walks. It was her act of defiance, for she felt that the dog was the long prayed for friend who was in league with her against her parents. The dog thus provided Miriam with a tolerated identification with an aggressive animal that supported her against the dangers which threatened her.

My impression that Miriam would benefit from having a dog of her own was discussed with her parents. I indicated that no prior agreement with Miriam for the care of the dog was to be a prerequisite, for I felt that eventually she would, on her own, accept such responsibility. Initially, it seemed to me, it was unwise to burden an emotionally disturbed child with unwanted responsibilities such as walking, feeding or combing the pet. I felt that at the beginning a pet should be enjoyed and not become another super-ego threat. I suggested that the Levs permit Miriam to assert her autonomy and that she be given the right to make provision for the dog. The dog was to stay in her room, and she could rearrange her furniture to make the dog more comfortable. If she wished to, she was to be permitted to sleep with the dog. Since this was a doctor's prescription, Mr. Lev. reluctantly agreed to secure a dog.

May I add that a trying period followed for the dog, Miriam, and her parents. The dog made a hole in a chair, chewed the family's best shoes, and had many accidents. Many a time, Mr. Lev. wanted to get rid of the dog, but he met the opposition of both Mrs. Lev and Miriam. Mrs. Lev constantly fussed over the dog. At one time when she brought him to the office, the dog had diarrhea, and Mrs. Lev wiped him. Miriam noted that the dog was loved, no matter what he did, and she learned that she too might be "bad," rebellious and impertinent and still be loved. She learned to accept her own "badness" and to feel that she could still be accepted. The realization that one may do "naughty" things at times and yet be loved was the crucial point in Miriam's improvement.

Another patient, David, aged seven, was an only child, the son of professional parents. His father was a research chemist and his mother a freelance writer. Both parents were extremely ambitious and stressed the need for "complete self-fulfillment in their marriage and work." Because nothing must interfere with their career plans, they had not wanted children. David was an accident. His mother wished she had never had him, and once she voiced this to one of her friends while David was playing and "not listening."

David was brought to see me because of his nightmares and refusal to go to school. His parents boasted that David had everything a child might need, a room full of toys, a junior encyclopedia, a microscope, a bicycle. But David had no love. Since his parents felt that a dog was messy and too hard to care for, he was not permitted to have one.

As part of his treatment (I treated the parents also), Jingles (my dog), David and I would visit the neighborhood grocery and candy stores where David had a chance to buy cookies with which to "bribe" Jingles to become his friend. By welding an alliance with the dog, David was trying to master his fears.

In the comfortable reality of the dog's and my presence, David began to learn that the outdoors was not as dangerous as he had fancied. Gradually, there was a concomitant decrease in his fear of going to school. At first, David would ask me to punish Jingles for "being bad" and scaring birds or chasing a chipmunk. I pointed out to David that naturally Jingles also had certain hates, fears, and spite, and Jingles acted on these impulses.

This discussion about Jingles' "badness" led to David's expressing his unacceptable feelings about his parents. He said that he wished they were dead and that he could live alone like Robinson Crusoe on a deserted island. He also confided that many times he dreamed of drenching his teacher in gasoline "like you do it in Vietnam" and setting her on fire. David now was able to express his emotions more fully as he found they were acceptable.

The parents finally consented to secure a dog for David. Eventually, he no longer needed to use his fear of school as an unconscious device with which to chain his mother to her home, and he no longer needed to control his parents and make sure that he was around in case they decided to separate while he was at school. He knew that whenever he came home his pet was there to greet him.

Nightmares now appeared at more and more infrequent intervals. David no longer needed to run into his parent's bedroom, displace his father, and with terrifying screeches, cling to his mother. His dog was there to protect him, to crawl into his bed if need be, and help him fight off the unwelcome intruders. Having mastered his pet, David was now able also to master his fears.

Sometimes the pet does not function importantly until later in the therapeutic process. This was true of John, an adopted child of seven, who was very much disturbed by the fact that his real mother had deserted him. He had threatened to kill his sister Helen (also an adopted child) and himself because he felt that they were both very bad or they would never have been surrendered for adoption.

In spite of the fact that Mrs. B. had read many stories to John which explained the fact that an adopted child was a preferred child because he had been chosen, while with a natural-born child the parents had to take potluck, John was not convinced. He did not accept this explanation, for he felt that it was not possible for his adoptive parents to love him since there must have been something inherently wicked about him which brought about his desertion. He was sure that he had been taken on approval and that as soon as he misbehaved he would be returned.

Although my cat slept in her basket on the table, a few sessions passed before John noticed her. Eventually, he began to fondle her and later he wanted to feed her. He asked many questions about the cat. Finally, he wanted to know where the cat came from. I explained that we had picked her up in the ASPCA from an abandoned litter of kittens. I emphasized that we love this cat very much and that my two sons often fight over the privilege of having her in their room at night.

At first John found it difficult to accept the idea that a cat that had been abandoned by her mother and her owner could still be loved and accepted by others. After several sessions, during which he constantly returned to this subject, he began to consider the possibility that he was actually loved by his adoptive parents. John's recovery seemed to commence with the discussions of our "adopted" cat.

DYNAMICS OF PET PSYCHOTHERAPY

In his use of pets a child goes through a maturational process. A pet that is adequate at one time may no longer be acceptable or useful at another. The differential meaning of a pet to a child has to be considered carefully, for there is a certain "lawfulness" within which pet therapy operates.

In this connection we also find that as the need decreases for the pet as the third member of the therapeutic threesome, there is almost always an accompanying better adjustment in school and at home. The child finds that he is more free in playing with other children, he develops a greater trust in adults both at home and in school and can concentrate better on his school work.

Frequently there is also a change in themes, not only in terms of the psychodynamics of the situation but also in terms of the length of time the child spends in therapy. In the beginning, the child just strokes or talks to the animal and engages in imaginative play in which the pet does not participate at all but only submits to being handled at the whim of the child. The child at this point disregards the therapist entirely. In the next stage, the pet is the center of the child's fantasied activity and is made by the child to participate in the role assigned to him.

Sometimes children cannot acknowledge the fact that they would like me to share something with others. When the child can offer a gift to the therapist via the dog, it may represent a major step in treatment. Overcoming the child's resistance and his inability to both receive and give gifts indicates that the child is ready both to offer love and accept it (Levin and Wermer, 1966). The child begins to realize that in order to have friends and be liked one must be able to give up apart of one's innermost being in exchange. Figuratively speaking, the Biblical story of giving up part of yourself, the rib, for female companionship, illustrates this.

By giving a gift, the child is beginning to deny his own infantile strivings which is indicative of a steady growth toward maturity. Sharing with the pet is the beginning of an active stage of relating to the therapist and to the child's peers. The children do not hesitate to say, "Jingles is hungry," or "the dog wants to eat." The child raids the refrigerator and we prepare a meal in which we all partake: the dog, the child, and the therapist. In preparing food for Jingles and for himself and later in washing up, the child can engage in what appears to him to be constructive activity in preparing food. When a child can take care of the dog, he can identify himself with the role of the therapist and possibly of the parents. He can regress and joyfully sublimate his anal drives: his drives to mess around and then clean up the dishes. He can prepare hot food for himself and for the dog and be permitted to engage in vicarious fire-setting activities. Under supervision, the child may light as many matches as he desires and put out the gas as often as he wishes. This very often serves as a release. The family food scene may be reactivated with the child forcing the pet to eat. The child may scream, curse or pout while engaged in preparing the meal or serving it to the pet. The experiences the child has had at home at meal times will probably be reactivated and worked through. Some children make a ritual of the meal. Repetitive patterns appear over and over again. They come with crackers and cookies, "force" Jingles to eat, and repeat patterns they have learned at home.

The child who has been on the receiving end almost all of his life now can be on the dispensing end. He can give and share with the pet. Others, in their rebellion against the compulsion of their homes, place the food on the floor and both child and dog eat. The child smells the food, makes animal noises, licks his hands. Later, the child assumes a more comfortable position at the table, with Jingles sitting at the head.

At this point, one must try to avoid at all costs playing the role of a parent. Nothing remotely resembling parental behavior should be in evidence. During a meal, a child may have everything he wants or not at all. Occasionally, I alone play or eat with the dog while the child plays the role of an interested observer. Later, however, the need for the dog's presence may disappear and the child no longer invites Jingles to participate in the session. Eventually the preparation of a meal may become an important ego building asset. The child proudly indicates to the parent that he (or particularly she) has actually prepared a meal in which all participated.

One of my former patients liked to visit the neighborhood candy store and attested out my acceptance of him by asking me to buy little knick-knacks for which I would give him an allowance of fifty cents. Jingles was usually taken along. This child who at the beginning of our therapeutic relationship looked at the dog from a distance and was afraid to approach him, finally, after many half-hearted and tentative trials, leashed the dog. The roles were reversed. Now he took the dog to the same candy store, had whispered consultations with Jingles as to what kind of cookies the dog wished to have, and bought these, presumably for Jingles. Actually the cookies were eaten by the child, but the impression that the child tried to convey was that he was the dog's master and could order Jingles about. This mastery of the dog showed him concretely and vividly that he could be liked and yet be the master of the situation. This helped the child to discover that he was wanted and liked in reality and that he was not "tricked" by the therapist. Playing with the dog offered the child a symbolic token that his wish for increased independence was approved and was considered as not threatening the therapist.

Even more important was the establishment of the fact that the dog was now his friend and ally and not mine. Further, taking the dog to the candy store and using his allowance of fifty cents involved making decisions. What kind of decisions should he make? Ability to make decisions and stick to them enhances the child's status in his own eyes.

Many disturbed children cannot tolerate monotony. Because of their inner restlessness, created by their inner emotional turmoil, they look for new activities which may momentarily quench their anxieties. Some of these children are aware of this need and are very much embarrassed at their lack of control. These boys and girls welcome the appearance of a companion who is just as restless as they are and on whom they can project their own desires. Jingles, they would say, wants to do this or that. Jingles was restless and wanted to explore every nook and crevice of the office or to follow the delicious smells of the outdoors. The need to "save face" was also satisfied by the dog.

Sometimes a fearful child identifies with a pet of whom she was originally afraid. Abbate (1967, p. 19) describes the treatment of Janie, a two-year, eleven month-old child. In the first session she meets the therapist's dog and although obviously frightened she protects herself by identifying with the aggressor, the lion. Janie denies this fear by making roaring sounds and by stating, "Oh, no. I am a roary, roary lion. I can scare anyone." Through this "hostile" identification, she finds it easier to face the world. In a sense she becomes strong and accepts herself unconsciously as a strong and fear-inspiring animal who can stand up for herself and is not afraid of anybody.

The child who comes to the therapy situation with the fear of dogs or cats and manages in the course of treatment to overcome it has undergone tremendous emotional growth and maturity. He now may perceive his home as a friendly, tolerable place and find that his parents and peers, similarly to his pet, are friendly and well disposed toward him.

ROLE PLAYING

The animal may assume different roles to a child. At one time the pet is protective while at others aggressive, and it may be benign and malevolent in turn. A dog is particularly well suited to this role because he is a member of a pack and considers the human beings with whom he lives as members and one of them as the leader of the pack (Smythe, 1958). A child patient is automatically included in this charmed circle. A dog likes to be useful, and he is happy when he is occupied (Smythe,

1959). These qualities make him an ideal pet and a very effective aid in child psychotherapy.

Actually, the therapist is in the nature of an auxiliary service. The therapist, child, and pet may crouch on the floor barking like dogs or mewing like cats. After a while, the child begins to people his fantasied world with other activities in which the pet, while actively participating, plays a role subsidiary to that of the therapist. Finally, the pet is no longer needed in the therapeutic interchange.

The technique of "behavior rehearsal" (Gittelman, 1965) may also be employed in pet psychotherapy. The child and the therapist accompanied by the pet, act out the traumatic situations which are provocative of an angry outburst or outright aggression. Since the animal is the hero, the child can make him engage in activities which would be forbidden to the child and thus gain unconscious feelings of gratification without developing actual guilt.

TRANSFERENCE

It is well known that transference, as we understand it to exist with adults, cannot exist with children (Freud, A. 1951). First, the active face-to-face relationship between a child and his therapist does not permit the development of a deep transference. Furthermore, children have parents who are with them and who control their destiny. The parents are thus not introjected, shadowy figures who control the patient through unconscious remote control. It is to be remembered, however, as was indicated by Sigmund Freud (1955) and Brill (1945) that the animal may in this context also become a transference object.

A deep transference to a therapist would, therefore, presents a threat to a child and might bring about unnecessary conflicts. The establishment of a beginning relationship with an animal is less threatening and thus leads to the establishment of a comfortable, nonthreatening reality-oriented therapy with the child.

In certain clinical situations, having a pet with whom the child can ally himself is very helpful as this frequently permits the therapist to play an impartial role. The therapist does not take the part of the child to the chagrin, embarrassment, and resentment of the parents and at the same time does not antagonize the child who has already obtained an ally in the pet in his fight for autonomy.

Occasionally parents become hostile when they find that strangers are successful in the very areas in which they have failed. An improvement in a child may force a parent to face his or her own guilt in the genesis of the child's difficulty and some immature parents cannot face it. However, this does not happen very often, when the competitor for the child's affection is a dog. The parent does not feel threatened when he sees his child playing with a pet and the pet assuming such a big role in the therapeutic constellation. He can rationalize the child's improvement in terms of the fact that he needed a certain pet to play with. Some parents have a desperate need to save face, preserve appearances, and make believe that their relationship with their own children remains undisturbed and that no interloper has invaded these sacred precincts. The parent does not feel displaced by the therapist in this situation and parental rivalry with the therapist, which sometimes precipitates the removal of the child from treatment, is bound to occur less frequently.

Of course, we realize that these parents have their own problems which we should help them to resolve through psychotherapy. However, until parental problems are tackled and alleviated, it is most important that the child remain in treatment. If the child is not removed from therapy, it becomes much easier later on to handle the parents' fears, guilt, etc., through therapeutic intercession.

INTERPRETATION

I do not subscribe to the (Klein, 1955) use of interpretation with young children. Frankly, I do not see how it is possible as the concepts presented to the child are beyond his conceptual level. Furthermore, what is even more important is that many children reject any attempt to interpret their behavior. They freeze up and stop participating. This may also be due to the fact that the interpretation may sound to them like the previously heard lectures and admonitions of well-meaning parents and authority figures. The child was burnt and hence does not want to accept these admonitions. A different approach is needed. Our focus is not on how the child got the way he is but on how he is functioning and what we can do to help him function better.

Generally speaking, working within any therapeutic relationship, one must have a general orientation. What is one looking for in treatment? What are the goals? What does one know of the patient's reactions? We must always bear in mind that the therapist may be a somewhat threatening figure about whom the child has heard before he came for treatment.

The child knows that the parent has spoken about him to the therapist. He wonders about what was said, and is most anxious that the therapist "doesn't tell on him" to his parents. Introduction of a dog at this point, an animal which is sympathetic, listens, and obviously cannot tell, may be crucial. The child grows in his ability to tolerate and to consciously experience emotions formerly denied. When working with young children, there is little need for interpretation and quite a bit of need for emotional reexperiencing.

My experience with pets has made me reject very reluctantly the maxim that if a child talks and develops "insight," healing occurs, or that if a child discusses his day in great detail, we have been successful in penetrating his inner defenses.

The child is interested in the present and possibly in the future, but he is not so much interested in the past. He wants, when he cares, to resolve his present situation and is not particularly concerned with the genesis of his difficulty and the methods of resolving them. To be sure, in the course of treatment he will tend to resort, driven by repetition compulsion, to earlier behavior, and thus, in a sense, he will disclose some of the factors which contributed to his nuclear neurosis. I do not subscribe to the belief that everything that happens in pet therapy has deep symbolic meaning. A motor release in an acceptant therapeutic atmosphere is helpful in releasing tension and in speeding up recovery. On the other hand, I feel that something very significant may occur even though the child merely plays with the pet and does not utter a word throughout the hour. Appearances are very often deceiving, for in therapy, things are very often not what they seem to be. Healing does not always occur where one would think it should . . . and it sometimes does occur in the most unexpected places.

For the very disturbed child, reality and fantasy are almost indistinguishable and what the child does in the therapist's office may, in his unconscious mind, be equated with a fantasy experience. It seems to me that as good results may be achieved without interpreting, since the conscious and unconscious material is so interchangeable.

If interpretation is called for, I always attempt to interpret in terms of the child's reality experiences, and I shy away as much as possible from all fancied and farfetched explanations. As a matter of fact, when the child's repressed emotions are coming out, both he and I become aware of the importance of what transpired and little interpretation is necessary. This comment is based upon my belief that in therapy one is not trying to eliminate certain undesirable thoughts or emotions, but trying to synthesize both acceptable and unacceptable drives and have the child become aware of the fact that the so-called unacceptable part of himself is acceptable. This, as can be seen from the above, is much more easily done through identification with an animal.

Since some of these children have an inadequate perception, it is most difficult for them to understand how a dog can smell and hear things they cannot perceive. Why does a dog smell? Why don't children smell as much? What smells, etc., do children like and dislike?

At this point we may have a little discussion about feelings to illustrate how some people perceive and feelings that others do not. Just as the dog, in concentrating on a very faint, but to him most important, scent forgets what to the child appear to be more important things, so we may perceive just one little insignificant item out of a totality and forget the grand picture in front of us. This gives the child an opportunity to discuss some of his sensations and vaguely to grope as to whether they are as important and meaningful to others as they appear to him, and what their meaning may be in the interlocking play of ideas and emotions.

The use of animals as a medium of therapy is largely nonverbal and the success of pet therapy depends to a great extent on the therapist's ability to convey through posture, facial expression, and tone of voice his positive attitude toward the child. Some children become interested in the dog's phallus. Why does the dog lick himself perpetually? Is he dirty? Does he like it? Are people that way too? A natural jumping-off point is then provided for a realistic discussion of dog and human sex activities. Clarification regarding masturbation and the problem of birth is sometimes brought about. Very frequently masturbation guilt may be alleviated when the child observes the cat masturbating against a sweater or pillow without the therapist remonstrating against it.

Why does the dog fight with other dogs? Why does he run after other dogs? This may help the child to think in terms of sibling rivalry and jealously. Sometimes children attempt to imitate the dog's elimination activities, and we discuss differences between boys and girls.

When a pet is used in psychotherapy, the need for language is reduced to a minimum. The child's difficulty may date from his preverbal level before he mastered speech. Thus in his nonverbal communications with the animal and with the therapist, it is much easier for him to recapitulate his previous emotional state of trauma (Ekman and Friesen, 1968). It seems that even to a verbal child it is not as frightening to convey his fears and terrors through nonverbal communication or play as through words. As was noted in another connection, this is so because probably language is "identified with demands and prohibitions of a specific level of the child's libidinal development (Harrington, 1960).

RESEARCH IMPLICATIONS

It is of utmost importance to learn whether we have in pet therapy a tool which permits us to examine at great length and under magnification the elusive something which occurs in child therapy and promotes healing.[8] Specifically we would like to address ourselves to the following questions: What problems lend themselves to pet play therapy, with what children, in what families? What roles are played by the personalities of the child, the therapist and the pet? What relationship exists between the pet and the child? What role does the need for mastery, for dependency, the need for imitation play? How does the pet bring insight into the situation? How is the path toward the rocky road of self-maturation taken? How can a pet help and sometimes substitute for a therapist? Is the relationship between the pet and child similar to that between the child and therapist? How does the child identify with the pet? Is it a partial or complete identification? What role does the nonverbal behavior of the child play in pet therapy (Ekman and Friesen, 1968)?

What is the difference between children who can and who cannot use pets? Differences in families which can and cannot accept pets? What about the first reaction of the child and his pet? The writer believes that the utilization of computer techniques will permit a more expeditious evaluation of the role of the pet, his genetic background, the child who plays with him the child's family, etc.

NOTES

[1]Many of the terms used by Levinson to describe children who come from single-parent families or who are living in poverty are no longer used.

[2]This is especially true for children in residential treatment settings as well as for children who have been sexually abused.

[3]Levinson was a firm believer in the benefits of animal- assisted therapy for nonverbal populations. He believed that pet- oriented child psychotherapy had useful applications for autistic children.

In a highly novel study in Florida, Smith (1983) brought together eight autistic children and three trained bottlenosed dolphins for six sessions of water play. Although the utilization of captive dolphins in animal-assisted therapy programs raises ethical dilemmas for some animal ethicists (personal communication with Betsy Smith, May, 1995), Atlantic bottlenosed dolphins were also utilized in a study conducted by Nathanson (1989). In an effort to increase cognition for mentally retarded children, six young boys, ranging in age from 2 to 6 years of age were taught new vocabulary words through interaction with the dolphins.

Redefer and Goodman, (1989) also wrote about animal-assisted therapy with autistic children.

[4]Levinson had great love for children and spent the last years of his life working with autistic children at The Blueberry Treatment Center in Brooklyn, New York, a program which was founded by one of his students, Mira Rothenberg. In an article published in 1980, Levinson (1980a) discussed an aspect of autism which he identified as the "Blueberry Syndrome."

[5]Levinson was the first to coin the term "Pet Therapy" but modified this term throughout his career. The terms Animal- Assisted Therapy and Animal-Assisted Activities are the most commonly accepted terms. These terms were developed by a Task Force convened by the Delta Society in 1991. They are further defined in a handbook issued by Delta (1992). For an excellent discussion on the use of these terms see Burch, Bustad, Duncan, Fredrickson, and Tebay (1995).

[6]This is a frequent theme for Levinson. Utilizing a pet in therapeutic situations does speed up therapy and a relationship is established much sooner. This is also one of the benefits of the intervention.

[7]The idea that the utilization of pets with children in treatment situations could be "dress rehearsal for life" was a concept which may have initially been discussed by Levinson, but was more fully addressed in Cain's (1983, pp. 5–6) study of pets in the family system.

[8]Levinson was a researcher and strongly advocated for investigation into the efficacy of this newly proposed intervention. In almost all of his published works, Levinson called for research to further investigate the experience. Andrew Rowan, editor of the interdisciplinary journal *Anthrozoos,* has also written (1990; 1994) about this topic.

Chapter 5

PET-ORIENTED THERAPY IN RESIDENTIAL SETTINGS

There are four aspects to the use of animals in the treatment of children in residential settings. These are (a) the use of animals as treatment aides in residential treatment centers for emotionally disturbed children; (b) the use of animals with children in a hospital for somatic disorders; (c) the use of animals as children's pets and pals in training schools for physically handicapped, deaf, blind and mentally handicapped children; (d) the use of animals in schools or classes for emotionally disturbed children (see Chapter Six). The above distinctions, however, are at present purely theoretical. Very little research in the use of pets was done in these areas, particularly in those of the deaf, the blind, and the mentally handicapped children.[1] We will discuss first the general principles which underlie all these programs, and later examine special aspects of some programs.

When pets are introduced into a therapeutic institutional setting, it indicates that the staff has rethought its role in the treatment of children and has come to the conclusion that the primary purpose of its organization is to help children and anything leading to that end should be encouraged. It also implies a recognition of the healing properties inherent in an association with nature and with our animal friends.

Generally speaking, the introduction of pets into any treatment setting will change the dynamics of the interpersonal relationships between staff members and the child.[2] For instance, pets provide that continuity of contact for which there is such a need in treatment, particularly when one is dealing with children. The substitutions in trained pet aides are likely to be considerably fewer than the turnover in human aides. Frequently, the only recognition a child can get as a person and not as a patient comes from his pet. The pet may provide the child with a feeling of ego mastery as well as with an opportunity to make some choices which would lead toward the strengthening of the ego and the development of inner controls. However, we should recall that children who spend some time in a confined setting, whether it be a hospital, training school, or residential treatment setting, tend to develop many aggressive reactions and unless properly handled, these may be directed against pets and other animals, as well as against people.

In instances where the staff, after considering various plans, has decided upon the introduction of certain pets into a new setting, it should be done gradually. Children have to go through a considerable period of learning how to handle a pet and how to be considerate to a pet (Burmeister, 1949) so as not to hurt it. Unless this is done, the introduction of pets may boomerang.

Further, many problems incident upon the introduction of pets into any setting must be considered. Routine, which is so precious to most administrators and staff, will probably be disrupted. There is also need for insurance against damage done by pets, such as scratches, bites, damage to furniture, etc. Provision should also be made for medical and physical care for the animals. A budgetary provision is necessary for attendants whose sole function would be to care for the animals and for extra space. Consequently, the introduction of pets demands a considerable reorganization of routines and somewhat different philosophy of treatment of children.[3]

In many situations, a child who had good relationships with his peers, with adults and with his pets, loses this ability to get along with his human companions and human environment as the result of illness. Nevertheless, he often maintains a good relationship with his nonhuman companion, the pet. It is quite possible that the only meaningful relationship he has at this point is with the pet. The situation is analogous to that found occasionally with ambulant schizophrenics whose meaningful association is the continuity of functioning on the job.

When it becomes necessary to remove a child from his home for therapeutic reasons, the child's interpretation of the situation must also be considered. He may feel that his bizarre behavior and poor adjustment to home or school were not valid reasons for his removal. Instead, he may think that he is rejected by his parents who refuse from now on to accept responsibility for his care. He may consider the punishment for his misbehavior, with which he has been threatened, has now materialized. If, however, his pet is taken along, the child may realize that his parents still have confidence in him since the pet is sent along and that in reality he is not being penalized. This will help the child to work through the trauma of separation from his home.

It is further known that a child's removal from his familiar environment, regardless of how unwholesome this environment may be, threatens the child's sense of identity. By not permitting the child to take his pet, one maybe eliminating the child's only contact with reality. The pet provides not only an important link with the internalized past but also an anchor in the stormy ocean of the new relationships in the institutional setting. There is security in something familiar. As pointed out by Searles (1960, p. 412), retaining personal "possessions might be of real help in affording him some remnant of personal identity, some continuity in the sense of self, upon his being admitted to a ward peopled by strangers whose actions are bewildering to him." Having a pet may give the child some hope for tomorrow, some hope for a future seen in the light of his pet.

Later on, as the child develops new, emotionally satisfying relationships, as so often happens in pet-oriented child therapy, he may no longer wish to cling for dear life to his pet, his only anchor of security. An example of this may be seen in the following: "There are several children who will not be separated from some toy animal which they have brought from home and compulsively hold it in one hand, if possible, even during washing, dressing, or eating. Lessening of that clinging is usually the first sign that the child has overcome the shock of separation and has found new living objects for his affection" (Freud, 1944, p. 70). Before parents decide to place a child in a residential setting, they usually undergo a period of anxiety, uncertainty, and guilt which creates a very tense family atmosphere and cannot but be felt by the child as aggression directed against him.

At first when a child leaves home for a long-term stay in a residential therapeutic center or school, a great void is felt in the family. Before too long, however, other interests and family preoccupations gradually fill this void and eventually the child is left out of the family's thinking and planning. The pet then helps to serve as a living link between the family and the child. The pet can also make it easier, on discharge, for the child to become reintegrated into the family.

Parents of institutionalized children need consideration also. When visiting is restricted, as it inevitably is, it serves to reinforce the feelings of these parents that they were unable to manage their child—that is why the child was removed. This tends even further to increase the parent's guilt.

By bringing the dog with them or leaving the dog at the institution, the parents indicate that they are still responsible for their child's care even though he is in an institution. Bringing a pet with them on a visit may increase the participation and interest in ward activities. This is very important if one wishes to bring about a closer relationship between child and parent.

SPECIAL NEEDS FOR PETS AMONG RESIDENTIAL PATIENTS

We must base our care in hospitals on the understanding of the "nature of the young child and his emotional needs" (Robertson, 1959, p. 6). The very young child needs his mother and is completely dependent on the person who devotes time to his care. If a young child who has so much confidence and trust in his mother is admitted to a hospital he feels that the environment which he implicitly trusted failed him. This may have an unfavorable influence on his emotional development for the rest of his life. He is too young to understand the reason for his hospitalization or too involved in his emotions to want to understand. He becomes very angry at himself (thinks that he is being punished) and at those whom he had implicitly trusted before (Robertson, 1959). While frequent visits by parents are important, the availability of pets is also important.

Frequently, on admission to the hospital, the young child will go through a period of protests, i.e., he will cry, shake himself, and look eagerly for the sight of his mother. He then goes through the phase of despair. He becomes apathetic, makes few demands on his environment, and is in a state of deep grief for his mother. Finally, he enters the phase of denial when he pretends not to care for his mother. This, however, is caused by the child's inability to tolerate the intensity of his grief for his mother. Eventually, if he stays in the hospital long enough, it may appear that he not only does not need his own mother but does not need mothering at all. The best nursing staff in the world cannot give the child what he needs, which is one person to care for him all the time (Robertson, 1959; 1962). In the absence of that, a loving pet may help prevent the dangerous denials of feeling and resultant apathy. The child's return to health can be accelerated through the acquisition or retention of a loved pet, primarily because the pet can keep communication open with the "outside" world, and help to prevent the psychological complications that can and do sometimes develop as a result of institutionalization.[4]

Even for older high-school students, removal from home frequently is traumatic. Witness the case of Joseph S. (Lieber, 1963)

> The Family Court of the Bronx, N.Y. placed Joseph S., a sullen 13-year-old hooligan, at Lincoln Hall, a 900-acre residential school for wayward boys in nearby Westchester County.
>
> A classical by-product of the slum and broken-home assembly line,[5] Joe excelled at such neighborhood sports as playing hooky, stealing car parts, and smoking marijuana. By 12, he had already become a full-fledged member of the marauding "Black Falcon's Gang." At 13, he had overreached himself—into a gas station cash register.
>
> When Joe entered Lincoln Hall, he was a hulk of hostility and stony silence. At 16, he had become a well-adjusted cooperative, above average student. Asked to explain, he said,
>
> "It was a Labrador retriever name Lucky. She was one of three 'social worker' dogs assigned to my cottage and she helped break down the wall between me and other people. Before Lincoln Hall, people meant a mother who deserted me, kids who hated other kids, cops who chased me, and judges who sentenced me. Lucky needed me for food and affection—the first thing that ever did."
>
> Asked what treatment approach had helped in their rehabilitation, the story was always the same—only the breed of dog differed. With 14-year-old dope trafficker Victor C., for example, the canine crutch had been a pointer named Tinker. Carl R., convicted of mugging at 15, gives credit to Champ, the school's sad-sack spaniel, and so on down the line-up of juvenile delinquents. As one lonely boy said to me, "It's nice to have someone around besides people."
>
> Lincoln Hall is an accredited school that uses all the skills of education and modern social sciences. Staffed by the Christian Brothers, a Roman Catholic teaching order, it was founded exactly one hundred years ago in 1863, and has been using dogs as a psychological ally for over a decade. Puppies have been in power ever since one quiet night when somewhere on the school's sprawling acres, a monk walking in the moonlight overheard a young tough who had never uttered a word to the school psychiatrist pouring out his troubles to a Russian wolf-hound.[6]
>
> "Dogs help many of the boys bridge the gap when they first arrive here, hostile, sullen, and withdrawn" says Brother Anthony, the school's gentle-faced principal. "It is not uncommon for a new boy to relax only with his cottage dog for the entire first week of his residence. The boy feels at home with the dog—who seems to him the only living creature within touch who doesn't know and couldn't care less that his newfound friend has run afoul of the law" (Lieber, 1963).

Several alternatives are available in terms of handling the child's need for a pet. If the child has a pet, he may be permitted to take the pet with him to the institution. If a child does not have his own pet, one can be assigned to him so that he has someone on whom he can bestow affection. If neither of these is possible, a third alternative is to permit the parents to bring the child's pet with them when they visit the child.

Whenever decisions have to be made regarding the child and his pet, one must be certain that the staff will cooperate and that the pet will not be considered an oppressive and undue burden. Otherwise, the staff is likely to transfer its dislike of the pet to the child. Prior to admission, a careful estimate should be made of how much responsibility the child is willing to accept or can exercise in caring for the pet; what are the child's relationships with his peers and whether having the pet will enhance these or will lead towards a deterioration of his friendship with other children. It must be ascertained whether there are adequate provisions for the care for the pet and whether the custodial staff is willing to shoulder the added responsibilities incident to caring for the pet. Later on, frequent conferences will be needed to reconcile the conflicting interests of the children and the personnel in the problems of pet-child and pet-staff relationships. What needs should be met? Where does one set the limits? Which staff member has final responsibility?[7]

The indiscriminate assignment of pets to children while they are in residential centers is not recommended. Nor does this author suggest that pets will be useful for all children. On the contrary, some children will not benefit from having pets and for others it may be positively harmful. An aggressive emotionally disturbed child who vents his hurt and anger by torturing and killing pets may later develop feelings of guilt about his uncontrollable anger which may impede therapy.[8] There are also infantile and severely disorganized children who have difficulty with time and space orientation (so-called schizophrenic children) and who have severely impaired ability in relating to human beings, to whom a nontherapy-oriented assignment of pets can do damage. These children need routine and regular activities to strengthen their egos. The introduction of a free-wheeling pet may serve to disrupt these. However, even here, if the pet is trained and properly introduced at the crucial moment, it may help the child to establish a routine of regular activities.

Some institutions have recognized the fact that permitting children to keep pets may in some degree compensate them for having to leave home. It is beneficial that pets cannot be treated like inanimate objects, and the responsibility for them may be shared with an adult (Brill, 1964). The value of pets and the emotional surcease one may obtain from them will vary depending on the kind of pets. "A pet (unless it is a dog) is not necessarily company, but at least it is something of your own. What the lonely child misses is someone who specially belongs to him or give comfort and care. It is generally a hopeful sign if the lonely child, instead of getting depressed or aggressive, gives to a pet the mothering he wants for himself; and many a child who, in his isolation, has turned to excessive masturbation has been helped by being given an animal which he can tend and play with" (Brill, 1964, p. 68).

"Some children are preoccupied with larger animals, perhaps to an inordinate degree. It is unlikely that they will be greatly helped by being given such animals as pets, or by being allowed to ride or to tend them. Large animals of strength and agility may fill a child's mind because they seem to him to be so powerful, whereas he himself feels so weak in a shifting world of unreliable parental figures. It is as if he expected the animal to be on his side, helping him to cope with life. If he is actually faced with responsibility for looking after the animal, his daydream may be shattered, and those who afford him the opportunity may be disappointed that it has not helped. The adults concerned will then learn what the child partly knew all along: that the child cannot look after anything, not even himself and his possessions" (Brill, 1964, p. 68).

Pamela, a disturbed child of eleven in a residential treatment center, was extremely interested in horses.[9] She had a scrapbook with horse pictures and a horse fantasy playmate whom she hitched to her bed every night. Sometimes she imagined she was a horse and she behaved like one. After Pam was prepared by her case worker to enable her to go visit her mother, whom she had not seen for some years, she disappeared only to be found riding a horse. Through this action "she revealed that what she was preoccupied with was a strong exciting creature which could give her freedom and happiness; in short, the Mother of her dreams. The episode was probably precipitated by her anxieties that the mother she was going to meet shortly would be less satisfying than the mother of her dreams" (Brill, 1964, p. 69).

> To return to the small animals like rabbits, guinea pigs and hamsters which feature so largely in children's homes, it is worth considering whether these serve the function for which they are supposedly intended: namely, to give the children something more to love and care for. That they do not care for them is often the cause of friction between children and housemother, who may eventually con-

> clude that keeping pets serves no good purpose. While it is true that they scarcely serve the purpose for which they were provided, it cannot be overlooked that they serve another definite purpose. They reproduce, have babies, feed and suckle them, and manifest an intricate family life at a level which is of great interest to the children.
>
> The staff can use this opportunity to make contact with the children about reproduction and birth, the divergent roles of the parents and their functions in the little families. In this way the animal families focus the children's fantasies but, unlike Pamela's horse, they offer an opportunity to bring these fantasies face to face with realistic instruction and discussion (Brill, 1964, p. 70).

Burmeister (1967) mentions the case of a disturbed boy, Ray, in whose cottage was placed a dog, Roxie. "It was decided that Roxie would undergo an operation and this was discussed with the boys. Ray, at this point, was able to talk with his case worker about his own operation, one on his sexual organs, that he never understood before. This cleared up many doubts and fears about himself" (p. 25).

Institutions can become so confining to young inmates that a tremendous urge to run away builds up to dangerous levels:

> It was past ten o'clock in a well-run, residential treatment center, when a fourteen-year-old girl barged into the director's office with the announcement that she was going to run away.
>
> "You've got to let me go out for an hour and walk around some blocks, or I'll run away! I'm so sick and tired of this place, I can't stand it." The director knew well that Claire suffered keenly from the rejection of her mother, and that her feelings of guilt over the hostility which she felt toward her mother as the result were at times more than she could manage.
>
> The director said, "Before you go, just sit down here for a few moments, and tell me what happened upstairs." Claire sat reluctantly, poised for flight, on the very edge of her chair. She was offered a Kleenex from the box on the desk. Somehow, this offer of a tissue to an adolescent girl often brought forth a flood of tears and nose blowing, together with harsh words—"this awful place—no one understands—we're so cooped up—I've **got** to get out!" The cat, curled up in the "outgoing mail" basket, got up, stretched, and looked at the girl, who reached out and took the animal into her lap. Fortunately, the cat rearranged herself and settled heavily into Claire's lap. The girl stroked her and may have received a small degree of solace from the warm soft fur; the cat purred in response, with loud content. Claire talked of her immediate grievance but less defiantly and gradually she calmed. By eleven o'clock she was ready to go up to bed, and the director thought to herself, "It was the cat who did the trick" (Burmeister, 1960, pp. 134–135).
>
> Bill, a boy of twelve with a hard, tough exterior, had temper tantrums, used rough language, and had a general what-do-I-care manner. He gave the impression of a boy who was not interested in receiving love. As he came home each day

> at lunch time, a certain little scene was often repeated. Sitting, usually in the same place, would be a small white and brown nondescript terrier known as Spot, who had a real feeling of identification with his group. As Bill came along, obviously on the lookout for Spot, the dog ran to the boy, wagging not only his tail but his whole rear end, with the kind of welcome only a dog can give. Bill knelt down, gathered Spot in his arms and there occurred a mutual exchange of love and devotion such as Bill would never in the world allow himself to show toward another being (Burmeister, 1960, pp. 135–136).

Among others in the field, Burmeister (1960) has concluded that:

> Pets can and do make such a positive and definite contribution to the life of a children's home that it sometimes almost seems as if they should be paid members of the treatment team because of all they add to the interest, life, warmth, and often humor of the group. The question of whether or not to have a pet, how many, and what kind of pets, should not be left to chance. This part of the program should be as carefully planned and worked out as some of the other aspects of treatment. The question deserves the consideration of the entire staff (Burmeister, 1960, p. 136).
>
> Youngsters from crowded housing in big cities have never had the fun of living with a pet. A pet may become an important member of the institutional living group . . . Those children who cannot love other children or adults, and who are afraid to allow themselves to show feelings of affection, can permit themselves to love a pet. Such a child may lavish the care on a pet that he himself would like to experience (Burmeister, 1960, p. 136).
>
> A pet can be of great help to the new child coming into the group. The boy or girl may turn to the animal, to stroke him, talk, and play with him, before he is able to make contact with or accept overtures of friendliness and welcome from the cottage parent or other children, or even before he interests himself in the available toys. Pets in evidence may be reassuring to the new child and his perhaps apprehensive parents (Burmeister, 1960, p. 136).
>
> A pet introduces humor, interest, and in some youngsters, feelings of protectiveness. A mother cat with kittens or a dog with puppies may evoke tenderness such as the child has not experienced before. For the child whose thoughts are mostly absorbed by his own anxieties, and who is concerned with himself almost completely, interest in a pet may take him out of himself to a degree and may help him to be concerned with another living creature (Burmeister, 1960, p. 137).[10]

SUMMER CAMPS FOR EMOTIONALLY DISTURBED CHILDREN

Summer camps are a "natural" for the introduction of pets as aides in the treatment of emotionally disturbed youngsters. All the complications attendant upon caring for pets in year-round institutions are eliminated in a camp where the animals can live outdoors (if so desired) and where they require a minimum of attention.

Some years ago, the author had been attending psychologist and consultant to a well-known camp in the East for emotionally disturbed children. Although the visits to the camp were fortnightly, a great deal could be accomplished in this setting where the entire day was used, without interruption, for interviews and consultations.

It was during the summer of 1959, a time when my investigations into the use of pets as psychotherapeutic aides was gaining momentum, that the idea occurred to me to leave my dog Jingles at Camp Blueberry for several weeks. The director of the camp was very responsive to the suggestion.[11] The staff was consulted and it was agreed that this would be an uncontrolled experiment, the main purpose of which would be to record observations. With some misgivings about what the children might do to Jingles, I left my dog at the camp after my mid-summer visit. Jingles was accustomed to being with my office patients and I had to assume that he would respond well to the campers.

There were other dogs at camp: a doberman, two sheep dogs, a scotch terrier, and a dog of questionable and obviously mixed heritage. Jingles is also a mongrel, but he has a very distinctive appearance and personality. Jingles, with his size, foxlike appearance, red fur, bushy tail, and clever eyes, made an immediate hit. According to the director, Jingles had a strange quality of "utter independence coupled with the chameleon quality of melting into his environment, taking on the coloration best suited to him with each specific child—and that was rare." Even a highly qualified therapist sooner or later fails to respond to a need, but not Jingles. He changed his personality and fitted it to each child's needs.

Although it has been ten years in crystallizing, it is to Jingles' visit at Camp Blueberry that the idea for this book must be credited. For that reason the record of Jingles' stay at Camp Blueberry, kept in diary form by the clinical director, Mira Rothenberg, (1959), is so relevant to the theme of this book that large portions of it are reproduced here:

> The first day was uneventful except that the dog and the children eyed each other closely. Next day, Jingles went along with the children to the water and there a strange thing happened.
>
> "Hey, Levinson, come on into the water," yelled out Barry.
>
> I looked up at the child in surprise and then looked around. To all my knowledge, Dr. Levinson wasn't there. The child must be hallucinating! So I ask with quiet innocence, "Where is Levinson?"

"He there sitting on the sand," was the child's response.

"Huh?" I expostulated.

"Oh, there, Levinson, the dog, you know," was Barry's answer to my idiotic "Huh?"

But the dog was smarter than all of us. He responded to Barry's calling him by his master's name and joined the child gleefully in the water. Much laughter and amusement ensued. One of the staff suggested to Barry that the dog's name was Jingles.

Again the child summed it up for us with, "He Levinson, the doctor. He nice. So he, the dog, be called Levinson. Understand? 'Cause Jingles is mostly for Christmas and Levinson better for all year around."

From then on Barry had first claim on Jingles. Suddenly, and for the first time, Barry, with a concern that amazed us all, became aware of someone else, of a being other than himself. The feeling Barry expressed did not smell of jealously or fear. Despite the possessiveness Barry demonstrated toward Jingles, there was in it an aspect of real consideration and concern. Barry asked, for him, new types of questions: Did Levinson eat? Did he sleep enough? Maybe the sun is too strong for him; maybe the water is too cold. Sure I want him to be in the water with me, but I think Levinson wants to sit in the sun with Andy. I think he wants to by hisself now; I don't think he want no children, not me anyhow. I can't sleep until Levinson gets back in the house, 'cause what if he gets lost.

Billy, Jerry, Larry also voted that the dog they loved most was Levinson. Suddenly they began to attribute to the dog insights about themselves and other people. It was safe to give up the hardened defense and the "I-don't-care" attitudes; and it became safe to admit to love, to concern, to consideration, to health in relation to this small, scrawny, imperfect, almost-human dog. Much safer than in relation to adults.

"He snarled because he is angry, but he is really angry because he is lonely and that hurts him. Loneliness hurts something awful to Levinson," Simon would say.

"Here we go off and have us a good time and leave this poor little Levinson alone, just like my parents do to me!" Jerry would yell out.

"You think Levinson wants to be loved, or he don't, ha? Maybe he is scared if he is loved. Maybe it's because when he is loved so awful hard then there is nothing left to him. He is all loved up," Billy would say and then continue his monologue, "But I think he really does want us to love him, not only so hard. What do you say, Larry?"

"You've got a point there," Larry piped up. "If we could sort of love him very much but at the same time not so much—sort of make him feel like he's free, like we ain't gonna make mince-meat out of him."

Billy, "Gee, it sounds good, but how?"

However, successful as Jingles was in leading many of these boys to an understanding of their own needs and desires and to expressing their feelings (supposedly about Jingles), the victory of the summer for the canine guest therapist was Andy. Andy was afraid of food, of walking, of talking, of screaming, of fighting, of water, of air, of his own shadow—and last but not least—Andy was terrified of all dogs and any dog. When he saw one he screamed. When a dog accidentally brushed against him, this boy would swoon. If Andy saw a picture of a dog, the boy would turn his eyes the other way. Andy also avoided Jingles and the dislike seemed to be mutual. However, whenever Andy was crying or in one of his "no, no, no" moods, Jingles just happened to be around, sitting quietly on the side like a "brudder," heavy with concern and preoccupation and at the same time with philosophical-rather quizzical contemplation of Andy's sorrows.

"Take him away!" Andy would scream. "The dog . . . the dog," he'd point. "Take him away from Andy," and Jingles would quietly leave. And then one day in the middle of a "take him away" tantrum, as Jingles began to walk away, Andy suddenly yelled out, "No, don't take him away. Andy wants Levinson to stay with him."

And from that point on, the friendship grew. Andy began to eat more and more (the extras would go under the table where Jingles was sitting ready to eat whatever was dropped). When he went to the water he checked to see whether Jingles was around. When he went to sleep he had to make sure that his friend was in view. Andy never did this openly, however, never directly, always from the corner of his eye, always surreptitiously—as if he wasn't sure that he could permit himself to dare.

Lo and behold! One day, very tentatively, Andy touched the tip of the dog's ear. It was all very fleeting and Andy ran away immediately. But after that, every now and then, one could see him sneaking in a touch of the dog. Slowly, Andy began to lose his fear of the dog as such. No longer did he slip the food under the table secretively, but held it in his hand yelling, "Levinson, that's for you!" Eventually, Andy was able to stroke and pat the dog, quite openly and unafraid.

The amazing part of the whole thing was Jingles. Never did the dog show the same exuberance with Andy that he did with the other boys. Never did he overwhelm Andy or jump up to lick and kiss his face as Jingles did with the other children who were not afraid of dogs. When Andy shouted, "Levinson," the dog, no matter where he was, would suddenly appear and wait patiently at the child's side.

And then one day Jingles got lost. He ran after a car full of children going to town and then he vanished. The children in the car assumed that he had returned to camp as he usually did. Those in camp believed that Jingles had taken a ride in the car to town. Only when the group in the car returned from their trip after four hours and the boys who had remained in camp ran out primarily to greet Jingles, was the "calamity" discovered. The camp began to take on the semblance of the earth and its people a split second before buildings come tumbling down in an earthquake. It was as if a vital nerve in everyone was touched, even the most withdrawn.

The bigger boys (ages 9 to 12) organized searching parties and every few minutes a few would disappear, some very good plans and others with rather fantastic schemes to get the dog back from a "there"—seldom specific. Difficult and fraught with tensions as the situation was, it nevertheless permitted many of the boys to project upon the dog their own fear of abandonment. A multitude of fears and terrors were triggered by this incident.

"The night is coming on and he will be terribly lonely."

"He cries now. I can hear Levinson cry."

"Right out there in the dark forest a witch will get him."

"He is scared of the giants; they will eat him up."

"Maybe he will drown himself because he so unhappy."

"HE WILL DIE!"

And then the guilt and remorse began to pour out.

"Maybe he just ran away 'cause you weren't nice to him."

"You know it is because he smiled at you this morning and you make him an ugly face."

"Maybe we didn't give him enough food."

"Maybe he just stopped loving us."

Then Barry and Johnny were gone. An excited garbage collector yelled out from his truck that he had just seen two of our boys walking toward the big lake. When we caught up with them, a few frightened minutes later, Barry said, "We was gonna look for Levinson in the lake. Johnny don't talk, but he can swim real good."

And so it went. After a while, after many calls to neighbors and the police, the children were put to bed. It took three hours to get them to sleep. When all seemed under control and all the children asleep, I started out for a walk but as I passed the younger children's cottage, I saw there on the stoop of the porch an apparition in white pajamas trying desperately to stifle sobs. Barry, who couldn't care about a soul in the world, sobbed out, "But Levinson is cold and he feels so lonely and scared . . . Tell God I'm never, never gonna be nasty if he sends Levinson back."

As the tensions mounted for two days, the children did utilize more and more of their intelligence.

"Call the dog catchers," Larry said.

We did.

"Call ASPCA," Billy commanded.

We did.

Every farmer in the vicinity got a description of the dog, composed, printed and delivered by our children. Sunday, early morning, it all brought forth results. The ASPCA notified us the dog was found.

As the dog was brought back, there was no greater love, no more genuine tears, no greater joy and relief than that which accompanied Jingle's return. And Barry, huddled up under the porch was sobbing happily, "Thank you, God. Now I'm gonna be real good."[12]

Sometimes an incident involving a dog may occur in a camp for emotionally disturbed children which may mobilize the children, promote interaction, and thus expedite emotional healing. Boys who seemingly knew little about themselves or others, or the dynamics of human interaction, developed meaningful insights and new depths of emotional interrelationships. Regardless of the kind of protective masks these boys presented to the adult world, whether hostile or indifferent, overactive, aggressive or withdrawn, it was remarkable how quickly a bushy-tailed sensitive mongrel won their trust to the extent that most of them poured out to Jingles their loneliness, fears, and hunger for love.

It will be recalled that there were several other dogs at Camp Blueberry, none of which had ever elicited the kind of responses from the children that Jingles did. This is no accident. Undoubtedly Jingles was endowed with an unusual amount of sensitivity to and faith in people. There is no doubt, also, that Jingles had learned much in a psychologist's office and that he had become extremely adept in picking up cues and modifying his responses to the needs of emotionally disturbed patients.

The training of Jingles had been accomplished without a planned program. But there is no reason why dogs could not be trained for exactly the kind of job Jingles was able to do at Camp Blueberry.[13] If programs can be so successfully devised and executed for the training of "Seeing Eye" dogs, for the rescue dogs who go out in the mountains of Switzerland with their "Red Cross" uniforms; then it should be quite feasible to train what a reporter in *This Week Magazine* called "Seeing Heart" dogs (Lieber, 1963).

It is very exciting to contemplate the scale of rehabilitation of the emotionally sick such a program could implemented. Problems of supplying Seeing Eye dogs to the blind, where one dog can serve only one man, or where one man may need several dogs because of the rather brief span of a dog's life, would not apply. "Seeing Heart" dogs could help hundreds of youngsters in institutional settings; youngsters who, unlike the blind, have a much better chance of regaining their emotional-insightful health.[14]

A WORK PLAN INVOLVING ANIMALS

A suitable work plan for institutionalized patients, and one that can be implemented for part of the year in many residences, is farming. In such a program, as little farm machinery as possible should be used. Emphasis, wherever and whenever possible, should be placed upon the use of farm animals. The farm need not become a profitable enterprise. Primarily, the benefits derive from children learning how to handle animals, to develop a relationship with them and through them with nature which can expedite healing.

The introduction of animals in a setting which never had them requires knowledge, planning, and staff. Every animal must be introduced carefully with a full explanation of how he is to be handled and what to avoid. The staff should emphasize the fact that every animal has special needs which must be taken care of if the animal is to thrive. Farm animals can easily become pets. Pets should not be handled too much or too roughly. In this situation, the attitude of the staff toward the animals will make an indelible impression on the children and they will behave accordingly. It will greatly influence the children's kindness and consideration for pets.

Those who previously were unable to join in any communal effort may find themselves motivated by animals to participate in work committees assigned to the care of the animals.[15] The need to make choices and decisions for the institution's pets can strengthen weak egos and foster cooperation among the children.

The following quotation from Erikson, which describes problems of adult patients, could equally be applied to teenagers who also have a great need for constructive activities in hospitals for mentally ill and one of these activities could certainly be working with pets. "Hospitalized patients, having been committed, are ready to commit themselves. They expect 'to go to work,' both on themselves and on whatever task they may be asked to do. But too often they are met by a laborious process of diagnosis and initiation which emphasizes the absolute distance of patienthood from active life. Thus literally "insult is added to injury" in that the uprooted one, already considered expendable or abnormal by his previous group of affiliation, finds himself categorized and judged by those who were expected to show him the way through a meaningful moratorium. Many a man acquires the irreversible identity of being a lifelong patient and client not on the basis of what he "is," but on the basis of what is first done about him (Erikson, 1964, p. 97).

LONG-TERM PHYSICAL ILLNESS AND THE PET

Children who have been exposed to severe physical pain or who have been immobilized for a long time tend to engage in autistic fantasies. They are also prone to develop distrust for people, as if the people who minister to them and of necessity have to force them to through certain procedures were responsible for their pain. These children may internalize their feeling of hurt, pain and despair by rationalizing it with the explanation that they are being punished for having been "bad". Significantly, quite a bit of the child's ego strength is used up during such an illness to build defenses against reality threats stemming from his illness. Having a pet around who can give added strength and act as a sort of "alter ego" is very helpful.

When the child's physical condition improves, any restraints, no matter how mild, which may be exerted by the staff on these sick children because of medical procedures which still have to be observed or for other medical reasons, become an overwhelming threat. The child is forced to realize that he is not what he was before his illness set in and begins to worry about whether he will ever be well again. The conflict between the need to deny his continued illness and life's reality becomes unbearable. The child panics. His unverbalized fear expresses itself in severe temper tantrums, refusal to eat, constipation, etc.

Reaction formation may also occur; the child may become apathetic. The presence of a pet who stays with the child throughout these periods and who in a sense is a participant in the child's autistic fantasies may be the greatest antidote to apathy. At this time the fear of death is vary great. The pet, at this time, can serve as a talisman against the fear of death (Heiman, 1965).

The frightened child, to whom every movement may signify sudden pain or the threat of another critical medical procedure, finds it difficult to follow instructions and to do things and engage in activities which were formerly medically contraindicated. However, having a pet around provides the child with an incentive for engaging in these very activities. The need for independence overcomes the regressive dependency needs. He has to get out of bed to feed and care for the animal. This provides an exercise for larger muscles. Minimal movements necessitated by picking up, petting, or playing in bed with the animal help restore and maintain muscular strength and coordination (Hill, 1966).

When the child returns home and misbehaves, the mother may feel that she is less competent in handling her child than the hospital nurses were. She finds this very embarrassing and will not mention it, not realizing that her self-esteem and confidence have been dealt a blow and that the child is "reacting to the separation experience and not to any fault in her" (Robertson, 1959, p. 13). However, when the child comes home with his pet, these experiences may not be as painful and anxiety-provoking and the transition period will not be as prolonged.

PHYSICALLY HANDICAPPED CHILDREN AND PETS

Parents of handicapped children generally feel guilty about their supposed role in causing the child's disability. In their efforts to expiate their guilt, these parents frequently overprotect the child and do many chores for the child that he can very well do for himself.

Adopting a pet can solve many problems both for the disabled child and his parents. Interviews with parents of handicapped children evoked many interesting appraisals of the value of pets. One mother reported that when a handicapped child is unable to join the other children's games, his pet will provide him with some companionship and show him that he is loved for himself. Another parent said, "My boy enjoys playing with his dog. When he first got the pet, his pats were really slaps because he couldn't control himself. He soon learned and forced himself to control his movements so he could pet the dog gently without frightening it."

An insightful remark about sibling rivalry was made. "We got a dog specifically for the child so when his brother went to play the dog would stay with him and he wouldn't feel so alone". The value of pets in the learning process was commented on by several parents. "Our son taught his dog to sit and lay on command. In doing so he had to force himself to speak the commands and make the motions to teach the dog." "My son had a poodle. Through teaching the dog and talking to it, he had to learn many words he had not said before. He also used his muscles by taking care of the dog. But, most helpful to his emotional growth, he learned about death through the dog. We explained what had happened when the dog died. He missed his pet and was very lonely, but he had learned to accept death. He wants another pet now and we will be getting him one soon" (Robertson, 1959, pp. 10–11).

Frequently, physically handicapped children are unhappy, emotionally immature, are concerned with their own problems and feel that no one in the world can be as miserable as they are. They feel inferior and because of the overprotection extended to them by their parents, think that they cannot achieve even the goals which are possible for them. Thus, *National Humane Review* (1966) reported that pets served therapeutic purposes for "severely handicapped youngsters at the United Cerebral School in Denver, Colorado." These children had a variety of pets. Occasionally, physically handicapped children are so afraid of competition and are so unsure of themselves that they will not permit another child to play with their pet.

Animals are used extensively in the instruction provided for children in the lower grades of the University of Michigan Medical Center hospital school (Rx for the ill and handicapped, 1961, p. 415). The animals are used to provide lessons for child patients. "See how the cat cleans himself . . . cleanliness is important for boys and girls too." It is reported that children become so entranced with their new animal friends that they are reluctant to leave the hospital. Occasionally a child is permitted to take a pet home with him.

Another successful experiment is carried on by the Norwalk Hospital (Norwalk, Connecticut) There, every Tuesday they hold an "Animal Day." The animals presented usually include a rabbit, guinea pigs, turtles, etc. At the Orthopaedic Hospital in Los Angeles where one may find severely handicapped children, a "butterfly tree" is provided for the children where they can observe the process of butterflies emerging form their cocoons.[16]

At Bellevue Hospital in New York City animals are included in the nature curriculum.

STAFF–PATIENT INTERPLAYS

Everyone gives lip service to the fact that a child in an institutional setting tends to lose contact with the outside world because of inadequate social stimulation and the lack of emotion-provoking personal possessions. There is the danger of the creation of feelings of depersonalization. The child must be given something he can love and cherish; something that will bolster his self-esteem; something that will make him feel that he counts, that he is important, that his likes and dislikes are considered. He will then no longer feel like a lost sheep.

The child may establish various types of emotional relationships with the adults in charge depending upon his own reaction to them and their reaction to him. The adult staff of a residential center may play constructive emotional and sometimes even hostile roles in the child's mind, even though their actual participation in the child's life may be minimal or the role they play in the child's life may have nothing to do with the role assigned to them by the child because of his inner psychic needs. Where there are pets, however, the animal can remain the recipient of the child's affection, a constant love object in the swirling currents of love and hate inundating the child.

For instance, in an institutional setting, a child may develop a very good relationship with a member of staff or even with a minor caretaker. This, I feel, is positive, and should be encouraged. However, it creates an unconscious rivalry between the parent and the staff person which hinders the optimal participation of the parent and the child in the psychotherapeutic process. Furthermore, the child is conflicted. However, the presence of a pet to whom the child can transmit some of his feelings presents no threat to the parent and will tend to reduce parental guilt and create a more favorable atmosphere for rapid recovery on the part of the child.

Particularly does this become important when the time for the child's discharge arrives. The child need no longer be in conflict or feel that he is going to be in trouble because of the alliance he has formed in the institution with the therapist against the so-called bad parent. The alliance was formed with his pet. The pet is also going home. Conflict is avoided and the danger is obviated.

When a child comes to a residential setting which is uncongenial, he may withdraw for self-protection into his own more pleasant autistic world and isolate himself from his environment or he may adapt to it by internalizing the bad features of his environment. Either approach is psychologically an inappropriate method of solving one's problem.

To help the children grow and develop in an institutional setting, provision for extras should be made and one of these is a pet. This pet should be matched as far as possible to meet the child's needs. Experimental investigations are in order as to what kind of pets would be useful and in what situation. What kind of a mascot is most suitable for a boys' or girls' cottage?

Pet fairs should be organized. Prizes should be awarded to all children who take good care of their pets. Children who have these common interests will develop a feeling that they have things in common, will accept a group identity, will feel that they belong. Most likely most of these children had never felt that they have a common identity. As was pointed out by Burmeister, "Pets in a children's home become an interesting part of the family" (Burmeister, 1949, p. 148).

The child in an institutional setting, just like a child at home, should have his own personal corner for his possessions and a place where he can keep his own small pets such as turtles, guinea pigs, fish, or frogs.

However, animals cannot be crowded too closely together or they become aggressive. This is because their living space has been invaded. They need a certain territory for themselves in order for them to survive. Children, too, have territorial needs (Colman, 1968, p. 465). "Many of us can only work or relax in one part of the home or library, or have one area, perhaps a barstool, where we feel secure. Children often have their own 'secret place' even after they have given up their security blanket or their favorite doll."

All staff members should be fully attuned to the unusual sensitivity and perceptiveness of many patients. For instance, the case worker should never give the child an opportunity to serve that she is disdainful of his parent. This may come through in very subtle ways by throwing out the clothes that the child brought with him, by making him immediately take a bath on arrival at the school, and also by neglecting or disparaging the pet that he brings with him.

SUMMARY

There are far too few residential treatment centers for children, but even some that are available do not meet anything like desirable standards. No doubt all personnel is scarce, particularly trained personnel, and turnover is excessive. Values that may make a residential setting worthwhile are generally absent. Of course, there are too many children to take care of and some feel that half a loaf is better than none. This is highly fallacious thinking. When we have no facilities, we are aware of our lack and we do something about it. Why mesmerize ourselves into the sleep of the "just" by saying: "Yes, we may lack many essentials, but our children get therapy twice a week." There is still a feeling, it seems, in many residential settings, that the word "therapy" can cover up for a multitude of sins. No amount of therapy can make up for the lack of essential relationships, of warmth and concern among which are the life-giving presence of selected pets to which children can relate. Particularly must one be concerned with it since residential psychiatric treatment, no matter how expertly managed, does not seem to relate to subsequent "adjustment on discharge" (Davids, 1968; Eaton, 1967).

Some children in residential or long-term hospital placement express their hostility against themselves and the setting in which they find themselves by becoming apathetic and uninterested in their surroundings. These children need manifold visual and perceptual stimulation and success experiences. Furthermore, those children who have been emotionally deprived in early childhood have difficulty in establishing firm interpersonal relationships (Spitz, 1960) and particularly in engaging in a psychotherapeutic interchange. These children, however, who have been so often rejected and who reject themselves and have quite a bit of inner-directed hostility may obtain emotionally satisfying success experiences through associating with an animal friend—a therapeutic aide.

Efforts must be made to stimulate the curiosity of the child by ever-changing displays for fish, small animals, etc., which should make the institutional child ask questions. Even handicapped children profit from pets.

The deaf child can communicate with his pet. In this area he need not feel handicapped. This is also true of the blind and physically handicapped child.[17]

It seems to us that considerations of "physical hygiene," staff convenience, etc. should not supersede children's psychological needs.[18] A definite provision should be made for the ownership of pets by children who may profit from the association with pets. A pet may provide the link between the child and his home and later on ease the transition between the residential setting and the home.

Occasionally, a member of the professional or nonprofessional staff may himself have great interest in nature and in pets. Children who own pets may find it easy to develop a relationship with such a person. These contacts may prove to be more fruitful, both socially and psychotherapeutically, than the formal psychotherapeutic sessions with a skilled therapist.[19]

NOTES

[1]Due in large part of the early work of Levinson, this statement is no longer accurate as there is a growing and rich body of literature which addresses this domain. Shortly after this publication, Loney, (1971) wrote about the canine therapist in a residential children's setting specifically addressing issues pertaining to the companion animal's qualifications, recruitment, and training. Sam Ross, the founder and executive director of Green Chimneys Children's Services, has dedicated his life to creating a community where animals play an important role in the emotional healing process with children. Ross has written extensively (1981, 1983, 1989a, 1989b) about the usefulness of farm animals and companion animals as therapeutic adjuncts in the treatment of children in residential care.

In another work, Gionski (1985) uses case examples to illustrate and document her work with adolescent males in a residential setting. Mallon,(1991, 1992a, 1992b, 1994a, 1994b) has also written extensively about the efficacy of utilizing both farm animals and companion animals with children in residential treatment.

[2]Mallon's (1992a and 1994a) articles speak to the change in dynamics between children and staff when an animal is introduced into a therapeutic setting.

[3]A guide edited by Stephanie Senter (1993) for Green Chimneys Children's Services discusses the specifics of implementing an animal-assisted therapy program. Mallon's (1993b) chapter in the same text specifically discusses aspects of implementing such a program in a residential treatment program for children.

[4]Once again, Levinson's approach to working with the child and his or her family resonates with the ecological perspective of child welfare services as advocated by Germain (1973), and Laird and Hartman (1985).

[5]Many of the terms used in this description, popular at the time when Levinson originally wrote this work, are no longer used to describe children's families or environments.

[6]Although Lincoln Hall continues to operate, they no longer utilize dogs as part of their intervention with their population. Green Chimneys is the only residential child caring agency which utilizes dogs in their treatment approaches with children.

[7]These issues are important to consider and are addressed by both Ross (1989a) and Mallon (1991).

[8]Although the issue of abuse toward animals in residential treatment centers is commonly given as a reason why animals cannot be integrated into the therapeutic milieu, most studies have found (Ross, 1989b; Mallon, 1994a, 1994b) that abuse is minimal; in fact, in most cases the children are protective of the animals and children who do abuse are quickly stigmatized by other children as perpetrators. Tapia (1971) studied children who were cruel to animals and in a follow-up study, Rigdon and Tapia (1977) revisited this domain.

[9]There is a large body of literature on the efficacy of therapeutic horseback riding. For further information see Brock (1992), Lawrence (1984), and McCowan (1984).

[10]Utilization of animals can help promote empathy and provide nurturing experiences for children.

[11]The director of this camp, Mira Rothenberg, whom Levinson considered to be "the daughter he never had," recounted this story to this author in an interview conducted in her home on April 19, 1993.

[12]Mira Rothenberg confided that her only thought throughout this ordeal was "what am I going to tell Dr. Levinson—I've lost Jingles!" When Jingles was found, she too said a prayer in thanksgiving for his recovery.

[13]Currently the Delta Society's Pet Partner's program certifies dogs and other companion animals to be utilized in therapy and service programs with people.

[14]Samuel and Elizabeth O'Leary Corson adopted this concept of "feeling

heart dogs" from Levinson, conducting one of the earliest pet-facilitated psychotherapy studies using a colony of 20 dogs at Upham Hall Psychiatric Hospital in Ohio.

[15]The Green Chimneys Children's Services and School of Little Folk, in Brewster, New York, founded in 1947 is one of the few schools in the country which took Levinson's suggestion to heart. For almost 50 years, Sam and Myra Ross have been providing the highest quality residential care for children who cannot live at home with their families. With its mission of care and concern for all living things, this program has been described as a "living laboratory for animal-assisted therapy."

[16]The popular literature is replete with references to the utilization of pets in therapy with people. In large part due to Levinson's pioneering work, many health care facilities for children and other populations utilize animals as an integral part of the overall treatment process. For an overview of the usefulness of this intervention with various populations, see Phil Arkow's (1984, 1987) edited works on animals in the helping professions. In an early article, Brickel (1982) also provides a practical framework for understanding the usefulness of animal-assisted therapy.

[17]Unfortunately, there remains little conceptualization or literature in these areas. Bassing (1984), however, does discuss the usefulness of companion animals with the blind; Bergen (1984) wrote about companion animals for the handicapped.

[18]The obviously labor intensive nature of cleaning up after companion animals in residential programs and other hygiene related issues are frequently cited by health care professionals as exclusionary criteria for the utilization of animals in such facilities. Such bias impedes many practitioners from ever witnessing the benefits of the intervention (see Schantz, 1990, for a discussion about preventing potential health hazards incidental to the utilization of pets in therapy).

[19]Levinson's final point cannot be overlooked in that, in many cases, it is the personal interest of one professional which motivates a program administrator to consider the efficacy of this intervention.

Chapter 6

PETS PROVIDE THE "EXCEPTIONAL" CHILD WITH MOTIVATION FOR LEARNING

The setting in which teaching with the aid of pets is arranged will determine both the role of the teacher and the pets. Pets are frequently used with so-called normal children in an ordinary school setting or in a residential setting (David, no date; Eisley, 1968). However, pets may also be used most beneficially in special cases for exceptional children in public or day schools or in residential settings for severely emotionally disturbed or schizophrenic children. Our discussion will concern itself primarily with children who have severe emotional handicaps. We shall consider (a) the role of the teacher, (b) the teaching method involved, and (c) the role of the child.

THE TEACHER

If a program is planned to use pets in teaching emotionally disturbed children, it is essential that the teaching staff as a whole learn about the therapeutic value of pets and the various techniques that can be employed to make such a project work effectively. It seems to this writer that the following are the minimum qualifications for effective teaching of emotionally disturbed children via pets. The teacher should be comfortable with nature, like pets, and have an easy relationship with animals. He should be pet and teaching oriented.[1] A staff member in such a program must be able to exert flexible firmness in helping a child grope his way towards learning even what may appear to be very easy tasks. This would come about from an **emotional** awareness that the child may have an ambivalent attitude toward learning, that learning may represent a subtle threat to his precarious emotional balance and defense structure. A sensitive teacher, intellectually aware of the fact that the very symbols used in a learning task may represent some unknown dangers of a frightening discovery, will make haste slowly.

Knowing that it takes a long time to modify undesirable attitudes towards learning, the teacher in good mental health and with confidence in his own judgment will be able to help these children. Children are always looking for subliminal cues in testing out the teacher's attitudes toward them and toward the subject matter. It is important to understand that even a normal child, when frustrated by difficult subject matter, may direct his hostility to the teacher who to him personifies the difficulty. Paradoxical as it may seem, the same student may direct his love (if successful) to the same teacher. These ambivalent attitudes are even more pronounced with the emotionally disturbed child where these attitudes are quite palpable and evident. A teacher who feels that he should be successful with every pupil may face a subtle threat with a child who is resistant or difficult to teach. The anxiety generated can produce internally-directed aggression resulting in a depression. This anxiety, however, may also express itself in child-directed hostility. Since emotionally disturbed children are hypersensitive to such cues, they will find rejection even with a teacher who is trying very hard to conceal his emotions. Such a child then feels that he is accepted neither at home nor at school. The introduction of pets can assist both the teacher and the students. Animals, a constant source of interest to children, provide a diversion which dissipates tensions and relieves the anxieties of teachers. Primary grade children were very much interested in units dealing with the needs, identification, and habits of animals (Kamby, 1963).

Teachers must become aware of their own likes and dislikes. They must accept the fact that it casts no reflection on them to prefer one child to another. It is not unusual for a teacher to have a feeling of dislike towards a child who is difficult to teach or who fails to learn as readily as his peer. Realizing how normal such emotions are enables one to better control these feelings and act them out in a manner that is not harmful to the children.

The teacher of emotionally disturbed children is not a therapist. Sometimes it is difficult to separate one from the other, except that the teacher's emphasis is on school learning. He is working with the **conflict free** sphere of the ego (Hartman, 1955; Hartman, 1964). While he may recognize the source of the child's difficulties, the teacher does not address himself to it.

Yet it is difficult to separate reality problems from those affecting attitudes and emotions. Successful learning of subject matter by itself can instill more positive attitudes towards learning and school which in turn affect the child's adjustment. As in every teaching situation, the child's level of emotional development, his ego strength, his age[2] and learning readiness are to be considered (Pearson, 1954; Winnicott, 1953).

Sometimes the preconceived notions harbored by teachers that the presence of pets in a class of emotionally disturbed children does not lead to positive learning experiences nullifies their use. Some teachers even fear that the aggressive children will kill the pet thus creating anxiety not only for themselves but for the other members of the class. Further, since some of the smaller pets die rather frequently, they fear that this too may exacerbate child anxieties.

The writer feels that these misgivings are not based upon palpable evidence. Proper supervision would in most cases prevent wanton killing. The death of a pet from natural causes, on the other hand, may become, if properly handled, a wholesome learning experience.[3]

METHOD

In order to develop the interest of the children in the pet, it is suggested that the cage, terrarium, or aquarium containing the species being studied be placed on the science table with an appropriate display of relevant books, animal pictures, etc., nearby.

The pet is a powerful tool for more fruitful teaching. When a child is confronted with a living object, his interest and attention are captured.[4] Learning becomes reality-oriented, giving the child emotionally satisfying experiences. Subjects become meaningful that were difficult to master, deflated the ego and often ended in failure. The living lesson is exciting, self-fulfilling, and ego building. The child becomes deeply involved involving problems concerning his pet's care. Learning difficulties are aborted and what's even more important, the child begins through the pet to identify with his teacher and is motivated to learn, to experiment, to explore and gradually even to modify his behavior.

In a particular class for emotionally disturbed children, where they had an aquarium and a turtle terrarium, a certain learning environment and procedure were established. When a new child was introduced, the entire class would ago to a pet store and purchase either a fish or a turtle for the newcomer. Prior to the visit to the pet store and during the trip there was animated discussion about what kind of fish or turtle to purchase, weighing the merits of each student's suggestion. Pets can provide real impetus for the development of writing and reading skills.

The child should be encouraged to write succinct paragraphs about the life and habits of his pet as well as the activities they participate in together. These stories should be filed and be part of the regular reading assignment.[5] Frequently, schizophrenic children reject remedial reading materials which carry the usual stories about happy people (Goldberg, 1952), "Joseph spit at them. Stephen tore them to pieces because 'they have everything and I have nothing.'" However, they very readily accepted stories dealing with animals and enjoyed making comparisons with their own experiences. Various academic skills may thus be taught by utilizing the child's intense interest in pets (Conrad, 1969). Provocative thought and discussion questions come naturally to the teaching situation where there are pets. "Why do we want to keep the animal? How can we make it comfortable (Blough, 1954).

Where pets are used in teaching, provision should be made for each animal to have adequate and comfortable living space and a habitat as alike his natural one as can possibly be made. There should also be adequate, every day care with provision for sufficient and wholesome food, water, and air (Carin & Sund, 1964).[6]

In speech therapy, a pet is a "natural." The pet does hot berate the child who lisps or stutters or stammers or has other speech impediments. Children should be encouraged to engage in speech games with their pets where they can imitate the animal's sounds and movements and pronounce the pet's name. Skits written by children describing the habits and lives of their pets can be acted out. Occasionally the young actors tell their teacher that when acting they actually feel more like rabbits and dogs than children.

THE CHILD

One of the major problems encountered in teaching emotionally disturbed children is their lack of interest in subject matter and the difficulty of motivating them to learn. A pet that makes education interesting motivates them to return to the classroom and to learn.

Many children are afraid of exploring the unknown, the *sine qua non* of learning. Delving into forbidden subjects such as sex activities, which in the past they were penalized for, carries a threat which inhibits learning (Pearson, 1954). When a child in the presence of a respected adult, the teacher, is permitted to examine a pet, his drive for exploration may be reawakened with subsequently increasing achievement level. Similarly, the horror stories children may have heard or imagined about sex activities may be alleviated. Generally speaking, whenever a learning activity symbolizes a dangerous exploration and the investigation is undertaken in the company of a pet and accompanied by a trusted adult, the exploration is transformed from a dangerous to an adventurous one.

To the disturbed child, learning may represent another frustrating experience or possibly a method by which grown-ups torture the younger members of the tribe. The economically and emotionally deprived child may come from a home full of related but not sympathetic adults and a home with very few material possessions to touch or call his very own. Such a child may never have had a "transitional object" (Winnicott, 1953) and hence never developed a positive relationship with nature. Such a child, by developing a friendly relationship with the pet, may eventually develop a friendly relationship with the teacher.[7] Some children have had aversive experiences with teachers and with other authority figures and thus are afraid to accept teaching tips and help when offered to them. It is easier for a child to identify with and respect a teacher who appears to have functional skills in caring for the pet.

When the child has satisfactory learning experiences with the pet, he is ready to accept the school structure. Further, these learning experiences which help build his ego are later transferred into emotional learning such as attitudes of liking pets and interest in meaningful rather than theoretical life experiences. As we pointed out earlier, severely disturbed children have permeable ego boundaries and have difficulties in distinguishing between self and nonself. Learning through association with a pet may shore up their egos.

Not only does the child who works with his pet get motor release, he also gets recognition from his classmates for the skills exhibited in handling the pet. Children with a fear of animals may lose his anxiety by observing their classmates work with pets. Group identification may be built up by the children's organization of a pet club.

THE THERAPIST

While both the teacher and the therapist use the pet, their approach and aim differ. Both the teacher and the therapist may utilize subject matter in working with the child. The therapist, as was indicated previously, tries to help the child understand the source of his difficulty and to explore his feelings at some length. The teacher uses the pet to motivate the child toward greater scholastic growth. Wherever possible, the teacher should share his experiences with the therapist so that they can evolve cooperative plans of helping the child. Whenever necessary, limits should be imposed after consultation with the therapist. Each child's tolerance and emotional status will determine the limits and teaching schedule.

Making progress in subject matter and developing new skills are frequently as important in the personality development of a child as is the growth of insight into his problems. When the child sees that he is making progress with the aid of the pet, his anxiety level is reduced. Progress in one area makes one ready for growth in another.

Through their experimental use in a special class of emotionally disturbed children, the motivational value of pets in the learning situation was dramatically indicated. During the time spent with his pet, each child's general deportment improved, creating a better educational and mental hygiene climate. Learning about their beloved pets was a new and exciting experience.

In one situation, a proviso was made that the child must first learn how to care for his pet before he could have it. The child soon began to realize that the welfare and ultimately the very life of his pet depended upon how well he cared for it. This stimulated the child to learn as much as he could about his pet and its management. Not only did the child's general achievement level and his ego control increase but he began to develop feelings of compassion for the pets of his peers. The child learned that the pet came first and discovered the importance of deferring immediate gratification. As the child's thoughts began to dwell on the pet, his frustration level elevated (David, no date).[8]

Through association with the pet, the child learned that the world was not inimical and that assuming active responsibility for another creature as well as learning about its needs can also be pleasurable. This awareness of the pleasures of learning carried over to the child's other learning activities, activities which only remotely revolved around the pet. A most important by-product was the child's unconscious realization that one need not retreat into dereistic fantasies to obtain pleasure.

There also developed an easier interchange between child and teacher. Children did not resent as bitterly adult direction and instruction. This was an easy way to success with a pet. The self-gratification that resulted from the gradual assumption and successful discharge of responsibility for a pet is evidenced in the stories that follow.

Bob B., an only child, was nine years old when he entered the class. He had been expelled from several schools, having viciously attacked children and teachers. He was a very bright child with an IQ as measured by the WISC of about 135. He would not eat anything in the school, fearful that it was poisoned. He felt that he was worthless and had never done anything for anyone in his life. He insisted on bringing all food from home because that was the only food which was not poisoned. He trusted no one. He was capable of all school tasks. However, he would only do electrical experiments or what he chose to do. He loved dogs and owned one, but had nothing to do with its care. He longed for a hamster, but his mother was afraid of them and called them dirty, particularly when they "went to the bathroom."

A child had been killed in front of Bob's home and died in Bob's father's arms. The specter of this tragedy paralyzed Bob's family emotionally with the result that Bob was never permitted out of their sight, except for school—thus, they infantilized him.

At school Bob was permitted to adopt a hamster. This event had great therapeutic value for him. He learned that in order to survive without its mother, the hamster had to depend upon him and to trust him. This was something Bob had great difficulty with himself. He began to see that this was not altogether an impossible idea. For example, the hamster actually ate the food Bob gave him—and not just one kind of food, but any kind that Bob gave him. Bob could plainly see that the hamster was not poisoned, and it was food different from the cheese sandwich that he had been eating daily for months. Bob also saw that on rare occasions, when he was absent or unable to feed the hamster, others performed this task—and much to Bob's amazement the hamster did not die. Thus, he came to trust a tiny bit and to dispel slightly his food poisoning fantasy. In addition, Bob was very frightened at first that the hamster would fall off the table top where we were training the animal to become friendly with Bob. Bob was sure that if the hamster did fall, he would die. One day, the hamster did fall. And miracle of miracle, it did not die. Bob was surprised, pleased, and began to show some signs of relinquishing his catastrophic expectations of life. He began to take a few more chances himself. He even assured his parents that he was capable of taking care of the hamster; that nothing would happen to it if he cared for it; that his mother who considered it dirty and was afraid of it was not to take care of it; but that he would show her how to handle it. This turnabout of roles was good for Bob. For once, he was the capable one. Bob, who brooded over the belief that he was worthless because he had never done anything for anyone, began to feel a little more value as a person. He began to separate himself ever so slightly from parental hold.

Bob's mother learned to like the hamster and at least, out of respect for Bob, to refrain from calling it dirty. The acquisition of the hamster also had a beneficial influence on his school behavior. Because Bob was a violent, hysterical child, with frequent outbursts of kicking, spitting, biting, swearing, and running out of the school, it was difficult to retain him in a classroom without an aide for five hours a day, five days a week with four other disturbed boys. His hamster provided real therapy for him when he had been untractable by any other method.[9]

Buzz: Buzz was twelve years old. He was very bright with an IQ of about 125. He was very bitter, distrustful, uncommunicative with teachers, and had a long history of poor peer relationships in school.

Buzz, rejected by his father, was the oldest of five children. He preferred not to work in group, professing hatred and contempt for his classmates as well as for the teacher. He preferred to work alone.

Buzz had an abnormal EEG, walked on his toes, had poor fine-motor coordination in writing, and poor gross-motor coordination in terms of playing group games or running. However, he could bat a ball, much to his own amazement, and was an accomplished cartoonist, if not a weird one with respect to content.

Buzz's real name was Robert. His mother treated him like a peer—discussing only intellectual problems with him, and buying books for him accordingly. He never had a chance to be a little boy except in his relationship with a turtle which he named after himself.

Buzz was highly uncommunicative except when he wanted to brag or cut down another person. He found it exceedingly difficult to discuss himself without bragging or to relate to someone without being acutely, sarcastically derogatory and condemning. In naming his turtle "Robert," which was own his real name, he could talk lovingly about something for which he cared very much without being ashamed. It also gave him a neutral subject to discuss with a feared and hated teacher. Strange as it may seem, at times Buzz secretly longed to confide in his teacher. The turtle provided the legitimate excuse of "confiding to the teacher" and for becoming a little boy by just watching the turtle for periods of time when no academic or intellectual task was required. With this same child, it was also interesting to note that the only other time he "opened up" was when he asked if he might bring a litter of kittens to school which he did with great pride.

The sense of pride in possessing a pet which appeals to so many people is often a turning point in the behavior of emotionally disturbed children. David M. is an excellent example of a boy whose behavior changed radically as he developed pride in a pet.

David M.: David was seven when he entered a special class. He was extremely friendly, loving, intensely shy, inhibited, very depressed, and a complete nonreader. He was very bright, with an IQ of 125 as measured by the WISC. His father is catatonic, on medication, but constantly having exacerbations with prolonged stays in a state hospital. The father verbally and in actions rejected David in favor of the youngest child, also a son. The mother, an infantile but capable woman, infantilized David. David was a buffer in an extremely sadistic **and** masochistic marital relationship.

David's behavior in school was cooperative as long as it did not involve reading. He was enthusiastic and helpful. He constantly referred to himself as "no good," "crazy," and repeatedly said: "I wish I would die," or "I should not have not been born."

David wanted friendship and affection but thought they would think he was "different." Thus, he withdrew physically and in his reading. He often had projects which he wanted to show children in the regular class. They were always about animals, but he was too shy to actually take the step to "show them off," feeling that he was unworthy. David wanted desperately to return to a regular class. He felt that children in regular classes differentiated him from themselves on the basis of his being "some kind of nut." Children loved David, and he was very eager and able to make friends. He longed to reach out—and he could, particularly through animals. He knew a great deal about animals and had many at home. One of the factors involved in his depression was the move from his beloved farm to the city just before he entered kindergarten. Another unfortunate occurrence was the fact that his horse was killed on the highway in front of him.

David took great pride in showing hamsters to regular classes, explaining the feeding, breeding, and general habits and care of these little animals. He achieved respect and status among his peers in this way. David's class pet, which he took home when school closed for the year as well as on weekends, was a beautiful yellow parakeet, which he named "Buttercup." On occasion when "Buttercup" flew free in the room, David took great pride in retrieving his pet, which no one else seemed to be able to do.

In this child's family where the father was in and out of the state hospital frequently and where the mother, overwhelmed by the realities of a very bizarre and difficult situation as well as her own infantile reactions to the situation, the pet given to David was the means of maintaining his self-worth. David's mother had on occasions left the home, with him, for long periods of time. Just prior to David's getting his parakeet, his mother left for many months, this time without him. David went into deep depression. The pet bird not only gave him something to love, something which paid attention to him, something to learn about and exercise school skills, such as reading upon, but acted as well as a means of his relating to his mother when she finally did return. This was possible because David's mother had raised parakeets and loved them. Because David respected his mother's knowledge of his pet, he was able to relate to her more easily and handle his hurt better.

Randy G.: Randy was almost ten when he entered the class. He was an ingratiating, constantly smiling blond boy, highly effeminate, angry, and afraid of animals although he loved his own dog. He was highly distrustful of people, was rejected by his father, used as a maid and babysitter for four siblings by his mother who also infantilized him. Randy had enuresis, encopresis, and could not read—his main academic problem appearing to be difficulty in auditory discrimination of vowels. He avoided school tasks. His peer relationships were poor.

Randy was really afraid of a hamster. He wanted one, but he would jump when he touched the little animal, or when the hamster's sudden movements or fearful movements caused him to be afraid. Randy had been punished physically as well as having been deprived of his bike for a month because he used his allowance to buy candy and lied to his father. He liked his aunt's fiance, Bruce. Bruce was nice to Randy. Randy wanted to be like Bruce. Naming his hamster "Bruce" made it easy for Randy to converse with him, to verbalize his pleasant feelings. Randy became more trusting of his peers. The hamster let Randy pet and love him, and wouldn't bite Randy. Randy rebelled at having to clean up a baby brother's room which two minutes later was messed up again—something for which he was blamed unfairly. In caring for his own pet, he had a sense of satisfaction that his efforts were well spent. He would ask to clean the cage, stating that this was necessary for the comfort of his pet.

When Randy was asked what he had learned from having the hamster, his answers were couched in these terms:

"I learned how to take care of him. This means that I know how to take care of something. It gives me a feeling that I know how to do it."

"He trusted me a lot. he knew that I would feed him. I felt glad that he trusted me and I could do something for him. And—my father loved him. My father would say, 'Go get your hamster, Randy.' My father and I would talk. My father would say, 'If ever need any food or anything, tell me, and I will get it.' We would laugh."

Food had a great deal of meaning for this child. He could never get enough, and his mother, having difficulty making financial ends meet, often deprived this child of breakfast, indoctrinating him with the idea that he was not hungry. Foodwise this child probably did not need the nourishment because he was overweight; however, he had the feeling that he could not get enough. Therefore, giving food to the hamster was as important as was the common meeting ground of food on which he finally came to have a good rapport with his father. Now Randy goes on weekends with his father while his father snowplows.

We sometimes find that a child's relationship with animals may serve as a defense against affect. Fraiberg (1967, p. 235) describes how for self-protection, an eight-year-old child had emptied her relationships with her parents and siblings of affection, since they no longer served as "protectors" and made her relationships with them formal, denuded of emotion. She transferred her love to animals.

Nancy's love for animals and the range of her feeling for them was extraordinary. When I observed her with my own dog or neighborhood dogs and cats, she was entirely spontaneous and joyful. She had such gentleness and tact in her handling of animals that the most savage dog of my neighborhood greeted her as a friend

> and walked her to my door. The illness or death of an animal in real life or in a story brought forth genuine grief. She loved all animals, birds, lizards, turtles—worms! Why worms? She brought one in to see me one day, carefully cradled in her hand. "Wouldn't it be sad to be a worm?" she said. "It's so helpless; it can't protect itself at all. And then one day a foot comes down and on it and squashes it and that's the end." She was, we saw, identified with the small and helpless animals. In her love and solicitude for them, she was also identified with the protectors of helpless things (Fraiberg, p. 235).

PERIPHERAL LEARNING FROM PETS

When pets are introduced into the environment of emotionally disturbed children, there seems to be "increased awareness and acceptance of the realities of the physiology, anatomy, and functions of a living organism. For example, many of the emotionally disturbed children described above were keenly embarrassed about and preoccupied with such biological functions as moving their bowels, urinating, etc. Such natural functions had often given rise to exaggerated laughter, neologisms, and general out-of-control behavior more than would be expected from the normal amount of self-consciousness shown by the average youngster of the same age. Often the families of these children frowned upon even the discussion of the human body or its functions. The children often referred to the process of excreting as "dirty" and believed that words describing these functions couldn't possibly be in the dictionary. They often commented, "My mother does not want me to discuss such things." However, after caring for, reading about, and learning about a pet firsthand, these normal bodily functions assumed their appropriate place in a scientific discussion dealing with systems of the body, anatomy, nutrition, etc. The children came to discuss these things naturally and to use the appropriate terms for parts and functions of the body that they had either not heard of before or considered shameful and dirty to mention" (David, no date).

In a more generalized sense, these children developed, through association with pets, greater tolerance of their own physiological process. Not only did embarrassment disappear, but it was replaced by a mature, acceptant attitude toward those bodily discomforts to which the emotionally disturbed are certainly more subject. There was less "panic" reaction and a great deal more self-control.

SUMMARY

From an eminent teacher of nature education who employed various pets in the home, the school, and the camp, come words which put so succinctly some of the major points of this chapter. Bertha Chapman Cady " . . . would make a strong plea for a larger educational use of the child's intimate relationship with nature. In no way can his (the child's) whole-hearted devotion be won more easily than by showing a real interest in his pet. It may be nothing more than a helpless birdling, even the despised house sparrow fledgling fallen from its nest, a mongrel pup, or neglected alley cat, yet it is treasured by the child and on it he expends his whole-hearted affection."

To him, it possesses the physical, mental, and emotional virtues and frailties familiar in human society and his time and energies are spent in teaching it tricks so that it may become as nearly like himself as possible. He sees himself reflected in the animal. The pet must think and feel, and act as he himself does, must dress in human fashion, walk on its hind legs, eat at a table, drink from a bottle, dance and sing or play a drum, must go to bed, feel sorry or ashamed, and in every way possible conform to relations like his own, else the child is unsatisfied. And not only the child but the adult as well usually assumes this attitude toward the animal world. Notice the crowds about the monkey on the streets, in the zoo, in the theater, and the circus.

This determination to train the pets is often so strong in children that they will subvert the animal's instincts to such an extent that the value of the study of its life as normally lived, will be overbalanced by this dramatic element unless curbed and carefully directed. Imaginative tales of humanlike animals or moralizing through animal behavior will take the place of careful observation of actual performances and real life activities which one should recognize as full of significance in and for themselves. This is a danger we are falling into today by offering our children so many books with little or nothing in them but exaggerated, humanized behavior (Cady, 1930; David, no date).

NOTES

[1]An excellent model for this type of program can be found in Hialeah, Florida within the Dade County School system. Dr. Dick Dillman, a retired veterinarian, with funding assistance from the Kellog Foundation, worked together with the

Dade County School system to develop an animal-assisted activities program for youngsters who were identified to be at-risk for dropping out of school. Guided by Dr. Dillman and a teacher from the Dade County School system, groups of young people participate in weekly visits to a farm/ecological-science classroom at the Amelia Earhart Park to work with animals and nature as a structured part of their individualized educational plan.

[2]The age of the child is an important factor in utilizing this intervention. Kidd and Kidd (1990b) in their study of high school student's attitudes toward animals suggest that adolescents do not appear to be as attracted to this intervention as do young elementary school children.

[3]Illustrative of this point is Condoret's (1983) report about the utilization of animals in the treatment of an autistic child in a nursery school setting. The report noted that the child's first spontaneous interaction with a living being occurred when she observed the flight of a dove that was brought into a classroom. After that one instance, the youngster paid attention to the dove's successive flights, the class dog, other children, and her teachers. The change in the child's demeanor when she encountered the dove's flight is beautifully documented on videotape.

[4]Based on his own experiences with children and animals, this author agrees with Levinson's conclusions. The fear that a child might kill a classroom pet is an idea frequently verbalized by teachers. Most experienced teachers know that they will, in many cases, have to teach "gentleness" as well as care and compassion for all living things.

[5]Utilizing animals as part of the educational process is very clearly present in the approach taken by teachers at the Green Chimneys School for Little Folks. In addition to having animals present in the classroom, including dogs, fish, snakes, and birds, the students are encouraged by their teachers to utilize their relationship with animals in every part of their curriculum. As such, children write poems about them in the language arts sequence, draw pictures of them in art, and learn about their life cycle and care in science.

[6]This is one area where educators are cautioned to proceed with care. Since animals require care seven days a week and school is in session only Monday through Friday, provisions must be made for the care of the animal during the weekends and holidays. The selection of appropriate animals within the context of the environment, must also be a primary concern for the teacher. One school in New York City decided to care for a piglet in their classroom. During the weekends and holidays the children took turns "hosting" the piglet in their homes. This plan worked well for a time, until the piglet grew to such a size that she could no longer be transported by public transportation. The teachers decided at that point that the solution would be to place the piglet at the ASPCA. There were several problems with the selection of a piglet and with the teachers plan to place the piglet at the ASPCA. First, a piglet was not an appropriate animal to care for in an urban environment and clearly it was not an appropriate solution to give the piglet to the ASPCA which is not in the business of long-term placement of animals. Second, it is illegal in New York

City to house a pig within the city limits. Lastly, the full-grown size of the animal was not considered when it was brought to the classroom. Fortunately, there was a happy ending to this saga in that the piglet, who is now a 700 pound pig, was placed by the ASPCA at Green Chimneys Farm. For a complete literature review on animal-assisted counseling in elementary schools and an excellent discussion about practical considerations for utilizing animals in the classroom see Trivedi and Perl (1995). Burton (1995) also provides a very insightful discussion which focuses on utilizing a dog in an elementary school counseling program. Polt and Hale (1985) discuss using pets as "therapists" for children with developmental disabilities.

[7]Levinson (1968, 1978) noted many times in his work, and others (Gonski, 1985; Mallon, 1994a, 1994b; Ross, 1983) have concurred, that at times the relationship between a child and an animal may be more salutary than the relationship between a child and another human.

[8]Several authors (Gonski, 1985; Loney, 1971; Mallon, 1992, 1994a, 1994b; Ross, 1989) have noted the important benefit of teaching responsibility through the utilization of pets in learning situations and therapeutic situations with children.

[9]Hamsters and other smaller caged animals, including mice, rats, and gerbils, can be very useful in the classroom setting. The fact that they are small, can be easily transported, and handled by children make them ideal pets. Even when they escape from their cages, as they sometimes do, teachers and therapists can utilize these opportunities to process events with young people. One such opportunity presented itself in a life skills class for adolescents in a group home preparing for independent living or emancipation from foster care, when the house hamster escaped from her cage. For days the young people wondered where she went, why she left, and would she die or survive on her own? These were questions that obviously were ruminating in their own minds about their own experiences that they would have in the future. Several days after the escape, she was spotted by one of the young men peering out of a hole in the baseboard; she was quickly captured and returned to her home. Immediately upon arrival, the hamster ate huge quantities of food, greedily filling her pouches, almost to the point of bursting. She seemed happy to be back. One of the boys commented that sometimes people don't know how good they have it until they don't have it that way anymore. Another noted that in some ways the hamster was like some of their peers who left the group home prematurely or who ran away. These observations opened the door for the instructor, enabling him to initiate a discussion about leaving the program and being prepared for independence. A discussion that would not have occurred at that point without the hamster's help.

Chapter 7

THE PET AND FAMILY THERAPY

The role of the pet in the family will be dependent upon the family's structure, its emotional undercurrents, the emotional and physical strengths and weaknesses of each of its members, and the family's social climate.[1] As indicated by Bossard (1950, p. 390): "Household pets are an integral part of family life; they must be considered as a basic implement in mental hygiene."

We often overlook the fact that pets are important not only for children but for every member of the family. A recent book, for example (Borland, 1962; Steinbeck, 1962), illustrates how a relationship between a dog and his chosen master ripens into long-lasting love and friendship.[2]

Very often this love for animals may be seen as a substitute for the love of mankind. "More than we like to admit, folks say to us, 'we just love animals, but we certainly could do without the *people* in this world' " (Editorial, *National Human Review,* 1967).

However, most people can love animals as well as human beings. When one loves and has objects of love, he is engaging in activities which lead to positive mental health. Mental health is, in a sense, indivisible, and anything that strengthens the mental health of the individual strengthens the mental health of the family and *ipso facto* also of the community.[3]

A subtle change begins to occur in the family's dynamics and in its very subculture when a pet is adopted. There occurs a dilution in a family's interaction and a reconstruction of the family's psychological potential. It seems to bring about a certain attenuation of the symbiotic relationship between mother and child and a re-direction of these emotions towards the pet. This may be particularly true of the small family. The discussion of the pet's antics is a subject in which all members of the family may participate. The mere discussion of the child's responsibility for the pet, forces the child to think of himself more honestly in relation to his parents and his pet.[4]

In an acute family crisis which may be brought about by divorce, terminal illness or financial losses, the pet may act as a stabilizer because of its offer of love, affection, and unconditional acceptance. When an older child takes care of the younger child's or sibling's pet, it will help the older child communicate more easily with the younger child. The younger child can more easily identify with the older child and thus tend to, become more willing to accept authority. This will also help him to work through, via the pet, some of his own problems of responsibility.

Through the developing relationship with a pet the child learns what he can and cannot do on a realistic basis. He may develop a new idea of self, based upon reality, and grow toward emotional maturity.[5] Perhaps the child will learn that like his parents, he too has to undergo many inconveniences for the sake of a loved one (Bossard and Boll, 1966). He further learns that sharing a loved object, a pet, does not mean losing it or that the loved object loves one less merely because it also offers its love to others.

In their myths, the ancients intuitively recognized the role animals could play in family life and in family well-being: " . . . Laelaps, for so we are told the dog was called, later figured in the reconciliation of Procris and her husband Cephalus, proving thereby not sagacity but intrinsic worth" (Gates, 1931, pp. 405–06).

Pets not only become members of the family but sometimes attain a position even more important than human members of the family. Pets very often mirror family tensions and critical situations. "There is evidence to suggest that the patterns of illness cycles in schizophrenic families are not limited to the human members of the family. We have repeatedly observed that the pet animals of the schizophrenic family show fluctuations in both behavior and health coincidental with the fluctuations in the behavior and health of the human family members. The observable animal behavior seems to have a direct relationship to the behavioral trends within the family. There are families where phobic humans have phobic pets. In one family, the mother, father, and schizophrenic daughter all had a fear of leaving their house. The dog and cat also refused to leave the house and appeared to show fearful behavior when they were encouraged to leave. In our work with psychotic families, pets are regularly in the sessions which we hold in the family's home. The pets often seem to reflect the feelings of the family members" (Speck, 1965, pp. 298–99).

PET-ORIENTED, PET-CENTERED AND PET-DOMINATED FAMILIES

The writer can still recall interviewing an aged man who said with deep bitterness, "My wife won't make as much fuss over me when I die as she did over that damn dog." It is sometimes very difficult to remove a dog from the household even when it is imperative for medical (allergy) reasons. Glasser (1961, p. 715) reports that when he requested a patient to get rid of her dog, she replied, "Why doctor, we can't get rid of our dog. She doesn't know she is a dog; she thinks she is a member of the family." And in a case mentioned by Jungreiss and Speck (1965), the mother admitted that she was less upset about the death of her own father than about the demise of her dog.

Occasionally, a parent after the death of a favorite child may acquire a pet and take care of it as if it were his child (Friedman, 1965). We find that in cases where the husband dies leaving a dog, the widow may become overattached to the dog from feelings of guilt caused by real or imagined neglect of her husband during his terminal illness. The widow identifies the dog with her husband and makes up to him for previous neglect. She indicates that she treasures the dog as a living witness to her undying loyalty to her husband. However, in the case of the husband who is the survivor, the pet is often killed because it brings back painful memories (Krutzmann, 1967). Dr. Krutzmann prepared the following case: "A woman accompanies her elderly mother into the examination room. The old mother is obviously deaf. The animal presented for an examination is an eleven-year-old Chihuahua. Diagnosis is 'heart cough,' a progressive condition of congestive heart failure, with the most obvious symptoms being that of dyspnea and painful coughing. Upon explanation to the daughter, she informs me that all must be done to save the animal, since mother lost her husband only three weeks ago from a heart attack and that the loss of her pet would be too much for her to take. The elderly woman and her pet are now both on digitalis and enjoying their remaining years."

Even unpracticed observers can tell something about the family's dynamics from the behavior of a dog. Different pets play interchangeable roles in the family setting when circumstances call for it. When the dog took sick in the Island family which was undergoing family therapy, the dog was placed in the parents' bedroom, and a member of the family had to be with him. Since the dog seemed to be so important, one of the therapists suggested that the entire family go up to the bedroom for the session. However, Mrs. Island refused because she was afraid that it might upset the dog. During the session the family cat assumed the position that was usually occupied by the dog. "In previous sessions the cat always remained on the periphery of the family circle, but tonight it sat in the center of the group, repeatedly approaching the mother the way the dog had done" (Jungreiss and Speck, 1965, p. 70).

Sometimes the pet plays a central role in the family as may be seen in the following case (Stekel, 1959, pp. 149–150):

> A family, consisting of father, mother, and three boys, kept a cat, which served as a sort of emotional clearinghouse for the entire group. The cat was not only everyone's declared pet, but even more important, it was in some ways a house deity, and every member of the family curried her favor. At mealtime the cat sat on the shoulder of one of the members of the family and was given the choicest morsels. Most of the conversation revolved around the pet, her looks and her wants. The cat was an inexhaustible source of stimulation and joy. But for the cat, the group would have been at a loss, because the interpersonal relations in this family were strained, and communications was, at best, blocked.
>
> It appeared, however, that the cat had a special symbolic significance to each member of the family. To all three boys it represented the mother; to the mother, one of the boys.
>
> Be that as it may, the cat served as a repository for the longings and emotions of the entire family. The presence of the cat permitted also a discharge of the family's libido and aggression which could not otherwise be released on the persons for whom they were intended. Someone would dump the cat onto the floor, and say, "Scram, you low-grade hussy!" or, "A bum daffy-doodle beast that's what you are!" and in such fashion, the cat always serving as a lightning rod, emotions of love and hatred were vented by all members of the family.[6]

In some families children are treated as pets. For example, Searles (1960) traces the severe psychosis of some of the patients at Chestnut Lodge to the fact that their parents treated them as pets rather than as human beings. Foote (1956, p. 217) also notes: "Dogs are loved for being almost human, but children are rejected for being somewhat canine. Which is it that we most value, human or canine characteristics?"

We occasionally find that the pet becomes the center of family life much to the neglect of the rest of the family. A woman unhappy in her marriage and not finding the strength to terminate the relationship may transfer her affection from her husband to the pet. Taking care of a pet involves a lesser commitment for the future of the marriage than having a child, is less taxing in terms of time, emotions and finances. Eventually this pet begins to assume the role of a baby that never outgrew her mistress' protective and caring needs. A child eventually grows up, goes to school, develops other associations, but the pet is always a faithful, juvenile companion, happy to stay within the narrow confines of his home. A young couple may become so involved in their pet that they neglect each other in favor of the pet, with divorce the inevitable result. Occasionally, pets acquired before marriage may play the symbolic role of in-laws and unless the couple learns to adapt to the idiosyncracies of the pet, the marriage may not survive (Disney, 1967).

In many families the pet offers the only kind of companionship the child is able to find. When the pet is removed, the child's relationship with both his human and animal environment is broken; there is an explosion of the inner protective ego defense mechanisms leading toward the development of a psychosis. An extremely important precipitating trauma occurred, for example, in the following case reported by Searles (1960):

> A schizoid youth who had no friends was raising some ducks on his parents' farm, and loved to feed the ducks and to spend his time watching them. His mother, annoyed by the noise which the ducks made in the mornings, summarily had sent them away, with no regard whatsoever for their importance to her son. It was shortly after this that he developed an overt paranoid schizophrenia, which led to a series of prolonged hospitalizations (p. 160).

We frequently find disturbed parents who neglect their family and can devote themselves to one pursuit only—care either of an animal or of the inanimate environment such as plants and flowers. Occasionally disturbed parents who wish to warn their children about sexual transgressions may as a symbol castrate the family's pet (Jungreiss and Speck, 1965), or kill the pet when it becomes the central figure in their child's life.[7]

A recent newspaper report describes the suicide of a young woman who had been ordered by her parents to kill her pet dog. The parents had intended the destruction of the pet to serve as punishment for "spending the night with a man." Obviously it boomeranged. The daughter used the gun, given to her by her parents to kill the dog, on herself. Conscious as well as unconscious parental attitudes towards sex come out quite clearly in their treatment of the pet.

Dr. W. G. Krutzmann, veterinarian, remarks, "I have often observed the character and mental attitude of clients reflected in the behavior of their pets. A tense and high strung animal is often only so because of his owner's behavior in a similar manner" (Krutzmann, 1967).

From the notes of a veterinarian come interesting clues about the roles of pets in families of "deviants" (Krutzmann, 1967).[8]

> The homosexuals make good clients; prompt to have medical attention given to their pets and prompt in paying their bills. The male homosexual attitude varies; the feminine partner acting very worried, the more masculine partner[9] displaying a gleeful attitude about the whole incident of bringing in a sick or injured animal.
>
> Among the Lesbian couples there appears to be no difference in attitude. Their animal is sick, therefore it must be treated. One incident is noteworthy. A male Samoyed dog had jumped a fence and in the process lacerated his genital organs. The tear involved skin and underlying tissues from the sheath back to the scrotum. This was a great cause for alarm for the lesbians. Each time they phoned their main concern was whether or not his "privates" would be restored to normal.[10]
>
> Hypochondriacs sometimes become involved with their pets and insist that their pet cannot exist without one or another type of medication. They are constantly swallowing pills, capsules, etc. themselves and, of course their pets must do likewise. One sympathetic husband tried to persuade his wife to stop giving their dog urinary antiseptics prescribed by us. She insisted that every time she stopped the dog felt miserable. He wanted something less expensive after three years of the same medication (Krutzmann, 1967).

Long has it been the contention of this author that there should be much closer teamwork between clinicians and veterinarians (Levinson, 1965). Not only could veterinarians be helpful in selecting and training pets for psychotherapeutic use with families that are pet-less, but for their continuing supervision of the pet's training and health, they could provide the therapist with invaluable information. As a matter of fact, the veterinarian is often the first to see the evidence of severe emotional disturbance among their clients and would be doing their clients a yeoman's service by suggesting professional help with a teammate in the mental hygiene field. In a field where the shortages of professional services are so critical, a vast and much needed resource remains untapped. This whole area should be explored further and conscientiously pursued.[11]

> In another situation, a slight, quiet, untidy thirty-eight-year-old man whom we shall call Mr. C. was married to a bigger, stronger, older, better-educated, more articulate, demanding woman. The couple lived in the home of the wife's parents and owned a gentle, affectionate, playful, intelligent male German shepherd dog.
>
> Since Mr. C.'s work was manual, he would return every evening physically fatigued. Yet, every evening without fail, he and the dog would act out a

dominance-subordination psychodrama in which each played his role as unerringly, as ritualistically as professional actors on a stage.

The greatest pleasure, Mr. C. asserted, was to relax in an easy chair, stretch his feet out onto an ottoman and read the paper after supper. As soon as he assumed this restful position, Fritzy the dog began his act. The dog would push the paper with his huge nose, paw Mr. C.'s arms and legs, whine loudly for attention, and prance back and forth excitedly, looking under each piece of furniture in the living room.

At these signals, Mr. C. would give in. "Oh, you want your ball. O.K., we'll look for it." Slowly Mr. C. would draw himself out of the chair, while the dog became delirious with happiness. Then Mr. C. would get down on hands and knees and look all over the floor for the ball. Meanwhile Fritzy nimbly stole into another room, retrieved his ball from a prearranged hiding place and returned to the parlor. There he would proudly stand with the ball in his mouth, behind his kneeling "master," who was plaintively crying, "Where's your ball, Fritzy? Get the ball. Come, let's find it, Fritzy."

Of course, Fritzy can't talk but it is hard not to imagine a knowing grin on his massive countenance. Why doesn't Mr. C. sharply reprimand his dog? Why doesn't he say, "Find the ball yourself. You know very well where it is. Get it and let me rest." Perhaps Mr. C. really likes to play the game. Well, then, why does he keep complaining that the dog doesn't let him relax?

Is it possible that Mr. C. is secretly proud of his dog? Is it possible that Fritzy is the pupil who has outsmarted the master, and the master is now taking pride in the accomplishment? Could Fritzy really be the intelligent son Mr. C. never had? And could this be the real reason why he indulges the dog?

Is it possible that Mr. C. dominated physically and emotionally by his wife, owing the very roof over his head to his in-laws, engaged in a routinized, unimportant manual occupation, finds the dog his greatest pleasure in life?

In any event, no matter how much Mr. C. complains about what his dog "makes him do" he will never wish to alter the relationship. The slight discomfort of this ritualized psychodrama of subordination to the dog is negligible compared to the satisfaction of being needed by his pet, of playing an important role in the life of an important member of his family, a member who offers him besides dependency, untiring love and adoration (Antelyes, 1967).

Not only in homes where the emotional climate seems to promote dissension and poor mental hygiene, but also in the average home, can pets promote positive mental hygiene. Bossard (1944) reports a study of thirty-seven families that kept dogs as household pets. The approach was through observations, case studies, and interviews. He found the dog to be most valuable to the members of the families studied in many different areas of living and that the dog met each one's affectional needs.[12]

The writer's research studies indicate that the possession of pets is directly related to the socioeconomic level. The type of pet owned is largely dependent upon the age composition of the group and housing available. At middle and upper socioeconomic levels, the pet becomes significantly more often a member of the family. He is permitted more frequently to eat in the dining room and even to sleep in the same room with his master. In lower class families, significantly more often the pet assumes the role of the "working" animal in that he is the guardian of the home and the protector of the family. A preliminary survey made by the writer indicates that a larger number of white children own or have owned pets than black children. Further that children who have owned pets seem to be more favorably disposed toward animals than those who did not. A large animal such as a cat or a dog is ordinarily considered the property of the entire family. Pets such as turtles and fish are usually considered the property of the child.

A question may very well be raised as to whether there are any psychological differences between pet and nonpet owners. The question, as posed, is difficult to answer because so many nonpsychological factors enter into pet ownership which might contaminate any findings: Such factors as financial ability, opportunity to own a pet, place of residence, occupation, etc. Other major factors to be considered are the preferences of the spouse, or in the case of children, the parents. However, all things being equal (and they are never equal), pet owners appear to be more introverted, less active socially, more subject to mood swings than non-pet owners. However, the writer would not wish to infer any cause and effect relationships existing here. Possibly without pets these men and women would have been even more withdrawn. Occasionally we find some individuals who use their pets (large vicious-looking animals) as a means of keeping people away from their company.

With the introduction into the family of the pet and the necessity for the pet's training, the father, if he is interested in pets, generally comes into his own and becomes an active member of the family. He is no longer the absentee member about whom the family and the children talk in therapy sessions, but who never actively participates in them.

CHOICE OF PET

In choosing a pet for one's child, many factors have to be considered. First and foremost are the parents' feelings about pets. Unless this is satisfactorily resolved, the pet adventure may be predoomed to failure.[13]

The parent should resolve for himself how much inconvenience he can tolerate. Can he see hair shed on his rugs by the dog or can he tolerate the cat's successful efforts at scratching up the furniture? The parent will have to decide what his duties, responsibilities, and obligations are. These limits will have to be decided by each parent and family in light of their own needs and tolerances.

The next problem concerns the kind of pet that is wanted. Is it a dog, a cat, a bird, or what? Hereditary and environmental influences are important in your pet. What experiences did the pet have before he reached you? What do you know about the pet's hereditary qualities?

Then again, is your child ready for a pet? Does he appreciate the need for patience and gentleness in handling a pet? What about the child's personality traits, his personality assets and liabilities?

The parent should planfully select the pet he wishes his child to have. A pet is too important and plays too great a role in the child's personality development for its choice to be left to mere chance. The pet which would be most satisfactory for the child and yet create the least annoyance for the members of the family is the ideal pet. However, the parent should try to secure a pet for his child that the child was asking for all along, if this is at all possible. The child is much more likely to cherish and take good care of a pet of his own choice. If this is not possible both parent and child should sit down and reason out which pet is most suitable, considering the interests of the entire family.

We should be aware of the fact that what a child does with a pet may be of great importance to him later. Awakening his interest in nature, it may even be decisive in terms of vocational guidance and a career. Pet ownership should and must be a positive and worth while experience.

When a young child asks for a pet, he does not realize that a pet needs care even though this may be explained and the child seemingly accepts the responsibility of caring for the pet. When the novelty of having a pet wears off, the child may become negligent in performing his duties. In such a situation, particularly when one is trying to help a very young child, the parent is very strongly tempted to do most of the work himself. It is less time-consuming and not as wearing on one's "nerves." However, the parent should realize that teaching a child to care for a pet is similar to teaching him to engage in all the other chores of daily living, such as dressing himself, feeding himself, brushing his teeth, etc. Responsibility for the pet should be introduced gradually and the child should be rewarded for the effort he makes in caring for the pet.

Once the child has mastered and secured gratification from his ability to care for the pet, he not only relieves the parent from a major part of the responsibility for the care of the pet but also develops pride in his accomplishment and a feeling of self-worth.

In his handling of the pet, the child wants the animal to be as much like himself as possible. The pet must learn to behave and even feel, if possible, like the child. The child is thus trying to find in his pet the qualities he most admires and wishes he had. If the child taught the dog and dog wins the C.D. (Companion Dog) "degree" at a dog show, the child can identify with his pet's success. Girls who successfully take care of a pet develop confidence that when they mature they will be able to take care of a baby.

When we help an older child to take care of a sibling's pet, we thereby usually establish firm lines of communication between the two. The younger child begins to think of authority as beneficial and is more willing to identify with it and to accept orders. This in turn may help him, in working with the pet, resolve some of his own problems of responsibility.

When children see how difficult it is for their pets to master certain tricks, they become more tolerant of their own learning efforts and no longer need to feel that they are "stupid." Furthermore, when children have to write about their pets and calculate the cost of feeding them, essential skills in reading, writing and arithmetic become functional and are quickly learned.

Occasionally, some children have difficulty getting up early in the morning to go to school on time. The provision of a "requested" pet who has to be walked and fed before the child can have his own breakfast, in many cases serves as a strong motivation for early rising. In many homes where both parents work during the day, the provision of a pet which has to be taken out for a walk right after school, and thus does not permit the child to engage in delinquent activities when the school day is over, has led to a decrease in juvenile delinquency.

Children who have pets are not as eager to approach and pet strange animals, nor do they express as much fear of animals. As a result, the incidents of such children being attacked by strange animals is significantly lower. It seems that animals tend to sense fear in humans and will attack more frequently those humans who are afraid of them.

However, a word of caution is in place. If a pet is wished on a child who has many material possessions and many extracurricular activities like Sunday school, music and dance lessons, etc., such a pet can only become an unwished-for hindrance rather than a mental hygiene asset. In this situation, careful soul searching before the pet is obtained on the part of the child and the parents as to who will take care of the pet could avoid much unpleasantness later on.

In order for the child to become emotionally mature, he should be given an opportunity to make his own choices. In this connection, even a normal child may have an occasional desire to destroy a prized possession or hurt a beloved pet. Children may wish, in this manner, to indicate that they are masters of their own destiny and can select for destruction whatever of their own they may wish.

Lorenz's (1965, p. 79) statement that "a strong inherent affinity with nature" makes children gentle with animals can be disputed. The writer insists that parents should teach children to be gentle with pets. Children should be taught to be considerate of animals just as they are considerate of their friends.

One way a parent can teach children how to care for pets is through example. Help the child to care for the pet. Praise him liberally for what he is trying to do, not for what he accomplishes. In such an intimate learning situation, the child ordinarily forgets about his own inner problems and begins to pay close attention and cares diligently for the cats, dogs, birds, or fish which have been entrusted to him.

Simple principles of how to approach unfamiliar animals, should this become necessary, may be taught at this time. Thus, for example, when approaching a dog, the child should approach it quietly and in a manner visible to the animal. The pet should at all times be aware of the child's approach and will not then be startled into self-defensive biting. The child should permit the dog to sniff his hand. If the dog accepts this overture by wagging his tail and licking the child's hand, the child may begin by petting the dog below the chin and down the chest.

Parents should be aware of the fact that child abuse as well as pet abuse is widespread (Morse, 1968; Rice, 1968). Just as we have the syndrome of the "battered child," we likewise have the syndrome of the battered pet.[14] Unlike the child, the battered pet is ordinarily not brought in for treatment and dies unseen and unmourned (Morse, 1968). Certain cultures, societies, groups, and families encourage children to take out their aggression on animals. For instance, when the toddler in the Navajo society begins to investigate his surroundings, he grabs cats and dogs who are so unwary as to permit themselves to be caught. Parents seldom discourage a child's cruelties to animals. They will often join in laughter with children at a dog's yelp when it is kicked or has its tail pulled by the baby (Leighton and Kluckhohn, 1948).

To counteract this, even a young child can be taught through activities appropriate to his age to develop responsibility for other living things. These young children will start developing protective attitudes toward animals in their care and eventually this may transfer to the entire animal kingdom and even to human beings. Children who have learned to love animals will not abuse them as grown-ups (Joseph, 1956).

In order to effectuate the development of such attitudes one must try to impress upon the very young child the idea that pets are not toys to be played with or left alone as one's whim dictates, but are living things which experience pain, thirst, and hunger just as the child does.

A powerful motive toward the development of the protective and nurturant activities of the child is the implantation of the idea that the child owns the pet and that the pet will only acknowledge as his master the individual who supplies him with its basic needs for food, shelter, protection, and love. Furthermore, because of their sympathy for all living things these children will also tend to be less destructive and more careful of the shrubbery and small animal life in the forest. They will not needlessly destroy butterflies, or ants' nests, or tear flowers. They will have developed respect for all forms of life.[15]

It is then and only then that we can say the following with Coleridge (1772–1834):

He prayeth best, who loveth best
All things both great and small;
For the dear God who loveth us,
He made and loveth all.

A PLANNED PROGRAM

The second aspect of pet therapy is the planned introduction of the pet, as part of a psychotherapeutic program, into a home previously devoid of pets. In embarking upon such a program, the clinician must ask himself many questions. What is the role of the pet in the family? What changes occur in the family structure when a pet is introduced? What changes occur in the power relationships? What are the differences in the psychodynamics of families willing and not willing to accept pets? Must subculture, type of family, size of family, age of parents, age of siblings, cardinal order of children, and sex composition be considered in the choice of pets? What bearing does the possession of a pet have on the popularity and acceptability of children?

Psychologists are moving away from the medical model. We no longer consider that the child's "illness" exists in a vacuum, but examine the family environment in which the child lives, which to us may become a "constituent" of the problem rather than merely contributory to it (Boszormenyi-Nagy and Framo, 1965).

In his work with the family, Bowen (1965, p. 219) conceives of the family as an emotional unit, an "undifferentiated family ego mass." He states that at times "the active fusion may include members of the extended family network and even nonrelatives and pets."

Since most of a child's difficulties originate in the home environment, in the final analysis, this is where the difficulties must be resolved. With centrifugal social forces rampant in our society, members of the family often become alienated. The presence of an emotionally disturbed child may be a storm warning of something amiss; he may be the exploded safety valve indicating that very hot fires are burning under the seemingly placid surface of family living.

Very often the child's pathology is the lightning rod which prevents other members of the family constellation from developing difficulties of their own. Members of the family project their guilt, animosity, and unresolved conflicts onto the child who in a sense becomes the family's scapegoat. A child in such a family must have constant support, for he is the hostage of fortune. He cannot divorce his parents, nor can he prevent a divorce (which he so much fears) by his parents. Whether there is an actual or imminent estrangement in the family or whether the family is intact, a pet can be the source of constant support for the child.

Frequently, a choice has to be made whether a child is to be treated at home or sent to a hospital or a residential school. By removing the child, the disturbance within the family which may have caused the child's difficulty in the first place, may spread in the family, become solidified, and eventually militate against the child's return.

To avoid the feeling on the part of the parents that they are being blamed for the child's difficulty, the therapist may begin with the following queries on introducing the pet (Framo, 1965, p. 147):

> "What changes would you like to see in the family that would benefit you?"
>
> "What changes would you like to see in yourself that would make your life better?"

And later there are the natural questions about what they think of the pet; how the pet has adjusted; does the presence of the pet add to their problems; and if so, in what way; and how the parents now feel about the child and his pet?

The crucial point on which the decision may be hinging is the availability of a suitable pet with the necessary supportive psychotherapeutic assistance. It seems to me that in most cases the latter therapy is preferable. Assigning the pet to the home and having the therapist visit the home at regular intervals tends to lessen the loss of self-esteem on the part of the child; the child can also have a better concept of himself as a deviant but still not too sick a member of the family.

In family therapy, we attempt to focus on the problem which is of immediate concern to the family. This may later lead to a discussion of past crises which may or may not have been successfully weathered by the family. When a parent brings a child in for treatment, he often feels guilty, bewildered and lost. In many cases, a child's admission to a residential setting implies that the parent is a failure and therefore the parent abdicates his interest, responsibility and further care of the child. After all, everything he tried did not work. He is a failure and might just as well admit it to himself. However, introducing a pet along with parallel therapy signifies to the parent that he is still considered of some importance, that the locus of treatment is in his home and that he can still do something for his child. In other words, he is still needed, wanted, and is not a complete failure. Generally speaking, it is easier for the family to see that they are involved in the problem and that it is up to them to do what they can to help the child.

In family therapy, one can learn more easily how the family members interact and the meaning of the symptoms of both the "sick" and the well members of the family. The advantage of having a pet is also the fact that ostensibly visiting to learn how the pet is managing lessens the social stigma of the therapy hours.

However, one should not be under any illusion that the mere placement of a pet in the family makes the task of therapy easy. Many sessions have to be spent at the beginning of the family therapy to help the family adjust to the presence of a pet and to understand the role the pet must play in the therapeutic encounter and generally to adjust to the freer family interaction and communication.

In the family sessions one can observe very clearly the aspects of the nonverbal communication between family members and their pet. "When we entered the house that evening, the dog was barking furiously at us. For many months we have noticed that in this and other families the pet was the first family member to greet us at the door. We had also learned that a pet's behavior on any particular evening was a direct reflection of the feeling-tone of the family group" (Jungreiss, 1965, p. 62). To repeat, assigning a pet to a disturbed home without supplementary therapy may not be too helpful. It is not the pet per se, it is the use made of his presence that brings about the hoped for change in the child's behavior. Yet the parents may more easily develop insight and understanding of the child's reactions and their role in precipitating some of the symptoms they object to. The entire family is helped to see some of the dynamics of the situation.

Through pets we may reach the "unreachable." While some parents may give lip service to the need for help, they might unconsciously not wish help either for themselves or their children. They try to manipulate the therapists since they cannot accept the fact that the therapist may be helpful with their children when they failed. These parents are usually poorly motivated and claim no benefit in "talking therapy." They will gladly, however, accept a visitor who is coming in regularly to find out how the pet is getting along.

The mother may observe the therapist's handling of the child and the pet and develop strength through the sympathetic guidance of the therapist. She learns to accept and then to handle the child's teasing and temper tantrums. She learns how to impose limits on her child's behavior.

By talking to the pet and about the pet, the parents may help the child to freely verbalize his own problems in relationship to them, to the pet, and to his peers.

In these situations we found that the child usually uses his symptom both to control his environment, that is his parents and siblings, and to ward off what he considers to be awe-inspiring situations outside of the home. His anxiety serves as a signal, warning him of certain dangers and impelling him to substitute other experiences, which may not be as desirable even from the child's point of view, such as reading, watching television, and daydreaming. Introducing an active pet will assist the child to make an active search for the resolution of his fears through the acquisition of pleasant experiences with his friends and outdoors. Such action must be accompanied by intensive therapy for the child and supportive therapy for the parents.

Introduction of a pet into a family requires careful preparation. First, one must acquire the cooperation of both parents, and second, one must consider the fact that the pet is a dependent creature. It may arouse the feelings of warmth, love, and protectiveness or of antagonism and active dislike.

The success of a dog in a family depends quite a bit on his first introduction or initiation into the family. Puppies are sensitive. The dog wishes to attach itself to a master, to the individual who will always take care of him. When the dog is brought home, very little fuss should be made over him. Soon the dog will begin to explore its surroundings and make acquaintance with the members of the family.

Initially, in our discussion with parents we recommend that no rules be set or "deals" made with the child for the care of a pet. Eventually, the child will assume responsibility on his own. It is unwise at the outset to burden an emotionally disturbed child with unwanted responsibilities such as walking, feeding, or combing the pet. We feel that at the beginning a pet should be enjoyed and not become another super-ego threat. We further advise parents to permit the child to assert his autonomy by rearranging his furniture (if he so desires) to make the pet more comfortable, and even permitting the child to sleep with the pet.

In short order, parents may threaten to get rid of the pet. Responsibility for the pet's care and the extra financial outlay caused by the destructiveness of certain pets will quickly antagonize many parents. This comes about when the disturbed child reneges on his original commitment to care for the pet and uses this as an additional weapon in testing both his parents and the therapist. This must be discussed on a reality basis, indicating that being the parent of a disturbed child involves certain difficulties and responsibilities. Occasionally we discover that these parents, as children, were closely attached to a pet, suffered a loss and felt that if they were to become attached to a new pet, they would suffer another loss and undergo a traumatic bereavement again. Other parents feel anxious when face to face with a pet possibly because the pet's presence triggers some of their own unresolved psychosexual problems.

It can happen that a pet that is unwelcome to a member of the family will precipitate strife. In such cases, the pet becomes the symbol of the disliked child, and verbal and sometimes physical attacks against the pet are actually diversionary moves made against the child. We also frequently find that sibling rivalry expresses itself in the behavior towards the pet. If one sibling takes a fancy to an animal, the other will probably dislike the pet.

There are many psychotherapeutic functions of pets for adults also. A parent who is afraid of becoming a mother because she feels very inadequate and thinks that she will never be able to properly care for an infant may develop confidence by securing a puppy that must be taken care of. We have found situations in which mothers tended to isolate themselves from their children preferring that their servants take care of them. In many cases it was because the mother tried to protect herself from the awareness of her own fears and inadequacies in taking care of her children. Securing a pet may provide the necessary tactile stimulation and feelings of security.[16]

A child's pet may occasionally provide a vicarious vehicle with which a child may express his parent's unconscious drives and desires. The case of Glenda (Holmes, 1964) describes the psychodynamics of a girl, aged twelve, who was caught by her mother while engaged in sexual activities with her dog. This child, according to Holmes, "was unconsciously expected to behave in ways which would provide vicarious satisfaction of the mother's unfulfilled and unsettled sexual drive" (p. 219).

One of my patients, a married woman who was unable to conceive, felt that she needed a child so that she would have an outlet for her maternal drives. She was aware of my interest in pets and their value as mental hygiene agents. She bought a poodle and lavished quite a bit of care and money on his grooming and attendance at an obedience school. After two years, she became pregnant. When the baby arrived, the dog, which had already become part of the family, continued as an older sibling. In this situation, the dog accepted the baby and the two played happily together.

The introduction of a pet (together with psychotherapy) sometimes helps to change the somewhat unwholesome static relationship between mother and child to a dynamic, wholesome, forward moving one. We sometimes find a mother who is unable because of her basic rejection of her child to permit him to grow, to develop and to be more on his own. Such a mother sees her child as an extension of herself and tends to overfeed, infantalize and overprotect him. Inevitably a struggle arises between the mother and her child. The introduction of a pet may deflect the attention of both to the pet's antics, reduce mother's need for domination and thus bring about a relaxation in the home atmosphere.

In another case, a patient also saw her child as an extension of herself and treated him as a pet. She would force the child to eat, and yet, she was compulsively clean about his appearance. The child became a feeding and conduct problem. After numerous sessions with the mother, she finally agreed to secure a dog for her son. The mother then became very much attached to the dog and transferred to him the behavior she had heretofore exhibited toward her son. As her interest in the pet increased she was able gradually to release her stranglehold and too intense relationship with her child. The child was now able to move away from her enveloping presence and participate in peer activities. Sometimes when a parent is unhappy over the sex of his child, introduction of a pet of the desired sex may ease the family strain.

Frequently, when a woman remarries several years after the death of or divorce from her husband, it serves to take away from her son the status of the head of the family. The mother feels guilty (Fast and Cain, 1966), and the son resents the fact that he is displaced and that his mother does not seem to love him as much as she did before. Introducing a pet into such a family can ease the situation.

Speck (1965) thus describes a family therapy session in which the animals participated. "An interesting part of the sessions was the behavior of the animals. The dog sat in the center of the circle while the cat sat on the couch near Cass. It became very clear on several occasions that the cat was mimicking the dog's behavior" (p. 65)

Speck (1965) found that family members were not as guarded when discussing their animals' activities as when discussing their own activities. Talking about the behavior of family pets provides very useful psychotherapeutic material. In family psychotherapy the family pet may be employed as a means of resisting therapy or a particular therapeutic interaction. Thus in one case "whenever the father became too excited, his dog would bark and he would take her out behind the house for a few minutes" (Sonne, 1965, p. 257). On another occasion when a father was pressed by the therapist to be more assertive as a male and become the family's authority figure, the father became so upset that he released the family's tropical bird from its cage resulting in the disruption of the session for a quarter of an hour by the loose bird (Friedman, 1965).

We may recall that in ancient times a dog was often used as a substitute for the sacrifice of a man (Lewis, 1963). In some disturbed families, the spectacle of ancient times repeats and, figuratively speaking, an animal is offered as a sacrifice for a human being. Speck (1965) notes, "We have often noted that when tensions in a schizophrenic family rise, and the fears of sexual and aggressive drives become paralyzing, a family member may become ill. In families that have pets, the pet may become ill either in conjunction with another family member or members, or as a substitute for illness in one of the human members. At such times of duress, the pet may die. The author has observed a pet's death in a schizophrenic family at a time of crisis on seven occasions. The family then grieves over the pet and in the mourning process channels off their intense destructive forces. At times we advised a family to acquire a pet when we feared that a human member of the family may be injured or killed" (pp. 204–205).

In this connection one wonders whether we may not be able to resolve some of the problems of psychosomatic contagion by placing animals in certain sick families and seeing what happens to them. The role they play in the family and the consequent psychophysiologic disorders may give clues to family dynamics and help us resolve conflicting points in the theory of the causation of psychophysiologic disorders.

SUMMARY

The implications of this chapter are more far reaching than just work with pets. The entire complex of social issues in therapy is involved. We believe that the placement of a pet in a socially or emotionally disturbed home tends to bring about a more rapid process of healing in the home. As we all know, today we tend to treat patients not in isolation but in family groups and in relation to their family. Today we believe that an emotionally disturbed person is symptomatic of some disturbance in the social relations of the home and that there is a disturbance in the communication of family members. Bringing a pet to such a home may tend to restore balance.

NOTES

[1]For a complete discussion on the role of companion animals in the family see Cain (1983, 1985); Soares, C.J. (1985) and the edited work by Sussman (1985). Friedmann and Thomas (1985) identify the health benefits of pets for families.

[2]Elizabeth Marshall Thomas' (1993) and Desmond Morris' (1988) books on the behavior of dogs, confirms the deep and enduring relationship between dogs and their humans, while giving the reader a glimpse of the inner workings of the relationship that dogs have within their species. See also McBride's (1995) chapter on "The Human-Dog Relationship" and Bergler's (1986) book, both of which provide an excellent overview of the topic. MacDonald's (1981) article specifically addresses issues concerning keeping a pet dog in the home.

[3]Janet Ruckert's (1987) chapter entitled "Connected in Love" provides an

excellent argument for utilizing a companion animal to counteract loneliness by connecting with others.

[4]Beck and Katcher's (1983) chapters on "Pets as Family" and "Pets as Self" are wonderful complements to this discussion. Ian Robinson's edited book on the benefits and responsibilities of pet ownership will also illuminate several points made by Levinson.

[5]Animals can be useful in teaching responsibility to young people and in elevating their sense of self-esteem. See Heath and McKenry (1989) for a discussion about the potential benefits of companion animals for children.

[6]Although there is significantly more literature on the relationship between humans and dogs, there is some excellent literature on the relationship between humans and cats. Turner (1995) provides an excellent overview of "The Human-Cat Relationship". Subsequent to her best selling book about dogs, Elizabeth Marshall Thomas (1994) gives equal time to felines in her elegant exploration of species. Mertens (1991) has also written about the relationship between cats and their humans.

[7]Most of the available information on this issue is derived from retrospective research in which adults report on their earlier behavior. The evidence suggests that there is a link between cruelty to animals and later aggression against people. Carson (1972) has written about this from a historical perspective; Felthous (1980); Felthous and Kellert (1987); Kellert and Felthous (1985) and Kellert and Westervelt (1983) have also written extensively about this phenomenon.

[8]At the time when Levinson originally wrote this, gay men and lesbians were considered by the mental health community to be "deviant" and homosexuality was thought to be a disorder. In 1973, the American Psychological Association depathologized homosexuality. Obviously, this pejorative reference to gay men and lesbians is antiquated and inaccurate.

[9]In gay relationships there is no feminine partner, since both individuals are male, both are masculine. The notion of one man playing the feminine role and one playing the masculine role is an erroneous and stereotypical representation of gay people.

[10]While the representation of the lesbian couple is less pejorative, the author appears to unnecessarily accentuate the concern which the women had for their dog's recovery.

[11]The role of the veterinarian in this process was a popular theme for Levinson. The literature is replete with references about the role of the Veterinarian in working with both people and animals. Most notably, however, is Harris' (1984) chapter on "The Veterinarian's Role in the Human/Animal Bond". Michael McCulloch and William McCulloch, both of whom were well-respected by Levinson, wrote together (1981) and separately (McCulloch, M.J., 1983; McCulloch, W.F., 1982) about this topic. Blume (1982) also wrote about this topic, emphasizing that veterinarians are responsible for not only the health of their animal patients, but for the welfare of their human clients as well. In a recent work, McNicholas and Collis (1995) also discuss the role of the

veterinarian in the Human-Animal bonding process in their chapter on Coping with Pet Loss.

[12]From a contemporary perspective, Allen (1995) explored the role of pets in coping with life changes and transitions. Covert, Whiren, Keith, and Nelson (1985) explored the experience of pets and early adolescents within the family system. Haggerty, Gerace, and Summers (1989) studied pet-care management in child-rearing families.

[13]Kidd and Kidd (1984) note that an extremely important aspect of the human-animal bonding process is the choice of the right animal to fit the need. If the wrong type of animal is selected, there will be no bond and a good animal will be destroyed or abandoned. Further, the human will receive no benefit and may acquire a sense of guilt over the failure of the selected animal to meet his or her unrealistic expectations or may build up resentment over the amount and kind of care which the animal requires.

[14]The American Humane Association (1993) has played an important role in bringing national attention to the connections between child abuse and animal abuse. Ascione (1991, 1993) and Ascione, Thompson, and Black (1995) have also made significant contributions in raising the level of consciousness about this topic. Ascione's (1995) paper presented at the 7th International Conference on Human-Animal Interactions provided insight into battered women's reports of their partner's cruelty to animals. In addition, Arkow's (1995) text entitled *Breaking the Cycles of Violence* is an excellent resource, which discusses the links between animal abuse and child abuse. Deviney, Dickert, and Lockwood (1983) have also documented the experience of caring for pets within a child abusing family; Boat (1995) recently wrote about the relationship between violence to children and violence to animals.

[15]This idea clearly resonates with the philosophy of Green Chimneys Children's Services whose Mission Statement incorporates the notion of "care and concern for all living things."

[16]See Beck and Katcher's (1984) chapter on "Touching and Intimacy"; Katcher, Friedmann, Goodman and Goodman's study of men, women, and dogs (1983); and Mallon's (1993a) study of men, women, and dogs at the ASPCA.

Chapter 8

THE CHILD AND HIS PET

One explanation of the millions of dogs, cats, mice, tropical fish and innumerable other pets which are treasured and owned by countless numbers of children is that "the love of animals by humans is one of the universals in the existence of both" (Bossard, 1950, p. 380).[1] As was indicated by Camuti and Alexander (1962), "a child's first important pet has something magical, mysterious, and unbelievably exciting about it." Hopefully, this magic will transmit itself to all of nature and the child's tremendous need to love or be protective of animal life will be a beacon of kindness encompassing all his fellow men.

Children often fantasize about animals and endow them with human characteristics. In the child's fantasy, the animals play different roles; disliked and restrictive parents appear as aggressive animals and tolerant parents assume the shape of more gentle animals (Bender, 1952).[2] Children are similar to the young of animals (Buss and Durkee, 1957). Indeed, some psychologists believe that it is easier for children to identify with animals than with human beings (Bellak, 1954). In fact, in their make believe play with pets children frequently assert that they themselves have become animals and accept their pets as equals (Stekel, 1959) and feel that they can easily communicate with their pets. This is one way a child acts out many of the normal problems of childhood.

The young child believes that his pet has the same experiences and emotions he has. Therefore, the pet also feels lonely, also gets occasionally angry, also feels sorrow and remorse, and also loves and hates and relates to him as he relates to his own parents. In the mind of the child, the pet also knows the difference between right and wrong and therefore can be held accountable for his misdeeds, as indeed the child knows and is responsible.

Children generally believe that a pet can speak animal language. Through the movements of his paws, arching of the back, mewing, or barking the animal communicates desire for food and for play. While the child may feel a sense of mastery because of his size and strength in relation to his pet, yet he obtains great satisfaction when his own pet is victorious in fights with other pets (Hall and Browne, 1904).

At the beginning of a child-pet relationship, the child may be afraid of the pet. However, through a process of identification the child may begin to love the pet (Freud, 1937). This identification with the pet is what makes the living animal so uniquely valuable to the child. This identification with the pet gives a child the possibility of incorporating the pet's strength. The child can now order his pet around and be its master (Bolton, 1948), and he can also feel that he can compete on a more equal footing with his parents whose mere size and apparent overwhelming strength are overpowering. "Probably the reason that most children take so readily and easily to animal pets as close companions stems from this need of the child to be close to a parent substitute that he can control and direct at will" (Caplan, 1951, p. 137).

Many children believe in a magic which helps them to overcome obstacles, feelings of loneliness, and inferiority. The pet may become one of the tools in the child's magical thinking, and in league with the pet, the child may overcome his adjustment problems.

One wonders why pets have eternally and universally made such good love objects. I believe that pets vary in their ability to fulfill the love needs of the child. A contact pet, i.e., a soft furry animal is much more conducive to feelings of love and security than a noncontact pet such as a goldfish. Even the monkeys ran to the cloth mother for protection when fearful (Harlow, Harlow and Hansen, 1963). The softness and furriness of the cloth mother seemed to have induced feelings of belonging and being protected.

A child's love and affection for a pet does not automatically transfer itself to human beings but can serve as a bridge. Here, as elsewhere, training and instruction are necessary. One must teach for transfer. There are many individuals like the pet owners in ancient Rome and Greece as well as modern Nazi Germany who have been kind to animals and yet cruel to people. Nevertheless, through associations formed around common interests in pets, humans develop an interest in each other, which may and often does lead toward the formation of friendships that finally generalize into a love of humanity.

Love for the pet drives the child's attention outwardly away from himself. He forgets his own immediate interests and becomes absorbed in the world of reality, of nature. Love for the pet also creates a relationship of mutual trust and confidence while building a bridge to the future and to greater self-awareness.

The possession of a pet which has been taught some tricks, may make the child a popular and valuable member of his peer group. His peers may wish to know where he secured the pet and how he cares for it, and this may be the first real recognition of the child by his peers.

Children, like grown-ups, have their "off" days. The child comes home from school in a dejected spirit. A pet dog can sense very quickly his master's moods. He is there to greet the child, to make him feel worthwhile and desirable. The pet offers infinite comfort to the child today and yesterday, in the United States as well as other parts of the world. "Ci-Nin curled up on my lap while I did my lessons; at bedtime, she followed me to my room, draped herself at my feet, and purred both of us to sleep" (Camuti and Alexander, 1962, p. 15).

The pet, in a sense, becomes the mirror in which the child sees himself wanted and loved not for what he should be, or might be or might have been but for what he is. The pet and his master look at each other and understand each other at a glance. The child learns that it is possible to communicate one's innermost feelings without words by mere gesture, glance, or even bodily posture.

Through trial and error in teaching his pet new tricks, the child discovers that he must at times learn to control himself. Through bitter experience, he learns that scolding will only serve to delay or impede the pet's learning. As he develops more tolerance for his pet's difficulties, he may become more tolerant of his own inability to master his lessons (Bolton, 1948). Teaching a pet can very well develop in the child a tolerance for working long hours at routine and seemingly unrewarding tasks while building within himself a tower of security for later trials that life will surely offer. Successes that he experiences in this area, as well as in other areas, will provide enough real satisfaction to prevent the child from seeking imaginary satisfactions in a fantasy world. Successful experiences in early childhood are the foundation stones of one's ability to meet and resolve life's problems.[3]

The child learns that even pets have to be trained to become more acceptable or desirable. He begins to realize that proper upbringing makes the pet a desirable companion and a welcome visitor. When the child sees that his dog will be loyal and join in a fight to protect him, the child begins to understand the nonjudgmental quality of loyalty to those one loves like family and friends. He learns that the pet is trying to be good because it wants to be loved, and this lesson the child may apply to himself. The child learns that if you want to be loved you must love (Lorenz, 1965). If you want affection you must be willing to share affection. By mastering the pet, the child realizes that he can handle reality, and the child develops ego strength and positive attitudes toward himself and the members of his family. The child learns to accept his pet as a being superbly adapted to getting along and thriving in its world, just as the child is endowed for his own. The child will learn to accept the pet as a sort of junior partner engaged with him in the business of living. An empathy for living things and a compassion for pets in distress can develop and will probably transmute itself into sympathy and understanding of the emotional suffering of the people with whom the child lives.[4]

Whether or not a child enjoys emotional well-being does not necessarily depend on the real or imagined handicaps which the child is suffering from but more importantly on the way in which he handles his handicaps. The child gets to know more about himself: his strength and weaknesses, his ability to love and hate. Forbearance for the pet's transgressions ensues from his relationship with his pet. The pet, in a sense, becomes the touchstone with which the child appraises himself and reality. In certain situations, the only way in which a child may be able to test reality is through the reactions of his pet. Thus Searles (1965, p. 260) reports that one of his patients "who throughout his childhood was told, 'You're crazy!' whenever he saw through his parents' defensive denial, became so mistrustful of his own emotional responses that he relied heavily, for years, upon a pet dog to let him know, by its reaction to this or that person whom he and his pet encountered, whether the persons were friendly and trustworthy, or hostile and ones to be on guard against."

The writer's clinical experience indicates that school phobia (Marks and Gelder, 1966; Pearson, 1968; Wickes, 1966) or separation anxieties are usually not as severe in the cases where the child has a pet of his own who is a cherished intimate friend and confidante. In most instances, school phobia is based upon the fact that there is an abnormally close relationship between a child and his mother or occasionally his father and the fear that the mother might disappear while the child is at school. Occasionally, immature parents who quarrel in front of their children may induce the fears of not finding the parent on return. The fact that there is a pet joyously waiting for the child's return from school may help to allay the anxiety and fear.

The child in his beginning relationship with the pet can see himself clearly. The pet is a mirror. If the child is kind to the pet, he can see himself as a kind individual; if the child is cruel, he again learns the bitter truth. A pet motivates the child to see himself in the role of a benevolent master, to be aggressive, and sometimes self-denying in caring for his pet. The child has to assume responsibility for the pet and plan for the pet's day. A pet that is to be well must be taken out at certain times, fed and occasionally even bathed.

We can also see here the development of what Erikson (19632) calls the principle of "mutuality." The child and the pet learn that they are mutually dependent upon each other. From this dependence later develops the strength to take, to give, and to share. The child learns to accept his animal self, the cause of his unconscious fears.

At one time the child may have loved and trusted an adult, but found his trust betrayed. However, when a child obtains a dog, he learns very rapidly that the dog does not betray its master and can be trusted. Eventually the child may again begin to transfer feelings of trust from his pet to the adult.

Sometimes a child observes his dog moaning and groaning in his sleep. Obviously the dog is having a nightmare. The child may be taught by his parents to pet the animal until such time as it quiets down. This may teach the child that occasional nightmares are not harmful and that he too may have them and overcome them without ill effects.

When a pet becomes sick the veterinarian will probably prescribe a strict regime for the animal. If when the pet is ill certain restrictions on activities are necessary like unpleasant medicines, eating unusual foods, etc., when the child becomes ill, he finds it easier to accept the doctor's orders and to play the role of the good patient.

A pet can establish, for the child, contact with nature, understanding and enjoyment of animals and the animal world. Fear of the woods and of the unknown, so common among young children, will tend to disappear, and love and respect for life in all its manifestations generally develops and remains a life long interest.

Frequently animals are spayed. The meaning of this alteration, differences in sex characteristics and why a male dog runs after a female dog in heat, can then be easily explained (Bossard, 1944). This in turn gives the child a chance to learn in a painless way the whys and wherefores of sex differences and perhaps gives him insight into his own emotions. The child may observe the dog licking himself, the pleasure that the dog is experiencing and the obvious unconcern of the adults. At this point the parents can discuss with the child the meaning of his own masturbation and dispel some of the anxiety and fear which has accumulated around it. The child can also learn that elimination and defecation are subjects which are easily discussed when they concern the pet. The dog is taken out for a walk so that he can relieve himself. Such a discussion leads easily to a consideration of the child's own elimination problems and the acceptance of these as being worthwhile and not dirty and unmentionable.

PET PREFERENCES

Several studies were made of the pet interests of boys and girls. The child's interests in pets may be seen in the fact that 24.7 million dogs and 20 million cats (Pet Census Needed, 1967) are well taken care of in the American home.[5] Bucke (1903) reports the result of a study of 2,804 papers written by boys and girls ranging in age from six to seventeen in which they discussed their pet animals. 42.86 percent wrote about dogs, 27.57 percent about cats, 6.28 percent about canaries, and 5.45 percent about rabbits, etc. A further analysis of the questionnaires indicated that the dog, horse and rabbit are favored by the boys and the cat, canary and parrot are favored by the girls. Bucke (1903) indicates that in early adolescent boys prefer dogs which are pugnacious, courageous, intelligent, and good hunters and girls prefer dogs which are graceful, beautiful, companionable, dependent, and dependable.[6]

In another study of the child's relationship with the cat (Hall and Browne, 1904), the child (N=804) who preferred the cat indicated that the fact of ownership made the cat so much more desirable as a pet. A contributing factor was also the fact that in approximately half of the cases the cats were liked because of the gratification the child felt in his role as a saver and adopter of a homeless cat. The cat was chosen as a favorite pet twice as often by girls as by boys. Lehman (1928) on the basis of a study of a checklist of 800 play activities voluntarily engaged in during a week by 5,000 subjects ranging in age from eight-and-a-half to over twenty-two, found that the dog was played with significantly more often than the cat.

Amatora (1960) studied the interests of 629 preadolescent boys and girls. She found that for 17.6 percent of the fifth-grade boys, animals were either the first, second, or third choice of interests and that for the sixth grade boys, the corresponding interests were only 12.2 percent. For 15.7 percent of the fifth-grade girls, animals were the first, second, or third choice of interests. These choices declined to 13 percent in the sixth grade. Boys were mainly interested in dogs, horses, birds, and cats and girls in horses, dogs, cats, and birds.[7] The present writer found a similar decline of active interest in pets among adolescents boys.[8] Apparently heterosexual interests are becoming of more import.

There are regional as well as urban-rural variations in the preferences for dogs. Large dogs are preferred in the suburbs and small dogs in the urban areas. In a study of dog preferences of city college students in Hartley and Shames (1959) found that liking for dogs is a generalized phenomenon which extends to all breeds. However, there are preferences based on sex. City college men preferred boxers and city college women, the Pekingese. The present writer found that the dog is preferred significantly more often than any other animal by most groups. This common impression is very well portrayed by Kipling (1912).

Pussy will rub my knees with her head
Pretending she loves me hard;
But the very minute I go to bed
Pussy runs out into the yard.
And there she stays till the morning light;
So I know it is only pretend;
But Binkie, he snores at my feet all night,
And he is my Firstest Friend.

PLANNED PLACEMENT INSURES SUCCESS

From the Berkeley Humane Society (California) comes a group of very telling tales about the role animals, particularly cats, play in the lives of children. Louella Cole Lowie, Ph.D., supervised the placement of cats from the adoption room of the Society. Dr. Lowie's chief interest was in adult cats and specifically in those who were to be placed where they would serve a recognized human need. Most prospective owners fell into five classifications: (a) the elderly, (b) the lonely, (c) small children, (d) the handicapped of all ages, and (e) those who are caught in emotional crises (Lowie).

Selecting the right cat for each individual child requires careful thought, according to Louella Lowie "For babies and little children kittens are not suitable. Kittens are inveterate and indiscriminate scratcher, and they will certainly scratch the baby along with the furniture. It is therefore best that a child's first cat should be an adult who has already learned what may or may not be scratched or bitten. Spayed females are especially good because they often regard the baby as their own and are extremely protective toward him. They are no good as 'watchdogs,' but they make fine nursemaids!"

"The selection of one animal rather than another should depend upon the needs of the small child for whom the animal is chosen. Older children should pick out their own cat or kitten, under guidance, but parents have to make the decision for babies and little ones." (Lowie, p. 16).

The contribution to the welfare and happiness of their owners was remarkable. Following are some instances that deal particularly with the effects of these cats upon the children who became their foster parents.

Little Billy, a nine-year old deaf child who went to a special school during the day, was greatly isolated out of school hours. The boy wanted a cat, but his mother—a working woman and a widow—had no money to buy one. She came to the shelter to ask if she might pay for the animal at the rate of a dollar a month, but take it home immediately. This was, of course, granted. Knowing little about cats, she asked me to select the cat I thought best for her son. I picked out a gentle, three-year-old, neutered male with a merry disposition and the playful habits of a kitten. He was not a particularly handsome cat, but his jovial good nature and outgoing friendliness more than compensated for his lack of dramatic beauty. From the moment of his arrival Billy had a friend. When the boy comes home from school he plays with his cat until dinner time, spends the early part of the evening looking at television with the cat snuggled up beside him, and then goes to sleep with his arms around its neck. On Sundays he and his mother take the cat on a leash to a nearby park and have a picnic. Other children soon come flocking about, and the mature cat plays contentedly with all of them. Billy's ownership of the animal has not only brightened his daily life but has provided him with a point of contact with other children and has won for him a respected position among them. He is no longer the isolated child he once was.

Mrs. Wheeler's ten-year-old daughter was a frail, slender child, who had been in the hospital with rheumatic fever. She was sent home with strict instructions that for at least a year she must live a quiet life. Dolly could read, she could do simple household chores like wiping the dishes, she could play quiet card games, she could watch television, but she could not join in the activities of other children nor could she go to school. Her mother was sure Dolly would be too active for her own good if she had a lively kitten to play with, but that a grown cat might do a good deal to make the hours go by happily. We selected a very handsome, soft, fluffy, gray Maltese, a neutered male about a year and a half old. Twice a day Dolly put the harness on her cat and set out for a leisurely stroll around the garden. It did not take long for the animal to learn that he was not supposed to romp, and after two or three days he settled down to walking sedately beside his child-mistress. It is easy now to persuade Dolly to take her after-lunch nap because her cat not only lies down beside her but also purrs her to sleep. The child is happy, and her doctors are happier. They expect her to make a complete recovery, to which the cat is making a significant and vital contribution.

Louise is a twelve-year-old girl whose leg was badly shattered in a traffic accident. After months of treatments to save the leg, she was sent home to recuperate and to learn again how to walk and to lead a normal life. During the first few weeks at home she made excellent progress, but then she began to get bored with her exercises and to develop the conviction that she would never be normal again. The "cripple psychology" was more damaging than the remaining stiffness in her leg or the weakness of her muscles. Louise had a passionate interest in animals, and so her mother had decided to give her a cat for her birthday, with the idea that perhaps a pet would encourage the girl to take more interest in life. At the time the mother came to the Shelter, we had a very interesting and affectionate white cat with only three legs. She had been in an accident but had recovered completely and was able to walk, run, jump, and climb on her three legs. Moreover, she was the epitome of courage; she did everything a cat could be expected to do, would attempt climbing feats that even a four-legged cat would avoid if possible, and generally told the world that she was only a cat with three legs but not a cripple. Louise's mother was so taken with the little creature's attitude that she took Friskie home with her. She felt that his recovery and courage would stimulate her daughter to keep on trying to become a normally active girl. Louise and Friskie are inseparable, and a great change in attitude has taken place. Louise has returned willingly to her exercises, in which Friskie plays a part, and she is sure now that she will eventually make a complete recovery. As she says, what a cat can do, she can do.

Billy Joe came running into the Shelter followed more slowly by his mother. He announced that this was his birthday and that he had been promised a cat; his mother had also agreed that he should select his own, provided he looked at every cat before he made his choice. I gave him permission to take each animal from its cage and play with it as long as he liked. While he was thus engaged, his mother explained to me that the boy had an emotional problem. He had had a very mild case of polio which had left him with a barely perceptible limp. However, he was greatly disturbed by his "lameness" and had convinced himself that the other boys in the neighborhood avoided him because he was a cripple. The mother hoped that possession of a cat might somehow take his mind off his troubles and help him to overcome his feelings of inferiority. A large, neutered, short-haired, four-year-old male, white underneath but with part of a tiger pattern on his head and back was the one he chose. The moment this animal walked out of his cage, Billy Joe cried out excitedly that this was the one. While Billy Joe played with Harry, I took his mother aside and told her that they could take the cat home then, and if her son subsequently tired of Harry, they could return him and take another. The cat never came back. The fact that Harry is the largest and strongest cat in the neighborhood seems somehow to compensate for the fact that Billy Joe is the smallest and weakest boy. The cat gives him something to brag about and be proud of. Harry is contributing his bit to the situation and delights the boy by meeting him at some point on the way home from school and walking along beside him. Other boys follow the pair home, and all of them play together. After dinner Billy Joe studies his lessons while Harry sits on the table beside his books, and later they go to sleep in the same bed. As the weeks go by, Billy Joe's limp becomes less and less, and while he awaits his return to normalcy he has a wonderful friend.

Freddie is a definitely dull boy of twelve. His reported IQ is only 78. Freddie has a fine home and is greatly loved by his parents, but as he grows older they are beginning to wonder how he can ever support himself. He will be able probably to finish junior high school, but then he would enter a trade school. The trouble with this plan is that no type of work taught in the local trade school has ever appealed to him. His one interest is animals, but because of his defective intelligence,[9] his parents have hesitated to let him have a pet of his own lest he do something stupid that would injure it—which would break his heart. However, Freddie's interest in animals seemed to be the only thing upon which one could build in helping him plan for a future vocation. As soon as Freddie started to handle the cats, it was evident that he was awkward and slow. In fact, he was not yet ready to have a pet. I therefore suggested that he come to the Shelter every Saturday morning for a while and work under my supervision until he could handle the animals properly. His intentions were good, but his technique was faulty. As soon as he had had a little training he proved to be good at this work and even to have a specific talent for understanding what an animal wanted. Although Freddie certainly wanted to have a cat of his own, he seemed from the first to be somewhat confused as to which one he really liked best, and I advised him to wait until he was sure. He had been working on Saturdays for nearly three months before he finally made up his mind. His selection was interesting in view of his own low-grade abilities and negative personality. It was a quite ordinary, grey-and-black tiger, definitely slow-witted, and aside from a general sweetness, seemed to have no personality at all. Freddie has a normal small boy's love for his pet and takes excellent care of it, and the cat responds with a gentle affection that seems to satisfy its owner. Probably one of our handsome long-haired beauties would overwhelm Freddie and give him more feelings of inferiority than he already has. This undemanding, colorless cat is just right for him. The boy has continued to work at the Shelter as a volunteer. If he were bright, he would probably become a veterinarian, but as matters stand, it is much kinder to train him as a kennel-man. Since he has begun this work at an early age, he should be competent to hold a job as soon as he is old enough to have one.

Geraldine was the un-favorite child in a family of five children. Both parents had been honor students at college; the two older sisters were pursuing the same path to academic success; and the two younger brothers had already passed Geraldine in school. Geraldine was not stupid; she merely happened to be the one person of normal intelligence in a family of high academic gifts and ambitions. Her inferiority had been so impressed upon her that she *knew* she would never be able to learn what she was taught in school. The child's clothes were hand-me-downs from her older sisters, as were her toys. As Geraldine approached her tenth birthday, she began to clamor for a cat. Her mother brought her to the Shelter one morning and told her to pick out the cat she wanted and be quick about it. Unfortunately, Geraldine was too unsure of herself to make any decision quickly. After a despairing glance at the array of cats, she sat down in a corner and cried. Her mother then started to select a cat for her, but I persuaded her that Geraldine would be much happier to choose her own, especially as it was to be a birthday gift. I suggested that she leave the child with me for the day, so that she would have enough time to look over all the cats and find the one she really wanted most. Mother was not too happy about this arrangement, but in the end she consented. Geraldine spent the day happily taking the cats one by one from their cages, petting and playing with them. In the end she chose a gray-and-black, neutered tiger cat about a year old, who had come into the Shelter as a gaunt, terrified stray, abandoned by its owners and left to shift for itself. When mother returned, she was not much pleased by her daughter's selection, but I pointed out that Geraldine would love the cat all the more if she gave it the food and care it needed and could experience the joy of watching it become contented. I emphasized also to the mother that she should make it clear to the other children that this was Geraldine's cat, not theirs; I even got her to admit that it would almost be the first real possession the child had ever had. In subsequent weeks, I made calls at the house, ostensibly to check upon the health of the cat, but really to make sure that the girl was not being gypped out of the only thing she valued as her own. Geraldine was for the first time doing reasonably good work in school, and she was happy at home. She has realized that she now occupies a position of respect in the family constellation, because she owns the cat. Her parents are delighted at the change in her. She is never going to reach academic heights, but she is growing up to be a cheerful, happy, normal girl. To be sure, any other possession might have had a similar effect upon her, with the exception that a cat is a responsive creature and deluges her with the affection she has needed and lacked all her life.

Ellen was a shy, already-withdrawn girl of sixteen whose father was ineffectual in personal relationships, although successful as a draughtsman. Her mother was a large, domineering, restless, dissatisfied German woman who had married an American soldier to escape the privations of post-war Germany but had come to detest life in America. Ellen was not deeply attached to her mother, but she was very dependent upon her. The girl was so withdrawn and quiet in school that her teachers had already sent her to the school clinic and had tried to interest her in school activities, but without much success. One day an old friend from Germany called Mrs. Oakley and asked her if she would consider going to Germany as chaperon for a group of American girls, since the scheduled chaperon had just entered a hospital and the boat was leaving in three hours. To Mrs. Oakley the offer was a godsend, especially as she and Ellen had had a small quarrel at breakfast time and she was as a result in a markedly bad frame of mind. She accepted with alacrity, packed a bag, wrote a note which she left on the table in the front hall and simply walked out. When Ellen returned from school she read the note and jumped to the conclusion that the morning's quarrel had driven her mother away and that she herself was therefore guilty. At six o'clock, Mr. Oakley came home from work to find Ellen sitting in a chair staring into space. When he could not rouse her, he sent for a doctor who treated her for shock, but Ellen did not make the expected recovery. For three days and nights she lay in bed without movement or reaction to stimuli; she would not even swallow food when it was put into her mouth. The doctor wanted to send Ellen to a hospital, but the family insurance did not cover mental illness. The only place to which Ellen could be sent was the state hospital for the mentally ill. As a last measure, the doctor asked Mr. Oakley to think carefully of anything or anyone who might be able to get Ellen's attention. At this point Mr. Oakley bethought himself of Ellen's love for cats and her sorrow that her mother would never permit her to have one. He called the Shelter, explained the situation, and asked me to bring him a cat. I selected a spayed tortoiseshell, whose outstanding characteristics were an intense desire to occupy the center of the stage, a firm determination to have her own way, a pestiferous ingenuity when she did not immediately get attention, and an endless patience. When I reached the house, I put little Dora down on Ellen's bed. Dora began by trying the usual cat tricks for gaining attention. She sat on Ellen's chest and slapped her face with her front paws, she kneaded Ellen's shoulders—prodding her toes into the skin—she crawled under the bed-clothes and played with Ellen's fingers and toes, she purred, she mewed, she ran up and down the bed, she turned somersaults, but all in vain. By this time, Dora was getting annoyed by the lack of attention. She then put on what she evidently considered her star act; she lay down on Ellen's stomach, facing the foot of the bed, and then switched her tail slowly back and forth just under Ellen's nose. For an hour there was no sound or movement, except for the steady swish of Dora's tail, but then came a response. Ellen lifted her hand to brush the tail away and opened her eyes. Dora could not have seen the awakening, but she obviously felt it. In a second she had reversed herself and begun to pat Ellen's face. Since Ellen was now accessible, I removed the cat while her father got some food into her, but soon she asked to have Dora brought back. Ellen still had a long way to go before she could accept the fact of her mother's desertion, and she needed psychiatric help to halt her tendency to withdraw from life, but she could now be reached and especially her feelings of guilt could be relieved. Dora remained on the scene and never stopped demanding attention long enough to let Ellen slip back into despair. It should perhaps be pointed out once more that one has to select the right cat to match the needs or the results are not likely to be of value. Dora was a success largely because she was self-centered, demanding, and pestiferous.

SOME PITFALLS

Needless to say, there are also some undesirable aspects of child-pet relationships.[10] Once in a while, a pet, because of its uninhibited sex activities, may seduce a child into similar activities which in turn may lead to the development of anxiety (Ford and Beach, 1951; Menninger, 1951). To get a surcease from these activities, a child may retreat into daydreaming or autoerotic activities. As has been pointed out before, this is just another reason why a disturbed child cannot be automatically helped by giving him a pet. A pet must be planfully introduced into the child's family and as the child is guided into learning how to master the pet, he will also learn how to master his anxieties.

Sibling rivalry may also erupt between the pet and the child (Chapman, 1946; Moskin, 1965). A new arrival in the family may disturb the pet who is accustomed to being the center of everybody's attention. The pet's displeasure may evidence itself in many ways: by attacking the nurse who takes care of the infant, by barking at the infant, by sulking and refusing to eat.

Chapman reports a case where a dog was in the household three years before the baby was born. The dog was dearly loved by both husband and wife. When the baby was born, Speckles, the dog, would start "begging for attention whenever the baby was fed, bathed, or attended in any way." "Speckles would get in the way whenever the mother or father started to do something for the baby. He became a pest, always asking to be petted and assured he was loved just as much as ever by his master and mistress." "Then the baby began to creep and was old enough to be left in a playpen for a few hours each day. The dog's jealously broke out in rebellion. Speckles would sit outside the pen a foot or so away, growling at the child. At times he would pace before the pen, glaring with almost human dislike at his rival" (Chapman, 1946, p. 135).

Children in the family have similar emotions but don't know how or feel free to express their chagrin and disappointment at the usurper. Where a pet is present in the home, it provides the parent with a "golden" opportunity to explain to the children the reasons why the dog behaves the way he does, indicating sympathy for and appreciation of the dog's devotion to the family and the dog's mistaken feeling of being deprived of its accustomed place in the heart of the family. The parent may then ask the children to reassure the dog by giving him extra care and love. Realizing that their parent does not think any less of the dog because of his behavior, children are more ready to accept and assimilate their own feelings. To realize that one's feelings and behavior are acceptable and will not be condemned is tremendously important and beneficial to healthy emotional development in children.

On the other hand, the child may become angry with his parents, siblings, or his peers and redirect his hostility towards his pet. Similarly a forbidden passion for his mother or sister may be acted out with the pet (Heiman, 1965; Menninger, 1952; Stekel, 1959). Stekel (1959) indicates that occasionally childhood experiences with animals develop into a "zoanthropic fixation." An illustrative case is given in Chapter 2.

THE CHILD AND HIS FEAR OF ANIMALS

Fear of animals is quite pronounced during childhood (Hagman, 1932; Jersild and Holmes, 1935; Jersild, Markey, and Jersild, 1933; Jersild, 1954; Pratt, 1945). We have all met children who are frozen with fear or breathlessly run away when, by chance, they meet a puppy or a cat. We are also familiar with the children who while in camp are afraid of butterflies and moths. Such children are quite often tense, are affected by minor annoyances, and may easily burst into tears or strike against those whom they consider their tormentors. Generally these children are more afraid of animals they rarely come in contact with, such as tigers and lions, than of ordinary domestic pets, such as cats or dogs. Country boys express more fears of wild animals while country girls seem more afraid of spiders and insects (Pratt, 1945). In a study of the animal and insect phobias of 139 adult patients, it was found that most started by the age of five and "none in adult life" (Marks and Gelder, 1966).

In a study of fears of children in which 398 children aged five to twelve reported on what they feared most and what was the worst thing that ever happened to them, 13.7 percent reported fear of animals, although only 1.8 percent had any fear-inspiring experiences in connection with animals (Jersild and Holmes, 1935; Jersild, Markey and Jersild, 1933). As the preschooler gets older, there is a qualitative change in the animals feared. This was indicated in a study by Jersild and Holmes (1935). Thus, whereas at age 24 to 35 months, 61.9 percent of children showing fear are afraid of a large dog, this decreased to 42.9 percent at age 36 to 47 months. However, in the case of a snake, this increases from 34.8 percent at age 24 to 35 months to 55.6 percent at age 36 to 47 months. It is to be noted that in subjects nine to eighteen years of age, the fear of animals decreased (Angelino, Dollins and Mech, 1956).

Foster and Anderson (1936), who made a study of 519 parental records of unpleasant dreams had by their children during a seven day period, report that 40 percent of the children aged one to four, 15.9 percent of the children, aged five to eight, and 9.1 percent of the children aged nine to twelve dreamed about animals. The earliest nightmares were about animals.

There is a diversity of opinions as to the origin of these fears. The fear of animals may be due to the fact that they unconsciously symbolize evil thoughts or may have become the projected image of an intolerable unconscious inner threat. Fenichel (1945) notes that animals we are afraid of are usually substitutes for human beings, particularly the father. When an animal symbolizes the father, it indicates that the individual in question perceives his father as "animal like, that is as a passionate, sexual, or aggressive being" (Fenichel, 1945). Wickes (1966) indicates that children develop fears of animals because the animal is associated in their mind with unethical activities or the animal may symbolize some characteristics which they dislike and fear they possess. Valentine (1930) feels that fear of animals is innate and Landreth (1958) indicates that psychoanalytic theory confirms that young children have universal innate fears. Jersild (1954, p. 865) feels that fears "of animals might occur as an unconditioned fear whether or not fear of the 'animalness' of animals as such is innate." However, Hebb (1958) asserts that any experience imprints a certain pattern in the nervous system. When the organism observes an incongruous pattern of the same phenomenon which cannot be reconciled with the information already coded about that pattern, fear results.

Many fears may be unlearned. Morris (1967) indicates that there is an "inborn susceptibility" to fear the snake and that it is not a learned response. These fears may be set up by such characteristics as different features of the animal or the fact that the animal is strange and forbidding.

Paradoxically enough, the brighter the child, the more, unless he is protected, may he exhibit the undesirable fears. He can better conceptualize, imagine, and visualize all the likely and unlikely misadventures which may occur (Hebb, 1966) when meeting an animal.

Whatever the reasons, the children who have fears of animals are usually unhappy children who experience tensions at home of which their fear of animals maybe symptomatic. These children are ashamed of their fears and would like to overcome them. Sometimes they cling to their parents and use their fears as clubs with which to dominate their mothers.

It is important to remember that the same experience with a pet which may be frightening to one child may be very pleasant to another. Children may learn to fear pets from reading about them in books or from seeing television or motion pictures depicting the animal in a fear-provoking situation. A great deal depends upon whether or not the child is secure and expects his next experience to be a pleasant one, and the circumstances under which the frightening experiences occurred. If the circumstances were pleasant, the parent was there and the child felt secure, he could very well accept even an unhappy experience with a pet. He might consider that his original feeling of discomfort in the presence of the dog was thrilling or even an adventure and he might develop a greater affection for the animal.

The important thing to consider is how the child handles his fear of pets. Does he withdraw from them or does he bravely try to overcome his fear by facing its source, the pet. The child must be able to erect a fine balance between his fears and his willingness to take a risk with new experiences. The path the child takes will depend to a great extent on his self concept.

Fear is contagious. If the parent expresses fear openly or even covertly, the child will see through the parent's subterfuge and will learn to fear animals through sheer imitation. The child will begin to realize that his parent can offer little protection against his fears and will tend to denigrate the general protective powers of his parent. Particularly does this hold true if the child wishes to be like his parent and looks to him for security. The virtues and failings of one's parents are adopted as one's own. Therefore, a child is more likely to adopt the attitudes towards pets of a loved protective parent than of one to whom he feels indifferent and who is not supportive.

A parent who wishes his child to like and enjoy his association with pets should teach pet acceptance by example. He should encourage and praise his child every time the child feeds, cares for, or plays with an animal.

If a child has such fears, the pet should be introduced gradually when the child is in a good mood and is in a familiar comfortable environment. Anything unusual about the animal or the circumstances under which the animal is introduced is bound to cause fear, and therefore, the parent should try to arrange matters in such a way that the child is rarely exposed to a frightening experience which he may associate with the pet. The child should be forewarned of the fact that he may meet a new or strange animal. From observing the behavior of adults, the child may also learn how to accept and react to sudden emergency situations involving animals. Frequent trips to the zoo where the child may meet fear inspiring animals under safe conditions may also lead toward the overcoming of fears.

In one instance, a child was frightened by a dog, and this fear has spread to other animals to such an extent that the child is afraid to go out alone. Properly guided, the parent may be instrumental, in helping the child to overcome his fear. He can read stories to the child about the dog's wonderful qualities, his exploits in the North, during the war, and his saving of innumerable lives of children and adults in the Swiss mountains. The parent may then take the child to a pet shop and show him a hamster or another small inoffensive looking creature at a safe distance. The child should have ice cream or be otherwise pleasantly engaged so as to begin to associate comfort and pleasure with the animal's presence.

For instance, if the purchase of a bird is contemplated it should be discussed with the child and his help solicited in the selection of an appropriate cage. The cage should remain in the child's room for a few days to give the child an opportunity to ask as many questions as he may wish about the cage, its future occupant, and the care the pet will need.

Prior to the installation of any pet, the parent may rehearse through pantomime the various activities involved in caring for the pet. The parent and child are taking a make-believe trip with the pet, and the child plays with the make-believe animal, takes it for a walk, grooms it, and feeds it. The pleasure involved in having a pet should be emphasized.[11] When the parent feels that the child has overcome his initial reserve and is favorably disposed towards the purchase of a small pet, the child should be accompanied to the pet shop to help in the selection of the animal. Whenever possible, the child should be permitted to choose his own pet.

Later, after the child has accepted the small pet and has had favorable experience with it, a larger pet may be obtained. Gradually, the child will lose his fear not only of his own pets but of other animals as well. This experience of having conquered a fear will enhance the child's confidence in his ability to deal with his problems and will enable him to compete with greater assurance against his playmates.

Occasionally, the child has to contend not only with his fear but also with the ridicule of it from a person he may admire, his parent. There may be conflict between the parents, such as the father wishing the child to be a model of bravery and to be more active, aggressive, and independent while the mother being more succorant, encourages the child to come to her for protection and to continue being her little boy. Helping the parents to resolve some of their ambivalent reactions toward their child and to each other may help the child to overcome his fears of animals.

Sometimes the common-sense methods of overcoming fears do not seem to be operative. In this case, when we examine a child's fear a little closer, we may discover that it is not connected with the animal or with the incidents that put the pet in what seemed to the child to be a threatening posture, but it may instead stem from the child's relationship either with his playmates, his parents, or possibly with an unconscious feeling of a threat from within. The child may feel threatened, wronged, or abused, and he tries to express his annoyance by hitting at his aggressors or by cursing them. However, this reaction is not accepted kindly by his parents. He is told that he is bad and that he behaves like an animal; he is then subsequently punished. The child learns that every time he tries to protect himself through aggressive action, he is made to feel worthless and is punished. He begins to feel that he himself may be worthless, and this idea becomes strengthened every time he meets an animal. Eventually, the child may begin to associate the idea of self-protection as an animal activity, and his feelings of worthlessness become associated with and symbolized by pets. The pet may come to symbolize evil thoughts or evil deeds. In this case, the fear has acquired the characteristics of a phobia and must be treated accordingly.

Freud (1955), in his classic discussion of the case of Little Hans, illustrates how a child's ambivalent feelings of love and hatred for his father developed into fears of horses. Hans was jealous of his father, wished to replace him, and wanted to secure his mother's affection. However, he was afraid that his father might retaliate and castrate him. He, therefore, directed his hostility toward the horse (who he previously learned could bite) and now he could safely love his father and enjoy his companionship. However, he developed a fear of horses because he was afraid of the retaliation of the horse.

To help a child in such a contingency, it first is necessary to learn what the pet symbolizes before any constructive measures for the removal of the fear may be undertaken. Then by helping the child to accept his hitherto unacceptable drives and by showing him that they are perfectly normal and even desirable, he will learn to accept them as part of himself. The child will then learn to tolerate the reflected wickedness in his pet, and he will not only overcome his fears of animals abut will become a self-assured individual.

QUESTIONS WORTH PURSUING

It would be most important to know at what ages pets are most useful to a child. How does the child see himself in relation to the pet? What are the intervening variables? Do we need different types of pets for different types of children? What role does the pet play in the development of affect? Will too early exposure of a child to a pet while there is no adequate stimulation from human beings bring about imprinting to the animal?[12]

NOTES

[1]Paul and Serpell (1992) look at the reasons why children keep pets giving particular attention to the influence of child and family characteristics. Blue (1986) explores the value of pets in children's lives.

[2]Kidd and Kidd (1985, 1990a, 1990b, 1990c) have conducted extensive research in the area of children's attitudes toward their pets. For a complete review of their work on companion animals throughout the human life cycle see Hart (1993).

[3]Promoting success in a child can lead to positive experiences in adolescence. For these reasons, utilizing animals with adolescents is an area which calls for further investigation. Although there is some literature in this area, most of the research has focused on utilization of companion animals with children rather than with adolescents. Davis (1987), Davis, and Juhasz (1995); Gage and

Christensen (1990) have all examined the experience of utilizing pets with early adolescents.

[4]The theme of empathy for all living things was explored by Ascione (1991) who looked at enhancing children's attitudes about the humane treatment of animals as a means to build empathy. One year earlier, Poresky (1990) developed the young children's empathy measure. In an inspiring work, Bustad (1990) wrote about the need for compassion.

[5]These figures have more than tripled. Scheib (1996) reports that in 1995, "cats officially became the most popular and populous pet in the U.S. outnumbering dogs 63 million to 54 million" (p.61).

[6]Kidd and Kidd (1990c) found similar results in a study they conducted with 300 boys and girls, 3 to 18 years of age.

[7]In a study conducted on the role of pets in the development of nurturant behavior, Melson (1989) concluded that gender had little influence on whether children became attached to pets. Melson also pointed out that, while children are traditionally thought of as recipients of nurturant behavior, they were seldom seen as being capable of nurturing others. Interacting with and caring for animals are sources of learning about and practicing nurturance that are equally accessible, in terms of gender role expectations, to boys and girls (Melson, 1990).

In a paper presented at Green Chimneys' People, Pets, and Plants Conference, Melson (1990) stated, "We have evidence that nurturing animals may be particularly beneficial to boys. This is because caring for babies and young children becomes associated in children's minds with 'women's work' or 'what mommies do', as early as three years of age; by age four or five, we find boys becoming less interested in infants and their care and more avoidant of experiences around baby care" (p. 6). Melson concludes that there was no such association in the minds of children with regards to caring for animals. Because such care is gender-neutral, thus, utilizing animals with children might prove to be a particularly useful training ground for the development of nurturance in boys. The influence of gender and further investigation into children's pet-related nurturing calls for further study. Its results could prove fruitful to facilitating nurturing experiences in young boys (See also Melson and Fogel, 1989).

[8]Kidd and Kidd (1990b) and Mallon (1994b) also found that interest in companion animals waned during adolescence.

[9]This pejorative description was a standard characterization to describe limited intelligence at the time Levinson wrote this.

[10]Offering a view which highlights some of the pitfalls of the relationship between humans and their animals, Shepard (1995) writes about why pets cannot fulfill our needs.

[11]Endenburg and Baarda (1995) provide an excellent discussion and overview of the role of pets in enhancing well being for children.

[12]Levinson was a researcher and as such always posed questions that he felt should be considered by others for investigation.

Chapter 9

THE THERAPIST AND HIS PET

The effectiveness with which a child's therapist utilizes pets will greatly depend upon his previous experience with pets, how comfortable he feels with them, his ability to impose controls both on the pet and the child, his personality traits, and his philosophy of treatment. The therapist who has pet aides has one advantage in that the child patients can develop admiration for him both because of the love the pets have for him, and because of the skillful way in which he handles the pets. This in turn may lead to earlier identification with the therapist, more rapid achievement of therapeutic goals and a consequent reduction in the number of sessions spent in therapy.[1]

Competence in individual psychotherapy is not sufficient for being effective in pet-oriented psychotherapy. Other qualities are necessary. The therapist should be able to empathize with the child and develop a "third ear" for subliminal cues both from the pet and his child. In this connection, we wish to confirm the observation made by Pearson (1968, p. viii) that many child therapists have a lack of "inner flair" in dealing with children, a lack which may be attributable to lack of experience in being emotionally involved with a child, living with him and being responsible for his care. The experience of being a parent or in *loco parentis* is invaluable. The trials and tribulations which a so-called normal parent goes through in dealing with his own "normal" children are very helpful in understanding the positive and negative features of abnormal child behavior and give one additional insight in dealing with emotionally disturbed children.[2]

Some child psychotherapists feel uncomfortable when they are no longer able to offer facile interpretations and to interact on an intellectual level with the child. We find that some child therapists are unable to use pets because unconsciously they feel that they are competing with the pet for the child's affection and this they cannot tolerate. Further, a therapist may feel that if the child begins to love the pet, the pet thereby robs the therapist of some of the child's love and this may make the therapist feel rejected and unwanted.

This is not true for Dr. H. Jon Geis who uses pets in a somewhat special way. When he was consulted about the use of pets in his extensive psychotherapeutic practice (a subject he elaborated upon earlier in this book from a different point of view) he had this to say:

> With regard to using pets for illustrative purposes with patients in psychotherapy, my latest and third cat, Juanita, is a cute tiger-striped little lady (as a scientist and therapist I allow myself to anthropomorphize when appropriate and *only* then!) who was extremely frightened of human beings when she came to live with me. Since she was then six months old she had most likely been frightened by her previous owners.
>
> As a psychologist I then set about deconditioning this fear according to principles of learning. The explanation of Juanita's change from a frightened young cat who shrank away when you approached to pet her to a very receptive cat who actually approaches now for petting and "smooths" up against my patients is quite analogous to the way I teach my patients to change, and I use Juanita as an example of how they will change when I explain psychotherapy to them in the first therapy session.
>
> You see Juanita there? When she first came to me she was very, very scared of being approached or touched by me or anybody else. So I gave her psychotherapy! I noticed that she would stay still for a moment if you scratched her back—she liked that, though she'd move away very quickly after your hand was there a second or two. I started scratching her back systematically whenever I had a chance and I would notice her begin to move away, so I'd take my hand away just *before* she actually did move away. So what happened was that she never really had a chance to connect my petting her back—what we can call the "stimulus"—to a negative "response," that is, moving away in fear.
>
> You see, you and other people *reinforce* your self-defeating behaviors and feelings by (1) acting in ways which keep supporting it (e.g., moving away in a fear response and (2) telling yourself some self-defeating idea, like "My God! That's *awful!*" Then, when you get away from the presumed "danger" you conclude, semi-consciously, that the object must indeed have been "dangerous" or you wouldn't have moved away and told yourself it was "awful."
>
> Another example of using an animal for illustrative purposes in psychotherapy was related to me recently by Dr. Ronald Schneider of Lehman College. Once while in a session with a very fearful, anxious woman patient he had heard a scream from his young son to "Come quick, Daddy. Help!" He moved quickly to the back porch, in view of the patient, where he found his son's small kitten hanging by the neck strangling, caught in a cord she had accidentally stumbled into. He calmly loosed the frightened animal and carried it back with him to the session, all the while stroking it to quiet its fears. He then smoothly moved back into the conversation with the patient as if there had been no interruption. The patient was dumbstruck. She remarked to the effect that "You were so calm in

doing that. I guess a person doesn't really have to upset himself about things, does he?" This is an excellent example, I think, of the use of the therapist as a role model. It is one of a number of ways in which we can use our household pets in creative ways.

The psychotherapist emotionally must be able to surrender part of his functioning to a pet. He must be able to permit the child to use the pet and not to feel slighted because of it. He should have awareness of his own conflicts so as not to intrude them on the children he is treating. The psychotherapist must face the following questions: Does he harbor unconscious sibling rivalry with the pet which may interfere with treatment? Is he somewhat jealous because the pet is becoming a friend of the child?

The therapist who wishes to use pets must also be willing to face, for a while at least, the fact that certain professional colleagues think that having pets assist in therapy with children is somehow demeaning and degrading to the therapist. These feelings must be worked out under supervision before the therapist can begin to work with pets.[3]

Probably the best type of therapist for a child is the individual who loves pets and who likes to commune with nature. The therapist should be emotionally mature and be acceptant of the so-called childish and immature traits within himself. He should be able to regress in service of his ego. This will permit him to become maximally aware of minimal cues from his child patients and to communicate with them on that level. The therapist should be a warm acceptant individual who has overcome difficulties of his own and who because or perhaps, in spite, of these difficulties became mellow, an individual who is sought by others because of the feeling of comfort and trust he can inspire. Children can "smell" phonies and distrust them. Singer adds that the therapist should be childlike, i.e., "characterized by activity and reflected in attentive involvement, openness to experience, readiness for surprise, willingness to stand uncertainty, and the capacity to shift flexibly the focus of perception and inquiry" (Singer, 1965, p. 69).

In selecting a pet to serve as a cotherapist, the clinician should be aware of the fact that different animals communicate and get feedback in different ways. The dog, for example, uses his sense of smell very extensively. Above all, the therapist should work with animals he is most comfortable with.

Another relevant factor is that a pet, unlike finger paints or a puppet, must be taken care of, for he is alive, requires active care, food, medication, exercise, compels attention and love.[4]

The type of animal the therapist will use will depend to a great extent on his personality and the type of practice he is engaging in. Most likely it will be a dog. The characteristics of the pet are most important in pet therapy. The pet selected must respond quickly and enthusiastically to a child's timid approach: the lack of such a response may be frustrating to a disturbed child and may make him feel even more rejected. The pet must be sensitive to the child's moods (be able to take some abuse good naturedly while engaging in rough play with the child), should like to play with the child, be intelligent, and be in excellent physical condition. Every child has his own needs and his own experiences which he brings to the therapy hour. The pet would thus present a different stimulus for the child, and the child is free to endow the pet with the qualities that he needs at the moment.

Each pet has his own behavioral and temperamental characteristics which must also be considered. For example, it is well known that breeds of dogs vary in temperamental qualities (Scott and Fuller, 1965) and in the rapidity with which they can learn to perform various tasks (Fox, 1965). The ease of learning and temperamental qualities, however, also differ within a breed. Even though dogs, just like people, vary in their temperamental and intellectual qualities, the vast majority of dogs can be taught certain routines and they will behave the way they have been taught to behave.[5] In this connection, note the qualities of the Seeing Eye dog (Hartwell, 1942). "Good looks, a remarkable intelligence, alertness, a keen inquisitiveness, gay disposition and a willingness to try anything and to keep trying it . . . loyalty, integrity, affectionate companionship and unshakable devotion" (p. 29).

The average useful life of a dog is about eight years. After that, senility may interfere with the dog's efficiency. Dogs, however, have been known to live for over eighteen years. It is worthwhile therefore to invest in good training for the dog since his usefulness will depend upon what he has learned (Finestone, Lukoff, and Whiteman, 1960).

The first prerequisite for the successful training of a dog is the dog's affection and unquestioned obedience to his master. This is rather easy to accomplish since dogs look for a leader of their pack (Smythe, 1965) and in this situation, the leader of the pack is the child psychotherapist. The psychotherapist can gain this confidence by treating the dog well and by being the only person who is permitted to feed the dog. Once the dog is a well-trained tool of the therapist, he will be able to ignore all outside distractions and attend exclusively to the commands of the therapist. Nay, even more, at this point the dog and his master will be able to communicate with each other without uttering a sound.

There are some general principles of dog training. For lack of space, we cannot discuss here the specifics in dog training. The reader is therefore referred to the following sources (Holmes, 1967; Koehler, 1967; Leedham, 1961; Liddel, 1956; Pearsall and Leedham, 1958; Saunders, 1965; Smythe, 1865; Whimhurst, 1955; Whitney, 1964).[6]

First, the dog must be treated with respect. Expect your pet to do his best and when properly trained, he will certainly not disappoint you (Borgese, 1968). Animals have some remarkable abilities which seem never to have been researched. For example, Rhine and Pratt (1962) feel that many of the unusual feats of animals such as travelling long distances over territories they have never seen before and their unerring ability to find their way home may be due to ESP. The ability of some animals to sense the mood of their owners and react accordingly may also be due to ESP. It is not important for our purposes whether the above speculations will be validated by further research. What is important is that these uncanny abilities do exist in certain animals. One of the jobs of the therapist is to search for these animals and to utilize them in psychotherapy.

The dog should be introduced gradually and gently to his new home. He should be fed before the members of the family are, have a regular schedule, and have a specific spot which he can call his own where he can sleep, relax and hide from the world. He should have adequate affection and play.

TRAINING A PET AIDE

Start training gradually and at the same time every day. Don't spend more than ten minutes per training sessions with your pet. Start with one or two words in giving commands, using the same tone and inflection. The dog becomes habituated not so much to the word itself as to the way it is said. The same word said in a different manner carries a different meaning to the animal. The dog may start moaning and whining. (As a matter of fact, it may be advisable to teach the dog to whine and to moan on command).

A dog can be conditioned to noise, screams, and sudden sham attacks by children. The dog should be taught never to attack a child, no matter what the provocation may be. He should be taught to be friendly and permit any child who may wish to do so to lead him by a leash. The dog should be trained so that he obeys the psychotherapist implicitly when taken on a home visit.

It is important for the therapist to be concerned with the health of his pet and to observe symptoms of aberrant, agnostic behavior. Animals—dogs, cats, etc., also get tired and they show their state by being irritable, disobedient and occasionally scratching or biting. The therapist should at this point consider whether he is exposing his pet to more frustration than the pet can possibly take.[7]

Since the pet will be with the therapist for a long time, it is most important that he be chosen with utmost care. Secure, if possible, the advice of an experienced veterinarian. Keep in mind the fact that the pet will become a member of your family.

Ordinarily, once you have selected a certain breed of dog you become so emotionally attached to his appearance and behavior that if there is a need to replace him, most people select a dog having the same appearance, hoping that his temperamental qualities will be the same as the previous dog had.[8]

The pet chosen as a therapy aide must appeal to the child and must fit the psychodynamics of the case. It seems to me, on the basis of my clinical experience, that children who have difficulties in relating socially to their peers prefer large animals; those whose difficulties are mainly intrapsychic prefer small animals. Young children prefer large animals; older children prefer small animals.[9]

Occasionally, the cat is preferred by some children who are undergoing oedipal conflict and are resentful of authority. Young withdrawn children who are not yet ready or do not wish to enter into an entangling emotional relationship also seem to prefer the cat. These children are emotionally "burnt," resent authority and being pushed, and therefore, they prefer a cat that is unobtrusive, independent, not demonstrative in its affection, and does not initiate or seek a friendship.

Most likely we will need different types of animals for different types of cases. This in turn may bring about the need for developing aptitude tests for the discovery of the various pets' aptitudes. This will also necessitate the training of pets for the part they will play and the training of therapists in the use of pets.[10]

The writer believes that eventually a pet will become the trademark of the child therapist.[11]

RESEARCH NEEDS

We must realize that while dogs and occasionally cats have been used as therapeutic agents, we have not as yet been able to realize their potential to the full. Before we can do that, we need to engage in a large scale program of dog selection. The possibility of using the working breeds as therapy aides should be investigated. I doubt if one type of dog or pet would be suitable for all purposes. I presume that different breeds of dogs could be used for different needs. We must select dogs who worked out well with children and breed these dogs selectively. This would be similar to the program which was so successful in the selection of dogs to be used as guides for the blind (Hartwell, 1968).[12]

We will have to determine through experimental research the best methods of training a dog to become a psychotherapeutic aide. Incidentally, we will also have to learn how to select and train therapists in this new field.[13]

For example, at Fortunate Fields, they train both the blind man and his dog. The blind man lives with his dog for four weeks. He learns how to take care of the dog, how to make him follow orders and also how to become sensitized to the clues the dog transmits to him as to the dangers ahead. The blind man also learns what his dog's capabilities and possible handicaps are such that he can make an allowance for them. The dog, on the other hand, gets to know his master, his peculiarities, and his virtues.

A survey should be made to learn how may child therapists would be willing to spend a few weeks in a school to learn how to use pets. How many therapists would be willing to use trained pets (dogs) if such were available? How many have the needed facilities and time for exercising the dog? Is there anything in their background which would inhibit such use—family, associate, etc.? A comparison of the differences between psychotherapists who do and who do not use dogs in their practice might provide interesting material.[14]

It is my hope that the many questions asked and suggestions implied in this book might activate and accelerate the use of pets in child psychotherapy.[15]

NOTES

[1]The speed with which a therapist engages his or her client was a theme which Levinson felt was important and one which he highlighted as a benefit of this intervention.

[2]Levinson was a devoted parent, who took great pride in his two sons, Martin and David. He was also a devoted grandfather and had many other "children" adopted by love.

[3]Although Levinson was clearly comfortable in his role as therapist and had worked out many of those feelings which he describes, many of his colleagues in the field continued to belittle his methods. While things have undoubtedly changed since Levinson's initial introduction of the intervention, even today, many professionals and researchers decry that the human-animal bond field is "too soft" a science to study.

[4]The fact that animals as adjuncts to therapy are alive and therefore are capable of interacting with the client, makes this adjunctive approach very different from other adjunctive approaches, i.e., art therapy, poetry therapy, play therapy, etc. In addition to this point, in a later article, Levinson (1978) makes a number of points about the benefits of the therapeutic role of animals that are most comprehensive and bear repeating: (1) The importance of the animal to humans is psychological, not "practical"; (2) A relationship between a human and animals can often be more salutary than one between two humans; (3) An animal can satisfy a human's need for loyalty, trust, and respect; (4) A relationship with an animal can be less threatening than a relationship with a human; (5) The arena in which one would work with a child and an animal is much broader than the therapist's office; (6) Animals can speed up the therapeutic process; (7) Animals can be around 24 hours a day if they are needed.

[5]The Pet Partners Program of the Delta Society and the American Kennel Club both have initiated temperament testing and certificate training programs for companion animals. Dunbar (1984) presents some excellent guidelines on temperament testing, temperament training, and companion animal selection. In addition, The Delta Society has written a comprehensive standard's manual describing all aspects of involving animals in treatment programs.

[6]Obviously, there are many other, more recent sources, among them are Fisher (1992); Fox (1975); Rogerson (1992); The Monks of New Skete (1978); and Volhard and Fisher (1983), just to name a few.

[7]Care should be taken by the human-therapist to avoid overstressing the animal. Animal-assisted therapy may be and should be fun for the animal, but it is work and as such animals should be permitted to rest and play between visits to avoid fatigue. See Iannuzzi and Rowan (1991) for guidelines on ethical issues in animal-assisted therapy programs.

[8]Although, most people select a dog having the same appearance, hoping that his temperamental qualities will be the same as the previous dog had, it is

an interesting point of information to note here that no one whom I interviewed could remember the names of Levinson's other dogs which came after Jingles.

[9]In certain settings, where appropriate, farm animals can be utilized in this capacity. See Diesch (1984); Mallon (1994b); Ross et al. (1984); and Senter (1993).

[10]Nielson and Delude (1989) examined the behaviors of young children in the presence of different kinds of animals. Although children responded to a wide variety of animals introduced to them, "the dog proved to be very popular, approximately 90% of the children in the sample looked at an approached the dog during his first visit" (p. 126).

[11]Although this prediction has not been realized, certainly the contributions made by Levinson and others have made it easier for many child therapists to utilize animals in therapeutic situations with children.

[12]Although this writer has observed that there is a reluctance to "name, names," in that most professionals in the human-animal bond field steer clear of identifying particular breeds that are useful in therapeutic situations, the labrador retriever and the golden retriever, in this writer's opinion, are clearly the most adept and natural of animal cotherapists. Coren (1994) wrote a controversial book entitled, *The intelligence of dogs*, which could certainly be useful as a guide.

[13]Few universities offer specialist certificates in the field of animal-assisted therapy. Most people become credentialed in their field of choice and then integrate animals into their practice. During their course work, however, they may do research projects about animal-assisted therapy. There are, however, a few colleges that offer special certification programs. Among them are: Harcum College in Bryn Mawr, Pennsylvania, and Mercy College, in Dobbs Ferry, New York, in collaboration with Green Chimneys Children's Services in Brewster, New York, both of which offer certificate training programs in Animal-Assisted Therapy. Dr. Besty Smith at Florida International University, in Miami, Florida, also teaches a very popular course in Animal-Assisted Therapy at the Department of Social Work, Florida International University. See also Daniel, Burke, and Burke (1985) for a complete discussion of educational programs for pet-assisted therapy in institutional settings.

[14]To this author's knowledge, this study has never been conducted.

[15]As a long-time proponent for research, one of Levinson's last published works (1982) initiated a discussion concerning the future of research into relationships between people and their animal companions. Although there is, without doubt, a need for those in the human-animal bond field to continue to monitor outcomes and to look for new ways to document these goal oriented measures, countless practitioners and researchers in a variety of disciplines have been stimulated and inspired by Levinson's work. In recent years, however, in an attempt to be more rigorous, there has been a movement toward proposing that animal-assisted therapy programs be based on client goals rather than developing client goals based on perceived benefits of contact with animals (Fredrickson, 1995).

This "need to quantify" largely comes from the managed care movement of the heathcare industry and is primarily aimed at producing measurable outcomes which can be quantified. While scientific rigor is essential in an evolving field, it would be lamentable to lose the more qualitative approaches that were so eloquently expressed by Levinson and some of the earlier pioneers in the field like the Corsons. However, as so aptly said by Rowan (1990): "the interaction of human and animal (and human and environment) raised many fascinating research questions that can be investigated using a variety of approaches. While there is a tendency to promote quantitative ("objective") over qualitative ("subjective") approaches because of an apparent belief that precisely measured quantities are more reliable and less subject to experimenter bias than are subjective insights, I would urge those conducting research in this area to make use of both approaches. I, for one, would be very sad to lose this mix and encourage a continued openness to all methods and disciplines to retain the enthusiasm and excitement that we all enjoy so much in this field (p. 72).

Wilson's (1994) commentary on developing a conceptual framework for human-animal interaction research (with comments by Allen, Lago, Marx, and Melson) presents a "challenge to build a scientific literature that has a unified theory base that allows evaluation of the impact and the process of the human-animal interaction in a wide variety of samples" (p. 22).

As professionals in human-animal bond field enter the next century, the groundwork first set by Levinson endures and stands firm as a strong foundation for an emerging field.

APPENDIX

RESOURCES

The following is a select list of resourses within the United States which either study or practice within the human-animal bond field. This is in no way a complete list, but one which may be useful as a starting place for readers.

American Humane Society
63 Inverness Drive East
Englewood, CO 80112
(303) 792-9900

Animal Medical Center
510 East 62nd Street
New York, New York 10021
(212) 838-8100

Canine Companions for Independence
P.O. Box 446
Santa Rosa, CA 95402
(707) 528-0830

The Delta Society
P.O. Box 1080
Renton, WA 98057-1080
(206) 310-2802

Center for Animals in Society
School of Veterinary Medicine
University of California
Davis, CA 95616
(916) 752-3602

Center for Applied Ethology and Human-Animal Interaction
Veterinary Pathobiology,
School of Veterinary Medicine
Purdue University
West Lafayette, IN 47907
(317) 494-0854

Green Chimneys Children's Services
Caller Box 719
Brewster, New York 10509
(914) 279-2996

Latham Foundation
Latham Plaza Building
Clement and Schiller Street
Alameda, CA 94501
(415) 521-0920

The Center for Animals and Public Policy
Tufts School of Veterinary Medicine
200 Westboro Road
North Grafton, MA 01536
(508) 839-5302

REFERENCES

Abbate, G. McLean. (1967). Notes on the first year of the analysis of a young child with minimum participation by the mother. In K.E. Geleerd (Ed.), *The child analyst at work* (p. 19). New York: International Universities Press.

Alexander, H.B. (Ed). (1916). *Mythology of all races* (Vol. X). North American: Boston, Marshall Jones Co.

Allen, K.M. (1995). Coping with life changes and transitions: The role of a pet. *Interactions, 13* (3), 5–10.

Allen, K.M. (1985). *The human-animal bond: An annotated bibliography.* Metuchen, N.J.: The Scarecrow Press.

Allen, T.J. (1967). Symbolism of animals. *The new Catholic encyclopedia* (Vol. I, pp. 547–548) New York: Catholic Press.

Amatora, M. (1960). Interests of preadolescent boys and girls. *Genetic Psychological Monograph, 61,* 77–113.

American Humane Association. (1993). *Protecting children and animals: Agenda for a non-violent future.* Englewood, CO: American Humane Association.

American National Red Cross. (1962, April 30). Personal communication.

Anderson, R.K., Hart, B.L., and Hart, L.A. (1984). *The pet connection: Its influence on our health and quality of life.* South St. Paul, MN: Globe Publishing Company.

Angelino, H.J., Dollins, V., and Mech, E.V. (1956). Trends in the fear and worries of school children as related to socio-economic status and age. *Journal of Genetic Psychology, (89),* 263–276.

Anonymous. (1962, May 22). (Quoted by permission).

Antelyes, J. (1967, July). Objectionable behavior in pet animals. *Veterinary Medicine/Small Animal Clinician,* 661–665.

Arkow, P. (Ed.). (1984). *Dynamic relationships in practice: Animals in the helping professions.* Alameda, CA: Latham Foundation.

Arkow, P. (1987). *Pet therapy: A study and resource guide for the use of companion animals in selected therapies* (5th ed.). Colorado Springs, CO: Humane Society of the Pikes Peak Region.

Arkow, P. (1994). Child abuse, animal abuse, and the veterinarian. *Journal of the American Veterinary Medical Association, 204*(7), 1004–1007.

Arkow, P. (1995). *Breaking the cycles of violence.* Alameda, CA: The Latham Foundation.

Aschaffenburg, H. (1966). Jackie. *Voices, No. 1,* 75–78.

Ascione, F. (1991). Enhancing children's attitudes about the humane treatment of animals: Generalization to human-directed empathy. *Anthrozoos, 5,* 176–191.

Ascione, F. (1993). Children who are cruel to animals: A review of the research and implications for developmental psychopathology. *Anthrozoos, 6,* 226–247.

Ascione, F., Thompson, T.M., and Black, T. (1995, September). *Childhood cruelty to animals: Assessing cruelty dimensions and motivations.* Paper presented at the 7th International Conference on Human-Animal Interactions, Geneva, Switzerland.

Ascione, F. (1995, September). *Battered women's reports of their partner's cruelty to animals.* Paper presented at the 7th International Conference on Human-Animal Interactions, Geneva, Switzerland.

Auld, F. (1968). Vicissitudes of communication in psychotherapy. In J.M. Shlien, (Ed.), *Research in psychotherapy* (pp. 169–178). Washington: American Psychological Association.

Axline, V.M. (1947). *Play therapy.* Boston: Houghton-Mifflin.

Aymar B. (Ed.). (1956). *Treasure of snake lore.* New York: Greenberg.

Bassing, J. (1984). Companion animals for the blind. In P. Arkow, (Ed.), *Dynamic relationships in practice: Animals in the helping professions* (pp. 171–187). Alameda, CA: Latham Foundation.

Beck, A. (1990). *The role of animal interaction with children and adolescents: A presentation of studies and practice.* Paper presented at the Center for Applied Ethology and Animal/Human Interaction, West Lafayette, Indiana.

Beck, A., and Katcher, A. H. (1983). *Between pets and people: The importance of animal companionship.* New York: G.P. Putnam's Sons.

Beck, A., and Katcher, A.H. (1984). A new look at pet-facilitated therapy. *Journal of the American Veterinary Medical Association, 184* (4), 414–421.

Beecher, M. W. (1957). *Parents on the run.* New York: The Julian Press.

Bellak, L. (1954). *The thematic apperception test and the Children's Apperception Test in clinical use.* New York: Grune and Stratton.

Bellak, L., and Adelman, C. (1960). The Children's Apperception Test (CAT). In A.I. Rabin and M.R. Haworth, (Eds.), *Projective techniques with children* (pp. 62–94). New York: Grune and Stratton.

Bender, L. (1952). *Child psychiatric techniques.* Springfield: Charles C Thomas.

Bender, L., and Rapoport, J. (1944). Animal drawings of children. *American Journal of Orthopsychiatry, 14,* 521–527.

Bergen, B. (1984). Companion animals for the handicapped. In P. Arkow, (Ed.), *Dynamic relationships in practice: Animals in the helping professions* (pp. 191–207). Alameda, CA: Latham Foundation.

Bergler, R. (1986). *Man and dog: Psychology of a relationship.* Oxford: Blackwell Scientific Publications.

Berl, M.E. (1952). Therapy at the zoo. *Quarterly Journal of Child Behavior, 4,* 209–212.

Beston, H. (1928). *The outermost house: A year of life on the great beach of Cape Cod.* New York: Doubleday, Doran and Co.

Bikales, G. (1975). Dog as significant other. *Social Work, 20,* 150–152.

Bishop, J.A. (1927). *Just dogs.* New York: G. Howard Watt.

Blough, G.O., and Campbell, M.H. (1954). *Making and using classroom science materials.* New York: Dryden Press.

Blue, G.F. (1986). The value of pets in children's lives. *Childhood Education, 63,* 84–90.

Blum, G., and Hunt, N.F. (1952). The validity of the blacky pictures. *Psychology Bulletin, 49,* 238–250.

Blume, B. (1982). The ties that bind: Research on the human-companion animal bond has important implications for veterinary medicine. *Northern News, 57*(1), 20–28.

Boat, B.W. (1995). The relationship between violence to children and violence to animals. *The Journal of Interpersonal Violence, 10*(2), 229–235.

Bolton, L. (1948). We sent our child to the dog school. *Parents Magazine, 26*(10), 48.

Borland, H. (1962). *The dog who came to stay.* New York: J.B. Lippincott.

Borgese, E. M. (1968). *The language barrier: Beasts and men.* New York: Holt, Rinehart, Winston.

Bossard, J.H.S., and Boll, E.S.. (1966). *The sociology of child development.* New York: Harper.

Bossard, J.H.S. (1950). I wrote about dogs: A mental hygiene note. *Mental Hygiene, 34,* (pp. 385–390).

Bossard, J.H.S. (1944). The mental hygiene of owning a dog. *Mental Hygiene, 28,* (pp. 408–413).

Boszormenyi-Nagy, I. and Framo, J.L. (Eds.). (1965). *Intensive family psychotherapy.* New York: Harper and Brothers.

Bowen, M. (1965). Family psychotherapy with a schizophrenic in the hospital and private practice. In I. Boszormenyi-Nagy and J.L. Framo (Eds.), *Intensive family psychotherapy* (pp. 213–244). New York: Harper and Row.

Bowlby, J. (1982). *Attachment* (2nd ed.). New York: Basic Books.

Boyd, N., and Mandler, C. (1955). Children's responses to human and animal stories and pictures. *Journal of Consulting Psycholology, 19,* (pp. 367–371).

Brickel, C.M. (1982). Pet facilitated psychotherapy: A theoretical explanation via attention shifts. *Psychological Reports, 50,* 71–74.

Brill, A.A. (1945). The university of symbols. *The yearbook of psychoanalysis, 1,* 63–78.

Brill, K., and Thomas, R. (1964). *Children in homes.* London: Victor Gollancz Ltd.

Brock, B. (1992). Recreational riding. In B.T. Engel (Ed.), *Therapeutic riding programs: Instruction and rehabilitation* (pp. 527–528). Durango, CO: Barbara Engel Therapy Services.

Bryant B.K. (1990). The richness of the child-pet relationship: A consideration of both benefits and costs to children. *Anthrozoos, 3,* 253–261.

Burch, M.R., Bustad, L., Duncan, S.L., Frederickson, M., and Tebay, J. The role of pets in therapeutic programmes. In I. Robinson (Ed.), *The Waltham book of human-animal interaction: Benefits and responsibilities of pet ownership* (pp. 55–69). New York: Pergamon.

Burmeister, E. (1949). *Forty-five in a family: The story of a home for children.* New York: Columbia University Press.

Burmeister, E. (1960). *The professional houseparent.* New York: Columbia University Press.

Burmeister, E. (1967). *Tough times and moments in child care work.* New York: Columbia University Press.

Burton, L.E. (1995). Using a dog in an elementary school counseling program. *Elementary School Guidance and Counseling, 29,* 236–240.

Buss, A.H., and Durkee, A. (1957). The association of animals with familial figures. *Journal of Projective Techniques, 21,* 366–371.

Bustad, L.K. (1979). How animals make people human and humane. *Modern Veterinary Practice, 60,* 707–710.

Bustad, L.K. (1990). *Compassion: Our last great hope.* Renton, WA: Delta Society.

Bustad, L.K., and Hines, L.M. (1984). Historical perspectives of the human-animal bond. In R.K. Anderson, B.L. Hart, and L.A. Hart, (Eds.), *The pet connection: Its influences on our health and quality of life* (pp.15–29). South St. Paul, MN: Globe Publishing Co.

Cady, B. Chapman. (1930). *Animal pets: As study in character and nature education.* Ithaca, N.Y.: Slingerland-Comstock Co.

Cain, A.O. (1983). A study of pets in the family system. In A. H. Katcher and A.M. Beck (Eds.), *New perspectives on our lives with companion animals* (pp. 72–81). Philadelphia: University of Pennsylvania Press.

Cain, A.O. (1985). Pets as family members. *Marriage and Family Review,8,* 5–10.

Camuti, L.J., and Alexander, L. (1962). *A Park Ave. vet.* New York: Rinehart and Winston.

Caplan, G. (Ed.). (1961). *Prevention of mental disorders in children.* New York: Basic Books.

Caplan, H. (1951). Some interview techniques in child psychiatry. *Journal of Pediatrics, 38,* 128–140.

Carin, A., and Sund, R.B. (1964). *Teaching science through discovery.* Columbus, Ohio, Charles E. Merrill.

Carson, G. (1972). *Men, beasts, and Gods: A history of cruelty and kindness to animals.* New York: Charles Schribner's Sons.

Chapman, J. (1964, April). Baby meets dog. *Parents Magazine, 21*(4), 135–135.

Clark, K.M. (1977). *Animals and men: Their relationship as reflected in western art from Prehistory to the present day.* New York: William Morrow and Co.

Cock, W.H. (1937). *Animals and a future life.* London: Mortiboy's.

Cohen, S. (1931). Animals. *The universal Jewish Encyclopedia* (Vol. I, pp. 321–328). New York: Universal Jewish Encyclopedia Co.

Cohen, S. (1983). Words of comfort. *People-Animals-Environment, 1,* (1), 16–17.

Cohen, S., and Fudin, C.E. (Eds). (1991). *Problems in Veterinary medicine: Animal illness and human emotion.* Philadelphia, PA: J.B. Lippincott Company.

Coleman, J.C. (1964). *Abnormal Psychology and Modern Life.* (3rd ed.). New York: Scott and Foresman.

Colman, A.D. (1968). Territoriality in man-a comparison of behavior in home and hospital. *American Journal of Orthopsychiatry, 38,* 464–475.

Condoret, A. (1983). Speech and companion animals: Experience with normal and disturbed nursery school children. In A.H. Katcher and A.M. Beck (Eds.), *New perspectives on our lives with companion animals* (pp. 467–471). Philadelphia: University of Pennsylvania Press.

Conrad, D., and Thier, H.D. (1969). The life sciences. *The instructor, (78),* (pp. 63–68).

Coren, S. (1994). *The intelligence of dogs.* New York: The Free Press.

Corson, S., and O'Leary-Corson, E. (1973). Proposal for research project designed to facilitate therapy of adults and adolescent psychiatric and psychosomatic patients and shorten hospital stay. Columbus, Ohio: Ohio State University.

Corson, S., O'Leary-Corson, E., Gwynne, P., and Arnold, E. (1977). Pet dogs as non-verbal communication links in hospital psychiatry. *Comprehensive Psychiatry, 18,* 61–72.

Corson, S.A., and Corson, E.O. (1978). Pets as mediators of therapy. *Current Psychiatric Therapies, 18,* 195–205.

Corson, S. A., and Corson, E.O. (1979). Pets as socializing catalysts in geriatrics: An experiment in nonverbal communication therapy. In L. Levi (Ed.), *Society, stress and disease: Aging and old age* (pp. 1–47). Oxford: Oxford University Press.

Covert, A.M., Whiren, A.P., Keith, J, and Nelson, C. (1985). Pets, early adolescents, and families. *Marriage and Family Review, 8* (3/4), 95–108.

Cronin, A. (1995, June 11). Primitive? Not the one who drew the lion. *The New York Times,* p. E2.

Cusack, O. (1988). *Pets and mental health.* New York: Haworth.

Dale-Green, P. (1963). *Cult of the cat.* London, Heinemann.

Daniel, S.A., Burke, J., and Burke, J. (1985). Educational programs for pet-assisted therapy in institutional settings: An interdisciplinary approach. *Veterinary Technician, 12*(4), 394-397.

David, H.P. (1955). Brief unstructured items; the projective question. *Journal of Projective Techniques, 19,* 292–300.

David, H.P., and Leach, W.W. (1957). The projective question: further exploratory studies. *Journal of Projective Techniques, 21,* 3–9.

David, S.L. (no date) Comments on the use of pets in the teaching of emotionally disturbed boys. Unpublished paper.

Davids, A., Ryan, R., and Salvatore, P.D. (1968). Effectiveness of residential treatment for psychotic and other disturbed children. *American Journal of Orthopsychiatry, 38,* 469–475.

Davis, J.H. (1987). Pre-adolescent self-concept development and pet ownership. *Anthrozoos, 1*(2), 90–94.

Davis, J.H., and Juhasz, A.M. (1995). The preadolescent/pet friendship bond. *Anthrozoos, 8*(2), 78–82.

Davis, S.J.M., and Valla, F.R. (1978). Evidence for domestication of the dog 12,000 years ago in Natufian of Israel, *Nature, 276,* 608–610.

Delta Society. (1992). *Handbook of animal-assisted activities and animal-assisted therapy.* Renton, WA: The Delta Society.

Dembeck, N.H. (1965). *Animals and men.* Garden City, New York: Natural History Press.

Des Lauriers, A.M. (1967). Psychotherapy with the schizophrenic child. In M.

Hammer, and A.M. Kaplan, (Eds.), *The practice of psychotherapy with children* (pp. 201–213). Homewood, IL: The Dorsey Press.

Des Lauriers, A.M. (1962). *The experience of reality in childhood schizophrenia.* New York: International Universities Press.

Deviney, E., Dickert, J., and Lockwood, R. (1983). The care of pets within child abusing families. *International Journal for the Study of Animal Problems, 4,* 321–328.

Diesch, S.L. (1984). Companion animals on the farm. In P. Arkow, (Ed.), *Dynamic relationships in practice: Animals in the helping professions* (pp. 257–270). Alameda, CA: Latham Foundation.

Disney, D.C. (1967). Can this marriage be saved? *Ladies Home Journal, 84*(4), 20–31.

Dunbar, I. (1984). Animal behavior: The animal's side of the bond. In P. Arkow (Ed.), *Dynamic relationships in practice: Animals in the helping professions* (pp. 83–105). Alameda, CA: Latham Foundation.

Eaton, L., and Menolascino, F. (1967). Psychotic reactions in childhood: a follow up study. *American Journal of Orthopsychiatry, 37,* 521–529.

Edgar, D.S. (1960). *Law for the pet owner.* New York: Oceana Publications.

Editorial, *National Humane Review, (51),* 3.

Eisley, L. (1968). Exploring animal secrets. *The Instructor,* 77(5), 117–119.

Ekman, P., and Friesen, W.V. (1968). Nonverbal behavior in psychotherapy research. In J.M. Shlien, (Ed.), *Research in Psychotherapy* (Vol. III, pp. 179–216). Washington: American Psychological Association.

Ellis, H. (1937). *Studies in The Psychology of Sex* (Vol. II, part I). New York: Random House.

Endenburg, N., and Baarda, B. (1995). The role of pets in enhancing human well-being: Effects on child development. In I. Robinson (Ed.), *The Waltham book of human-animal interaction: Benefits and responsibilities of pet ownership* (pp. 1–17). New York: Pergamon.

Epstein, I. (Ed.). (1935). *The Babylonian talmud. Abodah Zorah.* London: The Soncino Press.

Erikson, E.H. (1963). *Childhood and society,* 2nd ed. New York: Norton.

Erikson, E.H. (1964). *Insight and responsibility.* New York: N.W. Norton.

Erikson, E.H. (1968). *Identity, youth and crisis.* New York: Norton Press.

Evans-Pritchard, E.E. (1937). *Witchcraft, oracles, and magic among the Azande.* Oxford: Clarendon Press.

Eysenck, H. (Ed.). (1960). *Handbook of Abnormal Psychology.* London: Pitman.

Fast, I., and Cain, A.C. (1966). The step parent role: potential for disturbance in family functioning. *American Journal Orthopsychiatry, 34,* 485–491.

Felthous. A.R. (1980) Aggression against cats, dogs, and people. *Child Psychiatry and Human development, 10,* 169–177.

Felthous, A.R., and Kellert, S.R. (1987). Childhood cruelty to animals and later aggression against people: A review. *America Journal of Psychiatry, 144* (6), 710–717.

Fenichel, O. (1945). *The psychoanalytic theory of neurosis.* New York: Norton.

Finestone, S., Lukoff, I., and Whiteman, M. (1960). *The demand of dog guides and travel adjustment of blind persons.* New York: Research Center of the New York School of Social Work, Columbia University.

Fisher, J. (1992). *Dogwise: The natural way to train your dog.* London: Souvenir Press.

Foote, N. (1956). A neglected member of the family. *Marriage and Family Living, 18,* 213–218.

Ford, C.S., and Beach, F.A. (1951). *Patterns of sexual behavior.* New York: Harper and Brothers.

Fortune, R.F. (1963). *Sorcerers of Dobu.* New York: Dutton.

Foster, J.C., and Anderson, J.E. (1936). Unpleasant dreams in childhood. *Childhood in Development, 7,* 77–84.

Fogel, B. (1983). *Pets and their people.* New York: Viking.

Fox, M.W. (1965). *Canine behavior.* Springfield, IL: Charles C Thomas.

Fox, M.W. (1968). *Abnormal behavior in animals.* Philadelphia: W.B. Saunders.

Fox, M.W. (1975). *Understanding your dog.* London: Book Club Associates.

Fox, M.W. (1976). The needs of people for pets. In F.M. Loew (Ed.), *Proceedings of the First Canadian Symposium on pets and society* (pp. 25–30). Ottawa: Canadian Veterinary Medical Association.

Fox, M. (1981). Relationships between the human and non-human animals. In B. Fogel (Ed.), *Interrelations between people and pets* (pp. 23–40). Springfield, IL: Charles C Thomas.

Fraiberg, S. (1967). The analysis of an eight-year-old girl with epilepsy. In E.D. Geleerd, (Ed.), *The child analyst at work* (pp. 229–287). New York: International Universities Press.

Framo, J.L. (1965). Rationale and technique of intensive family psychotherapy. In I. Boszormenyi-Nagy, I. and J.L. Framo, (Eds.), *Intensive family psychotherapy,* (pp. 143–212). New York: Harper and Row.

Fraser, J. (1991). A lesson in healing. *Gazette, 109* (9), 88–93.

Frederickson, M. (1995). The role of animals in healing: Recent research on the outcomes of animal-assisted therapy. Unpublished paper.

Freed, E.X. (1965). Normative data on a self-administered projective question for children. *Journal of Projective Techniques and Personality Assessment, 29,* 3–6.

Freud, A. (1937). *The ego and the mechanisms of defense.* London: Hogarth Press.

Freud. A. (1951). *The psychoanalytical treatment of children.* (Translated from the German by Nancy Procter-Gregg). London: Imago Publishing Co., Ltd.

Freud, A. (1965). *Normality and pathology in childhood. Assessment of development.* New York: International Universities Press.

Freud, A., and Burlingham, D.T. (1944). *War and children.* New York: International Universities Press.

Freud, S. (1938). *The basic writings of Sigmund Freud.* (Translated by A.A. Brill), New York: Random House.

Freud, S. (1955). Analysis of a phobia in a five-year old boy. In *Collected Works* (Vol. 10). (Standard ed.) (Edited and translated by James Strachey). London: Hogarth Press.

Freud, S. (1960). *The interpretation of dreams.* (Translated by A.A. Brill), New York: Basic Books.

Freud, S. (1961). *The ego and the id* (Vol. XIV). (Standard ed.) (Edited and translated by James Strachey). London: Hogarth Press.

Fried, M. (1963). Grieving for a lost home. In L. Duhl (Ed.), *The urban condition* (pp. 151–171). New York: Basic Books.

Friedman, A.S. (1965). Implications of the home setting for family treatment. In Friedman, A.S., et al. (Eds.), *Psychotherapy for the whole family,* (pp. 240–254). New York: Springer Publishing Co.

Friedmann, E. (1995). The role of pets in enhancing human well-being: Physiological effects. In I. Robinson (Ed.), *The Waltham book of human-animal interaction: Benefits and responsibilities of pet ownership* (pp. 33–53). New York: Pergamon.

Friedmann, E., Katcher, A.H., Lynch, J.J., and Thomas, S.A. (1980). Animal companions and one year survival of patients after discharge from a coronary care unit. *Public Health Reports, 95,* 307–312.

Friedmann, E., Katcher, A.H., and Meislich, D. (1983). When pet owners are hospitalized: Significance of companion animals during hospitalization. In A.H. Katcher and A.M. Beck (Eds.), *New perspectives on our lives with companion animals* (pp. 346–350). Philadelphia: University of Pennsylvania Press.

Friedmann, E., and Thomas, S.A. (1985). Health benefits of pets for families. *Marriage and Family Review, 8,* 191–203.

Fromm, E. (1955). *The sane society.* New York: Rinehart.

Gage, M.G., and Christensen, D.H. (1990). Early adolescents' values about their pets. *The Journal of Psychology, 124,* 417–425.

Gates, A.M. (1931). Greek and Roman pets. *South Atlantic Quarterly, 30,* 405–419.

Gautier, J. (1957). *A priest and his dog.* New York: P.J. Kennedy and Sons.

Gay, M.C. (1950). *How to live with a cat.* New York: Simon and Schuster.

Geis, H.J. (1969, Feb. 15). Personal communication.

Geis, H.J. (1967, July 6). Personal communication.

Geleerd, E.R. (1967). *The child analyst at work.* New York: International Universities, 1967.

Germain, C.B. (1973). The ecological perspective in casework practice. *Social Casework: The Journal of Contemporary Social Work, 54,* 323–330.

Germain, C.B. (1978). General-systems theory and ego psychology: An ecological perspective. *Social Service Review,* 535–550.

Germain, C.B. (1981). The ecological approach to people-environment transactions. *Social Casework: The Journal of Contemporary Social Work, 62,* 323–331.

Germain, C.B. (1991). *Human behavior and the social environment.* New York: Columbia University Press.

Germain, C.B., and Gitterman, A. (1980). *The life model of social work practice.* New York: Columbia University Press.

Gessell, A. (1941). *Wolf child and human child.* New York: Harper.

Gheerbrant, A. (1954). *A journey to the far Amazon.* New York: Simon and Schuster.

Gittelman, M. (1965). Behavior rehearsal as a technique in child treatment. *Journal of Child Psychology and Psychiatry, 6,* 251–255.

Glasser, J. (1961). Allergic disease in general practice. *American Practice and Digest Treatment, 12,* 715.

Glenn, J. (1996, January/February). Wild at heart. *Utne Reader,* (73), 51.

Goldfarb, W. (1945). The animal symbol in the Rorschach test, and an animal association test. *Rorschach Research Exchange, 9,* 8–22.

Goldberg, I. (1952). Use of remedial reading tutoring as a method of psychotherapy for schizophrenic children with reading disabilities. *Quarterly Journal of Child Behavior, 4,* 273–280.

Gonski, Y. (1985). The therapeutic utilization of canines in a child welfare setting. *Child and Adolescent Social Work Journal, 2* (2), 93–105.

Gould, S.J. (1979). Mickey Mouse meets Konrad Lorenz. *Natural History, 88,* 30–36.

Haggerty, D.L., Gerace, L., and Summers, J. (1989). Pet-care management in child-rearing families. *Anthrozoos, 2*(3), 189–193.

Hagman, R.R. (1932). A study of fears of children of preschool age. *Journal of Experimental Education, 1,* (pp. 110–130).

Hall, S.G.; and Browne, C.E. (1904). The cat and the child. *Pedagogical Seminary, (11)* (pp. 3–29).

Halliday, W.R. (1922). Animal pets in ancient Greece. *Discovery, (3),* 151–154.

Hammer, E.F. (Ed.). (1958). *The clinical application of protective drawings.* Springfield, IL: Charles C Thomas.

Harlow, H.F. (1958). The nature of love. *American Psychology, 13,* 673–685.

Harlow, H.F., Harlow, M.K., and Hansen, E.W. (1963). The maternal affectional system of rhesus monkeys. In H.L. Rheingold (Ed.), *Maternal behavior in mammals* (no page numbers cited). New York: Wiley.

Harlow, H.F., and Zimmerman, R.R. (1959). Affectional response in infant monkeys. *Science, 130,* 421–432.

Harrington, J. (1960). The management of regression in the treatment of severely disturbed children. *Journal of Child Psychology and Psychiatry, 1,* 228–237.

Harris, J. (1984). The Veterinarian's role in the human/animal bond. In P. Arkow (Ed.), *Dynamic relationships in practice: Animals in the helping professions* (pp. 271–286). Alameda, CA: The Latham Foundation.

Harris, J.M. (1989). Children and pet loss. *Companion Animal Practice, 19*(3), 15–16.

Hart, L.A. (1993). Companion animals throughout the life cycle: The contributions of Aline and Robert Kidd. *Anthrozoos, 6* (3), 148–153.

Hartland, S.E. (1951). Totemism. *Encyclopedia of religion and ethics* (Vol. 12, pp. 393–407). New York: Charles Scribner's.

Hartley, E.L., and Shames, C. (1959). Man and dog: Psychological analysis. *Ninth Gaines Veterinary Symposium,* (pp. 4–7). New York.

Hartman, H. (1964). *Essays on ego psychology.* New York: International Universities Press.

Hartman, H. (1955). Notes on the theory of sublimation. *Psychoanalytic study of the child* (Vol. X). New York: International Universities Press.

Hartwell, D. (1942). *Dogs against darkness.* New York: Dodd, Mead.

Hartwell, D. (1968). *Dogs against darkness* (3rd ed). New York: Dodd, Mead.

Hassall, J.C. (1919). The serpent as a symbol. *Psychoanalytic Review, 6,* 296–305.

Haworth, M.R. (1966). *The CAT: Facts about fantasy.* New York: Grune and Stratton.

Hays, H.R. (1963). *In the beginnings. Early man and his Gods.* New York: G.P. Putnam's Sons.

Heath, T.D., and McKenry, P.C. (1989). Potential benefits of companion animals for self-care children. *Childhood Education, 7(4),* 311–314.

Hebb, D.O. (1958). *A textbook of psychology.* Philadelphia: W.B. Saunders.

Heiman, M. (1965). Psychoanalytic observations on the relationship of pet and man. *Veterinary Medicine/Small Animal Clinician,* 713–718.

Heiman, M. (1953). On the of animals. *The Psychoanalytic Quarterly, 22,* 147–148.

Heiman, M. (1956). The relationship between man and dog. *The Psychoanalytic Quarterly, 25,* 568–585.

Henry, J. (1952). *Culture against man.* New York: Random House.

Herzog, H.A., and Galvin, S.L. (1992). Animals, archetypes, and popular culture: Tales From the Tabloid Press. *Anthrozoos, 5* (2), 77–92.

Hill, B.H. (1966). Rx for apathy. *The National Humane Review, 54,* (1), 7–9.

Hodgin, J. (1962, July 9). Personal communication.

Holmes, D.J. (1964). *The adolescent in psychotherapy.* Boston: Little, Brown.

Holmes. J. (1967). *Obedience training for dogs* (Rev. ed). Levittown, New York: Transatlantic.

Hopley, C.C. (1956). Serpent and snake charming. In B. Aymar (Ed.), *Treasury of snake lore,* (pp. 49–59). New York: Greenberg.

Howells, W. (1948). *The heathens. Primitive man and his religion.* Garden City, NY: Doubleday and Co.

Hubbard, L.B.C. (1947). *Working dogs of the world.* London: Sidgwick and Jackson Ltd.

Huizinga, J. (1960). *Homo ludens. A study of the play-element in culture.* Boston: The Beacon Press.

Huxley, J. (1952). Foreword, In K.Z. Lorenz, *King Solomon's Ring.* London: Methuen.

Hyde, W.W. (1915–16). The prosecution and punishment of animals and lifeless things in the middle ages and modern times. *University of Pennsylvania Law Review, (64)* (696–730).

Iannuzzi, D., and Rowan, A.N. (1991). Ethical issues in animal-assisted therapy programs. *Anthrozoos, 4* (3), 154–163.

James, W. (1890). *Principles of psychology.* New York: Holt, Rinehart and Winston.

Jayne, A.W. (1962). *The healing gods of ancient civilizations.* New Hyde Park, NY: University Books.

Jelliffe, S.E., and Brink, L. (1917). The role of animals in the unconscious. *The Psychoanalytic Review, 4,* 253–271.

Jenkins, J.L. (1986). Physiological effects of petting a companion animal. *Psychological Reports, 58,* 21–22.

Jersild, A.T., and Holmes, F.B. (1935a). Children's fears. *Child Development Monographs,* (No. 20).

Jersild, A.T., and Holmes, F.B. (1935b). Some factors in the development of children's fears. *Journal of Experimental Education, 4,* 133–141.

Jersild, A.T., Markey, F.V., and Jersild, C.L. (1933). Children's fears, dreams, likes, dislikes, pleasant and unpleasant memories. *Child Development Monographs,* (No.12).

Jersild, A.T. (1954). Emotional development. In L. Carmichael, (Ed.), *Manual of Child Psychology* (2nd Ed.) (pp. 833–917) New York: Wiley.

Jones, E. (1959). *On the nightmare.* New York: Grove Press.

Jones, K. (1955). *Lunacy, law, and conscience.* London: Routledge and Kegan Paul.

Joseph, A. (1956). *A letter to the man who killed my dog.* New York: Frederick Fell.

Jowett, B. (1937). *The dialogues of Plato* (Vol. I). New York: Random House.

Joy, C. (Ed.) (1950). *The animal world of Albert Schweitzer.* Boston: Beacon Press.

Jungreiss, J.E., and Speck, R.V. (1965). The island family. In E. Friedmann et al. (Eds.), *Psychotherapy for the whole family,* (pp. 32–79). New York: Springer.

Kahler, E. (1960). The nature of the symbol. In R. May, (Ed.), *Symbolism in religion and literature* (pp. 50–73). New York: George Braziller.

Kamby, P.E., and Suttle, J.E. (1963). *Teaching elementary school science: Methods and resources.* New York: Ronald Press.

Kaplan, H.K., and Calden, C. (1967). An elaboration of the "projective question"-the animal test. *Journal of Clinical Psychology, 23,* 204.

Katcher, A.H. (1987). *The health significance of the living environment: A theoretical perspective.* Paper presented at the Center for the Interaction of Animals and Society, Philadelphia, PA.

Katcher, A.H., and Beck, A.M. (1983). *New perspectives on our lives with companion animals.* Philadelphia: University of Pennsylvania Press.

Katcher, A.H., and Beck, A.M. (1987). Health and caring for living things. *Anthozoos, 1* (3), 175–183.

Katcher, A.H., and Friedmann, E. (1980). Potential health value of pet ownership. *The Compendium on Continuing Education, 11* (2), 117–121.

Katcher, A.H., Friedmann, E.; Goodman, M., and Goodman, L. (1983). Men, women, and dogs. *California Veterinarian, 2,* 14–16.

Katcher, A.H., Segal, H., and Beck, A.M. (1984). Contemplation of an aquarium for the reduction of anxiety. In R.K. Anderson, B.L. Hart, and L.A. Hart (Eds.) *The pet connection: Its influence on our health and quality of life life* (pp.171–178). St. Paul, MN: Globe Publishing Co.

Kavanau, J.L. (1964). Confinement, adaptation, and compulsory regimes in laboratory studies. *Science, 143,* 490.

Kay, W.J., Cohen, S.P., Fudin, C.E., Kutcher, A.H., Nieberg, H.A., Grey, P.E., and Osman, M.M. (Eds). (1988). *Euthanasia of the companion animal: The impact on pet owners, veterinarians, and society.* Philadelphia, PA: The Charles Press.

Kellert, S. and Westervelt, S. (1983). *Childhood cruelty towards animals among criminals and non-criminals.* Unpublished manuscript.

Kellert, S.R., and Felthous, A.R. (1985). Childhood cruelty toward animals among criminals and noncriminals. *Human Relations, 38*(12), 1113–1129.

Kessler, J. (1966). *Psychopathology of childhood.* Englewood Cliffs, NJ: Prentice-Hall.

Kidd, A.H., and Kidd, R.H. (1985). Children's attitudes toward their pets. *Psychological Reports, 57,* 15–31.

Kidd, A.H., and Kidd, R.H. (1987). Seeking a theory of human/companion animal bond. *Anthrozoos, 4,* 140–145.

Kidd, A.H., and Kidd, R.H. (1990a). Factors in children's attitudes toward pets. *Psychological Reports, 66,* 775–786.

Kidd, A.H., and Kidd, R.H. (1990b). High school students and their pets. *Psychological Reports, 66,* 1391–94.

Kidd, A.H., and Kidd, R.H. (1990c). Social and environmental influences on children's attitudes toward pets. *Psychological Reports, 67,* 807–818.

Kinsey, A.C., Pomeroy, W.B., and Martin, C.E. (1948). *Sexual behavior in the human male.* Philadelphia: W.B. Saunders.

Kipling, R. (1912). The cat that walked by himself. *Just so stories for little children.* London: McMillan.

Klein, M. (1955). The psychoanalytic play technique. *American Journal of Orthopsychiatry, 1,* 223–238.

Klopper, B., and Davidson, H.H. (1962). *The rorschach technique: An introductory manual.* New York: Harcourt, Brace and World.

Koehler, W.R. (1967). *Koehler method of guard training.* New York: Howell.

Krutzmann, W.G.A. (1967, April 17). Personal communication.

Laird, J., and Hartman, A. (Eds.). (1985). *A handbook of child welfare: Context, knowledge, and practice.* New York: Free Press.

Landreth, C. (1958). *The psychology of early childhood.* New York: Knopf.

Langdon, S.H. (1931). *The mythology of all races* (Vol. V). New York: Cooper Square.

Lansky, L.M. (1968). Story completion methods. In A.I. Rabin, (Ed.), *Projective techniques in personality assessment,* (pp. 290–324). New York: Springer.

Lawrence, E.A. (1984). Human relationships with horses. In R.K. Anderson, B.L. Hart, and L.A. Hart (Eds.), *The pet connection,* (pp. 38–43). Minneapolis: Center to Study Human-Animal Relationships and the Environments.

Leach, E.R. (1964). Anthropologic aspects of language: Animal categories and verbal abuse. In E. Lennenberg (Ed.), *New directions in the study of language* (pp. 23–64). Cambridge: MIT Press.

Leach, M. (1961). *God had a dog. Folklore of the dog.* New Brunswick, N.J. Rutgers University Press.

Lee, D. (1984). Companion animals in institutions. In P. Arkow, (Ed.), *Dynamic relationships in practice: Animals in the helping professions* (pp. 229–236). Alameda, CA: Latham Foundation.

Leedham, C. (1961). *Care of the dog.* New York: Scribner's.

Lehman, K.Z. (1965). *Man meets dog.* Baltimore: Penguin Books.

Leighton, D., and Kluckhohn, C. (1948). *Children of the people.* Cambridge: Harvard University Press.

Levin, S., and Wermer, H. (1966). Giving gifts in therapy. *Journal of the American Academy of Child Psychiatry, 5,* 630–662.

Levinson, B. (1947). *A comparative study of certain homeless and unattached domiciled men.* Unpublished doctoral dissertation. New York University, New York, New York.

Levinson, Boris M. (1953–1954). In *Leaders in American science* (Vol. 1., pp. 202–203). Nashville, TN: Who's Who in American Education.

Levinson, B. (1958a). Some aspects of the personality of the native-born while homeless men as revealed by the Rorschach. *Psychiatric Quarterly Supplement, 32,* 278–286.

Levinson, B. (1958b). Culture and mental retardation. *Psychological Recorder, 8,* 27–38.

Levinson, B. (1959). The mentally defective child. *Yeshiva Educator, 3,* 3–15.

Levinson, B. (1962). The dog as co-therapist. *Mental Hygiene, 46,* 59–65.

Levinson, B. (1963). The homeless man: A psychological enigma. *Mental Hygiene, 47,* 590–601.

Levinson, B. (1964). Pets: A special technique in child psychotherapy. *Mental Hygiene, 48,* 243–248.

Levinson, B. (1965a). The veterinarian and mental hygiene. *Mental Hygiene, 49,* 320–323.

Levinson, B. (1965b). Pet psychotherapy: The use of household pets in the treatment of behavior disorders of childhood. *Psychological Reports, 17,* 695–698.

Levinson, B. (1966). Subcultural studies of homeless men. *Transactions of the New York Academy of Sciences, 29:* 165–182.

Levinson, B. (1968a). Household pets in residential schools. *Mental Hygiene, 52,* 411–414.

Levinson, B. (1968b). Interpersonal relationships between pet and human being. In M. W. Fox (Ed.), *Abnormal behavior in animals* (pp. 504–522). Philadelphia: W.B. Saunders.

Levinson, B. (1969a). *Pet-oriented child psychotherapy.* Springfield, IL: Charles C Thomas.

Levinson, B. (1969b). Pets and old age. *Mental Hygiene, 53,* 364–368.

Levinson, B. (1970a). Nursing home pets: A psychological adventure for the patients (Part I). *National Humane Review, 58,* 14–16.

Levinson, B. (1970b). Nursing home pets: A psychological adventure for the patients (Part II). *National Humane Review, 58,* 6–8.

Levinson, B. (1970c). Pets, child development, and mental illness. *The Journal of the American Veterinary Association, 157,* 1759–1766.

Levinson, B. (1971). Household pets in training schools serving delinquent children. *Psychological Reports, 28,* 475–481.

Levinson, B. (1972a). *Pets and human development.* Springfield, IL: Charles C Thomas.

Levinson, B. (1972b). Man, animal, nature. *Modern Veterinary Practice, 4,* 35–41.

Levinson, B. (1972c, Oct.). Pets and modern family life. *D. V.M. News-Magazine of Veterinary Medicine, 4*(10), 5–6.

Levinson, B. (1975a). Use of checkers in therapy, In C.E. Schaeffer (Ed.), *Therapeutic use of play* (pp. 383–384). New York: Aronson.

Levinson, B. (1975b). Pets and environment. In R.S. Anderson, (Ed.), *Pet animals and society* (pp. 223–243). London: Baillieire Tindal.

Levinson, B. (1976). Paper folding as a therapeutic device. *Perceptual and Motor Skills, 43,* 494.

Levinson, B. (1978). Pets and personality development. *Psychological Reports, 42,* 1031–1038.

Levinson, B. (1979a). *The animal companion and the emotionally handicapped child.* Paper presented at the Blueberry Treatment Center, Brooklyn, New York.

Levinson, B. (1979b). Dominoes as a therapeutic device. *Psychological Reports, 45,* 399–403.

Levinson, B. (1980a). The blueberry syndrome. *Psychological Reports, 46,* 47–52.

Levinson, B. (1980b). The child and his pet: A world of non-verbal communication. In S.A. Corson and E. O'Leary-Corson, (Eds.), *Ethology and non-verbal communication in mental health* (pp. 63–81). London: Pergamon Press.

Levinson, B. (1981). Human grief on the loss of an animal companion. *Archives of the Foundation of Thanatology, 9,* (2), 5.

Levinson, B. (1982). The future of research into the relationships between people and their companion animals. *International Journal for the Study of Animal Problems, 9,* 283–294.

Levinson, B. (1983a). The septuagenarian as a child psychotherapist: A change in career orientation at the end of the stream. *Psychotherapy, Theory, Research, and Practice, 20,* 251–253.

Levinson, B. (1983b). *A history of animal facilitated therapy.* Paper presented at the Green Chimneys People, Pets and Plants Conference, Brewster, N.Y.

Levinson, B. (1984a). Human/companion therapy. *Journal of Contemporary Psychotherapy, 14,* 112–123.

Levinson, B. (1984b). Foreword. Dynamic relationships in practice. In P. Arkow, (Ed.), *Animals in the helping professions* (pp. 1–20). Alameda, California: The Latham Foundation.

Levinson, B., and Mezei, H. (1973). The draw-a-dog scale. *Perceptual and Motor Skills, 36,* 19–22.

Levinson, B., and Oterweil, L. (1984). *Autism: Myth or reality?* Springfield, IL: Charles C Thomas.

Leviticus: 20:15–16.

Lewinsohn, R. (1954). *Animals, men and myths.* New York: Harper and Brothers.

Lewis, N.D.C. (1963–1964). Some theriomorphic symbolisms and mechanisms in ancient literature and dreams. *Psychoanalytic Review, 50*(4), 5–26.

Liddell, H.S. (1956). *Emotional hazards in animals and men.* Springfield, IL: Charles C Thomas.

Lieber, L. (1963). Someone besides people. *This Week Magazine.*

Lockard, R.B. (1968). The albino rat: a defensible choice or a bad habit. *American Psychology, 23,* 734–742.

Loney, J. (1971). The canine therapist in a residential children's setting: Qualifications, recruitment, training and related matters. *Journal American Academy of Child Psychiatry, 10* (3), 518–523.

Lorenz, K.Z. (1964). *Man meets dog.* Baltimore: Penguin Books.

Lorenz, K. Z. (1952). *King Solomon's Ring.* London: Methuen.

Ludwig, E., and Jamieson, D. (1981). Animals as a minority. *Humanity and Society, 5* (3), 246–255.

MacDonald, A. (1981). The pet dog in the home. A study of interactions. In B.

Fogle (Ed.), *Interrelations between people and pets* (pp. 195–206) Springfield, IL: Charles C Thomas.

Mallon, G. (1991). Rules and principles which guide animal-assisted therapy for children. Paper presented at the Green Chimneys People, Pets, and Plants Conference, Brewster, New York.

Mallon, G. (1992a). Dogs in the dorms: A study on the placement of dogs in the living units of a residential treatment center for children. Paper presented at the Green Chimneys People, Pet and Plants Conference, Brewster, NY.

Mallon, G.P. (1992b). Utilization of animals as therapeutic adjuncts with children and youth: A review of the literature. *Child and Youth Care Forum, 21,* (1), 53–65.

Mallon, G.P. (1993a). A study of the interaction between men, women, and dogs at the ASPCA. *Anthrozoos, 6*(1), 43–48.

Mallon, G.P. (1993b). Pets in residence. In S. Senter, (Ed.), *People and animals: An animal-assisted activities manual,* (pp. 35–75). Brewster: Green Chimneys Press.

Mallon, G. (1994a). Some of our best therapists are dogs. *Child and Youth Care Forum, 23*(2), 89–101.

Mallon, G.P. (1994b). Cow as co-therapist: Utilization of farm animals as therapeutic aides with children in residential treatment. *Child and Adolescent Social Work Journal, 11*(6), 455–474.

Mallon, G.P. (1994c). A generous spirit: The work and life of Boris Levinson. *Anthrozoos, 7*(4), 224–231.

Marks, I.M., and Gelder, G., (1966). Different onset ages in varieties of phobias. *American Journal of Psychiatry, 123,* 218–221.

Masters, W.H., and Johnson, V.E. (1966). *Human sexual response.* Boston: Little, Brown.

May, R. (1968). The significance of symbols. In May, R. (Ed.), *Symbolism in religion and literature* (pp. 11–49). New York: Braziller.

McBride, A. (1995). The human-dog relationship. In I. Robinson (Ed.), *The Waltham book of human-animal interaction: Benefits and responsibilities of pet ownership* (pp. 99–112). New York: Pergamon.

McCowan, L.L. (1984). Equestrian therapy. In P. Arkow, (Ed.), *Dynamic relationships in practice: Animals in the helping professions* (pp. 237–256). Alameda, CA: Latham Foundation.

McCulloch, M.J. (1983). Companion animals, human health, and the veterinarian. In S.J. Ettinger (Ed.), *Textbook of veterinary internal medicine-diseases of the dog and cat* (pp. 228–235). Philadelphia: W.B. Saunders.

McCulloch, M.J. (1984). Pets in therapeutic programs for the aged. In R.K. Anderson, B.L. Hart and L.A. Hart (Eds.), *The pet connection* (pp. 387–398). Minneapolis: Center to Study Human-Animal Relationships and the Environment.

McCulloch, W.F. (1982). The human-companion animal bond: Vital topic in veterinary education. *California Veterinarian, 36*(11), 29–32.

McCulloch, W.F., and McCulloch, M.J. (1982). The veterinarian and the human-companion animal bond. *Veterinary Economics, 22,* 18–22.

McNicholas, J., and Collis, G.M. (1995). The end of a relationship: Coping with pet loss. In I. Robinson (Ed.), *The Waltham book of human-animal interaction: Benefits and responsibilities of pet ownership* (pp. 127–143). New York: Pergamon.

Meller, W.C. (1911). *A brief for animal immortality.* London: C. Bell and Sons.

Melson, G.F. (1990). *Fostering inter-connectedness with animals and nature: The Developmental benefits for children.* Paper presented at the Green Chimneys People, Pets, and Plants Conference. Brewster, New York.

Melson, G.F. (1991). Studying children's attachment to their pets: A conceptual and methodological view. *Anthrozoos, 4,* 91–99.

Melson, G.F., and Fogel, A. (1989). Children's ideas about animal young and their care: A reassessment of gender differences in the development of nurturance. *Anthrozoos, 2,* 265–273.

Melson, G. F., Strimple, E.O., and Bustad, L.K. (1992, April). *The benefits of interactions of children and animals.* Paper presented at the Fourth National Health Policy Forum, Washington, D.C.

Menninger, K. A. (1951). Totemic aspects of contemporary attitudes toward animals. In G.B. Wilbur, and W. Muensterberger, (Eds.), *Psychoanalysis and Culture* (pp. 42–74). New York: International Universities Press.

Mertens, C. (1991). Human-cat interactions in the home setting. *Anthrozoos, 4*(4), 214–231.

Messent, P.R. (1983). Social facilitation of contact with people by pet dogs. In A.H. Katcher and A.M. Beck (Eds.), *New perspectives on our lives with companion animals* (pp. 45–67). Philadelphia, PA: University of Philadelphia Press.

Messent, P.R., and Serpell, J.A. (1981). An historical and biological view of pet-owner bond. In B. Fogel (Ed.), *Interrelationships between people and pets* (pp. 5–22). Springfield, IL: Charles C Thomas.

Morris, D. (1967). *The naked ape.* New York: McGraw.

Morris, D. (1986). *Dogwatching.* New York: Crown.

Morse, M. (1968). *Ordeal of the animals.* Englewood Cliffs, NJ: Prentice-Hall.

Moskin, J.R. (1965, March 28). Buttercup meets the baby. *Life, 29,* (pp. 114–116).

Mugford, R.A. (1980). The social significance of pet ownership. In S.A. Corson, and E.O. Corson (Eds.), *Ethology and nonverbal communication in mental health* (pp. 112–122). New York: Pergamon.

Mugford, R.A., and M'Comisky, J.G.M. (1975). Some recent work on the psychotherapeutic value of caged birds with old people, In R.S. Anderson (Ed.), *Pet animals and society* (pp. 54–65). Springfield, IL: Charles C Thomas.

Murphy, L.B., and Krall, V. (1960). Free play as a projective tool. In Rabin, A.I., and Haworth, M.R.: *Projective techniques with children.* New York: Grune and Stratton.

Nathanson, D.E., and de Faria, S. (1993). Cognitive improvement of children in water with and without dolphins. *Anthrozoos, 6* (2), 17–29.

Nathanson, D.E. (1989). Using Atlantic bottlenose increase cognition of mentally retarded children. In P. Lovibond and P. Wilson (Eds.), *Clinical and abnormal psychology* (pp. 233–242). North Holland: Elsevier.

National Humane Review. (1966). National Humane review attends a pet show for handicapped youngsters. *National Humane Review, 54*(2), 10–11.

Neiberg, H.A. (1981). Pathological grief in response to pet loss. *Archives of the Foundation of Thanatology, 9,* (2), 7.

Neiburg, H.A., and Fischer, A. (1982). *Pet loss: A thoughtful guide for adults and children.* New York: Harper and Row.

Netting, F.E., Wilson, C.C., and New, J.C. (1987). The human-animal bond: Implications for practice. *Social Work, 12* (1), 60–64.

Nise De Silvera. (1966, February 2). Personal communication.

Odendaal, J.S.J. (1993). Human-animal interactions—An academic quo vadis? *Anthrozoos, 6*(1), 2–3.

Oldfield, O.M. (1956a). The serpent as an amulet and charm. In B. Aymar, (Ed.), *Treasury of snake lore* (pp. 35–42). New York: Greenberg.

Oldfield, O.M. (1956b). The serpent as a phallic emblem. In B. Aymar, (Ed.), *Treasury of snake lore* (pp. 42–49). New York: Greenberg.

Papashvilly, G., and Papashvilly, H. (1954). *Dogs and people.* Philadelphia: J.B. Lippincott.

Patrick, T. (1964). *The thinking dog's man.* New York: Random House.

Paul, E.S., and Serpell, J. (1992). Why children keep pets: The influence of child and family characteristics. *Anthrozoos, 5*(4), 231–244.

Pearsall, M., and Leedham, C.G. (1958). *Dog obedience training.* New York: Charles Scribners.

Pearson, G.H.J. (Ed.). (1968). *A handbook of child psychoanalysis.* New York: Basic Books.

Pearson, G.H.J. (1954). *Psychoanalysis and the education of the child.* New York: Morton.

Pet Census Needed. (1967). *Journal of the American Veterinary Medical Association, 50,* 1144–1146.

Piaget, J. (1952). *The origins of intelligence in children.* New York: International Universities Press.

Piaget, J., and Inhelder, B. (1969). *The psychology of the child.* New York: Basic Books.

Pittman, F.S., De Young, C., Flomenhaft, K., Kaplan, D.M., and Langley, D.G. (1966). Crisis family therapy. In J.H. Masserman, (Ed.), *Current psychiatric therapies, 6,* (pp.187–196). No city or publisher cited.

Polt, J.M., and Hale, C. (1985). Using pets as "therapists" for children with developmental disabilities. *Teaching Exceptional Children, 17, 218–222.*

Poresky, R.H. (1990). The young children's empathy measure: reliability, validity, and the effects of companion animal bonding. *Psychological Reports, 66,* 931–936.

Poresky, R.H., and Hendrix, C. (1990). Differential effects of pet presence and pet-bonding on young children. *Psychological Reports, 66,* 931–936.

Poresky, R.H., Hendrix, C., Mosier, J.E., and Samuelson, M.L. (1987). The companion animal bonding scale: Internal reliability and construct validity. *Psychological Reports, 60,* 743–746.

Pratt, K.C. (1945). Study of the "fears" of rural children. *Journal of Genetic Psychology, 67,* 179–194.

Quackenbush, J.E. (1981). Social work in a Veterinary hospital: A response to owner grief reactions. *Archives of the Foundation of Thanatology, 9,* (2), 56.

Quackenbush, J.E. (1983a). Social work services for bereaved pet owners: A retrospective case study in a Veterinary hospital. In A.H. Katcher, and A.M. Beck, (Eds.), *New perspectives on our lives with companions animals* (pp.377–389). Philadelphia: University of Pennsylvania Press.

Quackenbush, J.E. (1983b). When the bond is broken. *People-Animals-Environment, 1,* (1), 18–20.

Quaytman, A. (1963). Animals as aids in child therapy. *Journal of Long Island Consultation Center, 3,* 29–35.

Rabin, A.I. (Ed.). (1968). *Projective techniques in personality assessment.* New York: Springer.

Redefer, L.A., and Goodman, J.F. (1989). Brief report: Pet-facilitated therapy with autistic children. *Journal of Autism and Developmental Disorders, 19,* 461–467.

Reed, C.A. (1959). Animal domestication in the prehistoric near East. *Science, (130):* (pp. 1629–1639).

Rhine, J.B., and Pratt, J.G. (1962). *Parapsychology,* (Rev. ed.). Springfield, IL: Charles C Thomas.

Rice, B. (1968). *The other end of the leash.* Boston: Little, Brown.

Rigdon, J.D. and Tapia, F. (1977). Children who are cruel to animals—A follow-up study. *Journal of Operational Psychiatry, 8* (1), 27–36.

Robertson, J. (1962). *Hospitals and children.* New York: International Universities Press.

Robertson, J. (1959). *Young children in hospitals.* New York: Basic Books.

Robin, M., and ten Bensel, R.W. (1985). Pets and socialization of children. In M.B. Sussman (Ed.), *Pets and the family* (pp. 63–79). New York: Haworth.

Robin, M., ten Bensel, R.W., Quigley, J., and Anderson, R.K. (1983). Childhood pets and psychosocial development of adolescents. In A.H. Katcher and A.M. Beck (Eds.), *New perspectives in our lives with companion animals* (pp. 436–443). Philadelphia: University of Pennsylvania Press.

Robinson, I. (Ed.). (1995a). *The Waltham book of human-animal interaction: Benefits and responsibilities of pet ownership.* New York: Pergamon.

Robinson, I. (Ed.). (1995b). Associations between man and animals. In I. Robinson (Ed.), *The Waltham book of human-animal interaction: Benefits and responsibilities of pet ownership* (pp. 1–6). New York: Pergamon.

Rogers, C. (1963). Psychotherapy to-day or where do we go from here? *American Journal of Psychotherapy, 17,* 5–16.

Rogerson, J. (1992). *Training your dog.* New York: Popular Dogs.

Ross, S.B. (1981). Children and companion animals. *Ross Timesaver Feelings, 23*(4), 13–16.

Ross, S.B. (1983). The therapeutic use of animals with the handicapped. *International Child Welfare Review, 3* (56), 26–39.

Ross, S.B. (1989a). Children and Animals: Many benefits—some concerns. *New York State Outdoor Education Association, 3,* 2–13.

Ross, S.B. (1989b). Thoughtful wisdom on PFT from the perspective of Green Chimneys. *The Latham Letter, 2,* 5–6.

Ross, S.B. Jr., Vigdor, M.G., Kohnstamm, M., Di Paoli, M., Manley, B., and Ross,

L. (1984). The effects of farm programming with emotionally handicapped children. In R.K. Anderson, B.L. Hart, and L.A. Hart (Eds.), *The pet connection* (pp. 120–130). Minneapolis: University of Minnesota Press.

Rossbeck, K.A., and Wilson, J.P. (1992). Does a dog's presence make a person appear more likable? Two studies. *Anthrozoos, 5*(1), 40–51.

Rothenberg, M. (1959). Jingles at Camp Blueberry. Unpublished paper.

Rothenberg, M. (1960, Feb.). The strange story of Johnny. *Harper's Magazine, 220,* (pp. 51–66).

Rowan, A. (1987). Editorial. *Anthrozoos, 1*(3), 135–136.

Rowan, A. (1988). *Animals and people sharing the world.* Hanover, MA: University Press of New England.

Rowan, A. (1990). Methods of searching for truth. *Anthrozoos, 4*(2), 71–72.

Rowan, A. (1992). The dark side of the "force". *Anthrozoos, 5*(1), 4–5.

Rowan, A. (1994). Research, quality, journal publication, and academic discourse. *Anthrozoos, 7*(1), 2–3.

Rowan, A. (1995). Medical disinterest in human-animal bond research? *Anthrozoos, 8*(3), 130–131.

Ruckert, J. (1987). *The four-footed therapist.* Berkeley, CA: Ten Speed Press.

Rx for the ill and handicapped, (1961). The "zoo" visits young patients. *Recreation,* (54), (pp. 414–415).

Rynearson, E.K. (1978). Humans and pet attachment. *British Journal of Psychiatry,* 133, 550–555.

Salomon, A. (1981). Animals and children: The role of the pet. *Canada's Mental Health, June* 9–13.

Sanders, C.R., Robins, D.M., and Cahill, S.E. (1991). Dogs and their people. Pet-facilitated therapy in a public setting. *Journal of Contemporary Ethnography, 20* (1), 3–25.

Sauer, C.O. (1952). *Agricultural origins and dispersal.* New York: American Geographical Society.

Saunders, B. (1965). *Complete book of dog obedience* (Rev. ed.). New York: Howell.

Savishinsky, J.S. (1974). The child is the father of the dog: Canines and personality processes in an Artic community. *Human Development, 17* 460–466.

Schaffer, A.R., and Emerson, P.F. (1964). Patterns of response to physical contact in early human development. *Journal of Child Psychology and Psychiatry, 5*(1), 1–13.

Schantz, P.M. (1990). Preventing potential health hazards incidental to the use of pets in therapy. *Anthrozoos, 4*(1), 14–23.

Scheib, R. (1996, January/February). Timeline. *Utne Reader,* (73), 51–61.

Schilder, P. (1950). *The image and appearance of the human body.* New York: International Universities Press.

Schildkrout, M.S. (1967, March 6). Personal communication. Schwartz, A.A., and Rosenberg, I.H. (1955). Some observations on the significance of animal drawings. *American Journal of Orthopsychiatry, 25,* 729–746.

Scott, J.P. (1962). Introduction to animal behavior. In E.S.E. Hafez, (Ed.), *The behavior of domestic animals.* London: Balliere, Tindall and Cox.

Scott, J.P., and Fuller, J.L. (1965). *Genetics and the social behavior of the dog.* Chicago: University of Chicago Press.

Searles, H.F. (1960). *The non-human environment.* New York: International University Press.

Searles, H.F. (1965). *Collected papers on schizophrenia and related services.* NY: International Universities Press.

Senter, S. (Ed.). (1993). *People and animals: An animal-assisted activities manual.* Brewster: Green Chimneys Press.

Sephath Emeth: Order of prayers for the entire year. New York: Hebrew Publishing Co.

Serpell, J.A. (1981a). Childhood pets and their influence on adult's attitudes. *Psychological Reports, 49* 651–654.

Serpell, J.A. (1981b). Pet keeping in non-Western societies: Some popular misconceptions. *Anthrozoos, 1*(2), 166–174.

Serpell, J.A. (1986). *In the company of animals: A study of human-animal relationships.* New York: Basil Blackwell.

Serpell, J.A. (1991). Beneficial effects of pet ownership on some aspects of human health. *Journal of the Royal Society of Medicine, 84* 717–720.

Shaw, C.R. (1966). *The psychiatric disorders of childhood.* New York: Appleton-Century Crofts.

Shepard, P. (1995). *The others: How animals made us human.* Island Press/Shearwater Books.

Shlien, J.M. (1968). Introduction and overview. In J.M. Shlien, (Ed.), *Research in psychotherapy* (Vol. VIII). Washington: American Psychological Association.

Siegal, A. (1962). Reaching the severely withdrawn through pet therapy. *American Journal of Psychiatry, 118* (2), 1045–1046.

Siegal, J. (1993). Companion animals: In sickness and in health. *Journal of Social Issues, 48* (1), 57–67.

Siegrist, H.E. (1951). *A history of medicine primitive and archaic* (Vol. 1). New York: Oxford University Press.

Simons, M. (1995, June 8). Newly found cave paintings in France are the oldest, scientists estimate. *The New York Times,* p. A18.

Singer, E. (1965). *Key concepts in psychotherapy.* New York: Random House.

Sloan, A., and Farqhar, A. (1925). *Dog and man: The story of a friendship.* London: Hutchinson and Co.

Smith, B. (1985). Project in-reach: A program to explore the ability of Atlantic bottle-nose dolphins to elicit communication responses from autistic children. In A.H. Katcher and A.M. Beck (Eds.), *New perspectives on our lives with companion animals* (pp. 460–466). Philadelphia: University of Pennsylvania Press.

Smythe, R.H. (1958). *The mind of the dog.* London: Country Life, Ltd.

Smythe, R.H. (1965). *Private life of the dog. Does it think?* New York: Arco.

Soares, C.J. (1985). The companion animal in the context of the family system. In M.B. Sussman (Ed.), *Pets and the family* (pp. 49–62). New York: Haworth.

Some current therapeutic use of animals in a hospital setting (1961). *Recreations, 54,* 415.

Sonne, J.C. (1965). Resistances in family therapy of schizophrenia in the home. In Friedmann et al: *Psychotherapy for the whole family,* (pp. 255–262). New York: Springer.

Speck, R.V. (1965a). Some specific therapeutic techniques with schizophrenic families. In A.S. Friedmann et al (Eds.), *Psychotherapy for the whole family* (pp. 197–205). New York: Springer.

Speck, R.V. (1965b). The transfer of illness phenomenon in schizophrenic families. In A.S. Friedmann et al (Eds.), *Psychotherapy for the whole family* (pp. 293–304). New York: Springer.

Spitz, R. (1960). Hospitalism—an inquiry into the genesis of psychiatric conditions in early childhood. *Psychoanalytic study of the child* (Vol. II and III). New York: International Universities Press.

Steinbeck, J. (1962). *Travels with Charley.* New York: Viking Press.

Stekel, W. (1959). *Patterns of psychosexual infantilism.* New York: Grove Press.

Stevenson, O. (1954). The first treasured possession: a study of the part played by specially loved objects and toys in the lives of certain children. *The Psychoanalytic Study of the Child, 9,* 199–217.

Steward, M. (1983). Loss of a pet—Loss of a person: A comparative study of bereavement. In A.H. Katcher and A.M. Beck (Eds.), *New perspectives on our lives with companion animals* (pp. 229–234). Philadelphia: University of Pennsylvania Press.

Stockard, C.R. (1941). *Genetic and endocrine basis for differences in form and behavior.* University of Pennsylvania, Wistar Institute of Anatomy and Biology.

Stone, S. (1937). Psychiatry through the ages. *Journal of Abnormal Social Psychology, 32,* 131–160.

Swingler, R.C. (1966, Feb.). Education values of classroom pets. *The Education Digest, 31.*

Tapia, F. (1971). Children who are cruel to animals. *Child Psychiatry and Human Development, 2* (2), 70–77.

ten Bensel, R.W. (1984). Historical perspectives of human values for animals and vulnerable people. In P. Arkow (Ed.), *Dynamic relationships in practice: Animals in the helping professions* (pp. 23–36). Alameda, CA: Latham Foundation.

The Monks of New Skete. (1978). *How to be your dog's best friend.* Boston: Little, Brown.

Thomas, E.M. (1993). *The hidden life of dogs.* New York: Houghton-Mifflin.

Thomas, E.M. (1994). *The tribe of the tiger: Cats and their culture.* New York: Simon and Schuster.

Thomas, N.W. (1951). Animals. *Encyclopedia of religion and ethics* (Vol. I, pp. 483–535). New York: Charles Scribner's.

Trew, C.G. (1940). *The story of the dog and his uses to mankind.* London: Methuen.

Trigg, H.L. (1962, February 12). Personal communication.

Trivedi, L. and Perl, J. (1995). Animal facilitated counseling in elementary schools: A literature review and practical considerations. *Elementary School Guidance and Counseling, 29* 223–234.

Turner, D.C. (1995). The human-cat relationship. In I. Robinson (Ed.), *The Waltham book of human-animal interaction: Benefits and responsibilities of pet ownership* (pp. 87–97). New York: Pergamon.

Tylor, E.B. (1958). *Religion in primitive culture.* New York: Harper and Brothers.

Valentine, C.W. (1930). The innate bases of fear. *Journal of Genetic Psychology, 37,* 394–420.

Veper, G.M. (1954). *Les procès des animaux au moyen âge.* Cour d'appel de Chambèry. Chambèry, 1954.

Verville, E. (1967). *Behavior problems of children.* Philadelphia: W.B. Saunders.

Volhard, J., and Fisher, G. (1983). *Training your dog: The step by step manual.* New York: Howell Books.

Walshaw, S.O. (1984). Contemporary perspectives on pets and people. In P. Arkow, (Ed.), *Dynamic relationships in practice: Animals in the helping professions* (pp.37–55). Alameda, CA: Latham Foundation.

Weigel, R.G., and Straumfjord, A.A. (1969, May 17). The dog as a therapeutic adjunct in group treatment. A paper presented at the annual meeting of the Rocky Mountain Psychological Association, Albuquerque.

Werner, H. (1957). *Comparative Psychology of Mental Development* (2nd revised ed.). New York: International Universities Press.

Whimhurst, C. (1955). *Obedience training for your dog.* New York: Dover Publications.

Whitman, W. Section 32. Song of myself in *Leaves of grass.*

Whitney, F. (1964). *Psychology: The basis of dog training.* Springfield, IL: Charles C Thomas.

Whittaker, J.K., and Trieschman, A.E. (Eds.). (1972). *Children away from home: A source book of residential treatment.* Chicago: Aldine/Atherton.

Wickes, F.G. (1966). *The inner world of childhood* (Rev. ed.). New York: Appleton-Century.

Wilson, C.C. (1994). A conceptual framework for human-animal interaction research: the challenge revisited. *Anthrozoos, 7*(1), 4–24.

Winnicott, D.W. (1953). Transitional objects and transitional phenomena. *International Journal of Psychoanalysis, 24,* 88–97.

Winnicott, D.W. (1965). *The maturational process and the facilitating environment.* New York: International Universities Press.

Wishon, P.M. (1987). An examination of childhood-companion animal interactions in facilitating physical, emotional and social well-being. *Early Child Development and Care, 29* (4), 417–433.

Wohlwill, J.F. (1966). The physical environment: A problem for a psychology of stimulation. *Journal of Social Issues, 12* (4), 29–38.

Yates. E. (1973). *Skeezer: Dog with a mission.* New York: Harvey House.

Zeuner, F.E. (1963). *A History of Domesticated Animals.* New York: Harper and Row.

AUTHOR INDEX

W

Y

Z

SUBJECT INDEX

R